ARSENAL ON THE DO

To my old man, Mervyn, for making sure it was McLintock, not Mullery. While 'resting in peace' I wonder if he continues to give Ray Parlour a hard time?

Arsenal on the Double

*OVERDRAWN, UNDER THE WEATHER,
OVERSLEPT, UNDERPANTS, OVER THE MOON,
UNDER THE TABLE – A TERRACE TAKE
ON A GLORIOUS SEASON 2001–02*

BERNARD AZULAY

MAINSTREAM
PUBLISHING

EDINBURGH AND LONDON

First published in Great Britain in 2002 by
MAINSTREAM PUBLISHING (EDINBURGH) LTD
7 Albany Street
Edinburgh EH1 3UG

ISBN 1 84018 683 6

A catalogue record for this book is available from the British Library

Typeset in Dante and UniversBQ

Printed in Great Britain by
Mackays of Chatham plc

Acknowledgements

My sister, Debbie Taffler without whom I would have still been procrastinating about putting this book together. Bill Campbell, Will Mackie, Kirsteen Wright and all at Mainstream Publishing for their patience in putting up with my pedantic behaviour. Everyone at Pentagram, especially Sharon Hwang for all her artistic efforts, above and beyond the call of duty, and Angus Hyland for his inspiration. Despite the costly fact that I may never again use my abstinence from alcohol as an excuse for not buying a round! My gratitude also for the assistance of Nick Turner and Steven Bateman. Not forgetting Douglas for my deliverance from the dangers of the dreaded parking ticket.

Tony Leen and everyone at *The Examiner* in Ireland who have laboured over the editing of my persistently late and all too lengthy diary pieces for four years. Special thanks to Brian Murphy, who goes to so much trouble posting me the paper without fail from Dublin each week, enabling me to get wound up over what's been edited out (not to mention the small matter of my being warmly welcomed into his family). And of course Con Murphy, without whose encouragement, none of this might have come to pass. Not forgetting my good pal Peter Denholm, since without his help we would have lost our seats in the West Upper years back.

Gooners Jonathan 'Nell' Moser, a patently useful pal, if only for the fact that he always carries on his person the Arsenal's previous five years' fixture lists/results. Brian Dawes and his match reports, bulging with blow-by-blow details. Chris Parry for his constant efforts maintaining www.arsenal-world.net. The hard work of Kevin Whitcher and Mike Francis which ensures *The Gooner* remains one of the country's foremost fanzines.

For their photographic contributions, Mark Hakansson and the Internet mailing list Gooners, George and Rex Kaldre, Daniel and Ben Godfrey, Richard Palmer, Paul Matz and IASA, Tommi Peuhkurinen, Karl Sinfield (WeLoveYouFreddie.com), Laurie, Billy & Sara Buchsbaum, Clockend Jen, Joe Wise and all those others who were kind enough to send me the photos which would have filled another book, but at least left us spending the summer poring over sunny memories.

The best publicist a son could wish for in my ma, Eunice Azulay. Doubtless I would miss out on far more fixtures during the worst of our British winters, if it wasn't for her part in my healthy constitution, permitted as a result of her chicken soup. My missus, Róna, and her long suffering during all those lonely hours, either widowed by my writing, or my wandering on the www. The majority of my most memorable Gooner moments wouldn't have been nearly so magical without her by my side to share them.

Contents

Introduction: Reasons to be Cheerful (Part One)

As such an avid Arsenal fan, some might find it strange that my most precious piece of sporting memorabilia is a scruffy old Spurs programme that has seen better days. With a horrific hoarding problem, I have accrued an enormous collection of sporting knick-knacks over the past 30 years. It is a constant source of contention between myself and my Dublin-born missus, Róna. I am particularly proud of a sizable selection of scarves – souvenirs I've amassed from almost every European game since the Gunners' return to continental competition back in 1991. Stuffed in a drawer amidst our ever-decreasing storage space, these hardly ever see the light of day. Similarly I don't dare get Ró started on what amounts to almost an anthology of the Arsenal amongst my massive T-shirt collection. The many and varied memories associated with each individual Gooner garment, even those that laud dead-loss departures from our team, leave me loath to dispose of any of them. Consequently, with our overcrowded cupboards, I can no longer wander past the stalls around Highbury buying whatever takes my fancy, willy-nilly, every other week. I might slip the odd one past Ró when her defences are down, but generally I adhere to a strict one-in, one-out agreement. Meanwhile I still find it difficult to downgrade a memento of the likes of Paul Merson to a mere duster.

I dread the day when she finally adopts my ma's method of dumping anything I haven't cast an eye over for donkey's years. When my old man passed away and Mum decided to move from the house which held all my childhood memories, it was about a year before it suddenly struck me to query the whereabouts of a whole heap of teenage tat. I understood Mum's motives. Doubtless, left to my own devices, I'd be lugging all that stuff around in the back of the motor for the duration, unable even to get rid of my *Soccer Stars* swaps. There was no point crying over what was little more than a cupboard full of clutter, especially when I couldn't get much past the cuddly toy on my imaginary conveyor belt, in a *Generation Game*-type test of my limited powers of recollection. More's the point, I could have kissed my ma for having the presence of mind to set aside all my most precious pieces of football ephemera. I can't see my 1970 Esso World Cup coin collection and assorted *Soccer Stars* albums fetching a fortune at Sotheby's (at least not for a few generations). Nevertheless the substantial sentimental value of these items, along with some of my most prized match programmes from the same period, just cannot be measured in mundane monetary terms.

ARSENAL ON THE DOUBLE

Like most of my age, I was introduced to the magic of the match-day experience thanks to my dear departed old man. It was a different era, long before the advent of all-ticket matches. Affordable prices and unreserved seating meant a young dad could wake up on any Saturday morning and make a spur-of-the-moment decision to open his offspring's eyes to a love of football. By contrast these days, unless you are one of the privileged few with a season ticket to top-class football in this country, it takes months of military planning, not to mention a mountain of cash, to take one's kids to a Premiership match. In an age when buzz words like 'quality time' and 'bonding' get bandied about so much, it is a crying shame that the vast majority of kids miss out on this enriching experience. Many only get to go to the odd game, if they are lucky, perhaps as an annual birthday treat. Football may have benefited from the fact that there is more of a family atmosphere at our modern stadia than existed at the frightening grounds of yesteryear, which were full of foreboding. Still our sport is increasingly priced beyond the means of your average parent. Especially when mum and daughter might be equally as keen as father and son nowadays.

Róna tells me that her dad used to take her brothers off to see Shamrock Rovers on a Sunday in Dublin. In those dark days one wouldn't have wanted to inflict the swearing and the none too salubrious surroundings on members of the fairer sex. Whereas, with the ubiquitous nature of the modern game, my contagious enthusiasm for the Arsenal has infected virtually all my 'out-laws' in Ireland (as I am wont to label a family relationship of choice, as opposed to a contractual one!). Fixture lists are studied at the earliest opportunity and plans are laid months in advance for the annual pilgrimages of two of Róna's sisters, Clionna and Grainne, to 'The Home of Football'. Religion may be the opiate of the masses, but the Arsenal can rapidly become one's religion and apparently Grainne now often lights a candle on the Arsenal's behalf, before our more important matches. Similarly, the solidarity of all our nephews has been cemented, counterbalancing the domination of the Red Devils in their classrooms across the Irish Sea. Their fervent interest has been fostered by means of occasional autographs, T-shirts and the birthday cards they've received as members of the Junior Gunners. Although with a phlegmatic father, who prefers fishing to football, none of us could comprehend the possibility that the four-year-old son of another sibling, Aisling, might be lost to Liverpool. Thank goodness with Róna's help, his mother seems to have set him straight. By pandering to his penchant for Freddie Ljungberg, the charismatic Swede with the 'go-faster' red stripe, Jake appears to have been successfully initiated into the Arsenal tribe, sporting his favourite 'Freddie's Gonna Get Ya' top.

The Junior Gunners do an admirable job at the Arsenal, in particular for all those kids whose only contact with their heroes comes courtesy of the cathode-ray. You can't possibly overstate the importance in the imagination of a child who believes such a big club has bothered to remember his or her birthday. I am often amused by the Arsenal-supporting parents whose priorities are such that the names of their progeny must go down on the three-year waiting-list for season tickets, not only before they bother about a school, but even before the birth. However with a lifetime of unlimited loyalty at stake, I am hardly naive enough to believe that the sugar-coated marketing strategies for the regeneration of a club's support are likely to be motivated by the milk of human kindness. The majority of our top clubs are less sporting and more economic institutions. The moneymen in their boardrooms view all these boys and girls in terms of potential income on their merchandising balance sheet. If the poor parents are unable to fork out a small fortune for their loved ones to see live football, they are sure to be coughing up not far short of a hundred quid for a nylon kit every couple of seasons (no matter how much the manufacturers try to dress up the latest high-tech fabric, to my mind it remains nasty artificial material).

It wasn't a birthday card which was behind my schoolboy betrothal and the start of a lifelong love affair. Mercifully my dad was a bit of a black sheep – otherwise, as a descendant of 28 generations of rabbis, we might never have been to a football match on a Saturday. The fact that we were slipping off on the day of rest, to worship at The Home of Football instead of the House of the Lord, to idolise some altogether more interesting gods, already made it an attractive proposition. With my uncle and cousins doing likewise, it became a badly kept secret in our family, although no one dared mention football in front of my grandfather, the rabbi, for fear of rubbing his beard in his brood's ungodly Gooner gabble.

In line with Desmond Morris's tribal themes, taking one's son to his first live football match in the late '60s was a masculine rite of passage for my dad. It certainly had a bigger impact than the manhood ritual of my bar mitzvah. With my little hand in his, I remember my old man dragging me past the enticing smell of fried onions wafting from the hot-dog stands (a forbidden food either for holy or hygienic reasons), towards the phosphorescent glow of the floodlights burning through the midwinter gloom. From the moment I first stood in the shadows of Highbury's magnificent art-deco stands and sensed the buzz of atmosphere building in the crowded streets, I was sold on this male-dominated domain.

It was a revelation as a child to discover this illicit place where adults apparently came to scream and shout their heads off, venting a whole week's worth of frustrations at the opposition, the referee and even their own team. Football's recent corporate makeover and the decline of its blue-collar crowd may mean that the frisson is not so frequent in the Highbury Library, but the forceful effect of the all too rare sound of 30,000 voices joining as one, enthrals me now, just as it did that first time. What tickled me most was that everyone was allowed to curse out loud, deferring to the odd indifferent female with the occasional 'Sorry Missus' –

to someone who often had a mouth like the Blackwall Tunnel, but twice as dirty! The epitome of this amazing anarchy was the sound of thousands effing and blinding, screaming out profanities that I would have got a slap for using at home. At times I could sense Dad's discomfort, no doubt fearing a diatribe from my mum for introducing the delicate ears of her precious son to such coarse language. Naturally the words were nothing new, I just wouldn't have dared express myself in this way in front of my elders (even as an adult, I was never comfortable coating off a w**ker of a referee when sitting beside my dad). Similarly Dad's admirable but somewhat lame attempt to limit his language, often involved the liberal use of his favoured: 'Fu . . . crying out loud!'

They may be a little vague now, but through the sands of time my earliest memories of The Home of Football include the thrilling sensation of being passed over the heads of a swollen crowd and escaping the crush, to sit in safety on the track beside the St John Ambulance men only a whisper away from the action. Knowing my father, it was probably a ruse to finagle his way to the front. When it came to limitless 'chutzpah' my old man was in a league of his own. A more vivid childhood flashback finds me shuffling through the turnstiles of the West Upper at Highbury, between the bugger's legs, hidden by the fulsome folds of his winter overcoat. Having outgrown this gambit, I never failed to marvel at how he always managed to come up trumps with tickets, despite his strict tenets of having no truck with the touts, or not paying over the odds.

As a salesman in the rag trade and with a gregarious good nature, Dad had a tendency for tongue-wagging which resulted in an endless amount of acquaintances. Many was the time my sister and I would be sitting in front of the television, taking the mickey out of his unbelievable boasts about his intimate knowledge of, or how he'd been out with, whoever happened across the screen. Yet over the years we learnt not to take his outrageous claims too lightly because every now and again we were left dumbstruck by some definitive proof. I had eight mates over to celebrate my birthday one year and Dad decided to take us all to see the Arsenal. Getting eight adjacent seats on the day would have been hard enough for any match. For Arsenal versus Manchester Utd it was well-nigh impossible. He left us outside Highbury in a heightened state of excitement to go and find his mate Sir Matt Busby in the famous marble halls. I will never know how he managed to procure a prime pitch for us, all the tickets together in two rows, for one of the biggest games of the season. It must have been a bit of an anticlimax for my football-mad friends who turned up the following year when my birthday treat was a trip to see *Tora, Tora, Tora* at the flicks.

Promises from my pop were pretty sacred and he must have felt like he had let us down when he failed to come up with FA Cup final tickets in 1970. Chelsea and Leeds played out a draw at Wembley, so the replay provided a perfect opportunity for him to redeem himself. I can still picture the envious little phizogs of my school friends, pressed up against the classroom window, as my sister Debbie and I were allowed to leave early for the long drive north to Manchester. Apparently the match itself was a memorable game, but more firmly imprinted on my mind are the strange events prior. Again he must have reckoned on Sir Matt coming to his rescue, but on the night Old Trafford was a neutral venue with no Mancunian involvement. Struggling in vain to find a friendly face, we were still walking around the ground as kick-off time approached. I wondered whether Dad would relent and turn to a tout as a last resort, or were we facing an interminably long ride back to London? Perhaps he was waiting for that time when, preferring to get something rather than nothing, the leeches who were left with tickets would let them go for less than the astronomic amount they'd been asking for earlier. Such thoughts didn't prevent the searing sense of disappointment on hearing the huge roar from inside the stadium, which was instantaneously recognisable as the signal for the end of the friendly formalities and the outbreak of hostilities. Somehow Dad always seemed to get away with it and, on this occasion, salvation came in the form of one of the local constabulary. He must have taken pity on my poor father and his two crestfallen kids, as he came over and conjured up three priceless tickets from his pocket.

I had plenty of opportunities during the subsequent decade to become a bandwagon-jumping glory-hunter, as Dad developed a connection at the Football Association. We became the sort of people that I constantly bemoan these days, turning up at virtually every Wembley final and depriving a true fan of one of the two teams of a ticket (at least we had a genuine love of the game, unlike many of the corporate liggers of the modern era, who will appear at the opening of a paper bag if it includes lunch and a free bar!). The extraordinary tales every year of those fans who are prepared to go to outrageous extremes to obtain a ticket, left me feeling incredibly privileged. They weren't all terrific games but, as testament to my presence at each, I continue to cherish all my Cup final programmes.

Our virtual season ticket at Wembley lasted throughout the '70s, during which time the Arsenal were involved in four finals. At all the other games, I would always support the underdogs on the day, but there was no question about where my true allegiances lay. It's embarrassing to admit now, but instead of the Arsenal, I could have just as easily been a follower of the forces of darkness from the wrong end of the Seven Sisters Road. In the days long before the TV tail began wagging the football dog, when midweek matches apart, all the games kicked off at three o'clock on a Saturday afternoon, the two North London rivals would always play at home on alternate weeks. You wouldn't dream of doing it now, but the old man would often take me to Highbury one week and to White Hart Lane the next, like many other football-loving locals at that time. I might be reluctant to admit it in some company, having done my best to erase the memories of this aberration, but I have some programmes which testify to the fact that we even travelled on the odd occasion to see Tottenham play away. I might have been very young at the time, but even without this proof I have never been able to forget the shocking sound that rang around a northern ground: the snap of ('Nice One') Cyril Knowles' leg. Or the frightening sight of Mike Summerbee in full flow up at Maine Road, as he ran towards the touchline where a Spurs player was about to take a throw-in and simply kneed him in the knackers (and the foreign players complain about the physical side to our modern game; they don't know they're born!).

In fact prior to 1971 it would have been easy for me to swear allegiance to the enemy. My dad was always a Highbury man at heart but I can't recall him exerting any pressure whatsoever to influence my decision either way. Which couldn't be said of everyone in my family, many of whom kicked with the wrong foot (including a taxi-driving cousin of my mum's who was renowned for his response, 'You know, when you come out of Spurs', whenever he was asked directions, no matter where you were starting from, or heading to!). One of my relatives would tease me relentlessly whenever we met, suggesting that is was nothing short of cruelty by my old man to make me sit through 90 minutes at the Arsenal. 'Don't you get bored there?' he would ask. 'Why don't you ask him to bring you to Spurs, so you can watch some real football?'

Even before the Spurs side captained by Danny Blanchflower won the first ever League and FA Cup Double in 1961 (up until then it was thought to be an impossible feat) they had the reputation for playing exciting, entertaining football, while the Arsenal were renowned for being a safe, solid but ultimately boring side which ground out single-goal victories. This was entirely accurate in 1970 and, as a lover of the game, my old man often sought respite from the dour deeds of the likes of Mclintock, Storey and Radford, in the flair footie from the feet of Greaves, Gilzean, Mullery and co. Although the thrills from this temperamental Tottenham team often came at a price, because even with gentle giant Pat Jennings between the sticks, they conceded costly goals. Whereas at Highbury if we didn't have the guile to get them in at one end, we usually had the grit to keep them out at t'other. It was the traditional tale of Tottenham's talented individuals compared with the famous Arsenal team spirit, where the sum of the parts was greater than the whole.

When playing football at school I wasn't eccentric enough to play in goal but, unlike the majority of lads, I was one of the weird ones who was far less interested in scoring goals than I was in keeping them out. As a defender, I soon learnt to appreciate a goal-saving challenge, as much, if not more than any goal-scoring feats and as a result I was destined to be a Gooner. The terrific Arsenal spirit was a prime factor in my preference, as were Highbury's padded seats, which were far less painful on my bony little bum after 90 minutes than the hard wooden ones at

White Hart Lane. Albeit there was something far less tangible to the attraction of the Arsenal.

Almost every player that has signed for the club has testified to the fact that his mind was made up from the moment he entered the portals of the famous marble halls and sensed the special aura about the place. From the bust of the great Herbert Chapman, to all the other amazing memorabilia lining the walls and dotted around the majestic art-deco building, all one's senses are assaulted by the Arsenal's aristocratic football heritage. I must visit the box office to sort out tickets at least once or twice a week during the season. Though I could just as easily see my pal in there, from one of the windows on to the street, I often find an excuse to climb the steps of the main entrance, to see him at the window inside the building. Those same steps that have worn shiny under the feet of all the greats in British football history and, after 30 years, I still get a thrill from following in the footsteps of the legendary players. Once inside, I often have to wait a few minutes before catching my mate's eye in the box office, but it is no hardship as I never tire of drinking in all that history whilst revisiting some of the Arsenal's greatest moments as represented by some of the pictures on the walls. The building is steeped in so much history that am I always half expecting an appearance of the ghost of Herbert Chapman, come to give me a guided tour!

As a child, I might not have been familiar with the finer points of the two teams' histories and that by comparison to the aristocratic Arsenal, the Lilywhites were flashy johnny-come-latelys. Yet even in the slightly more plush surroundings of the Arsenal's stands, compared to Tottenham's strictly functional terracing, I certainly had some sense of the intrinsic differences. A team with few stars but oodles of the famous Arsenal team spirit; the squad suited and booted at all times, in an age of awful hairstyles and calamitous casual clothes; a boardroom full of double-barrelled old Etonians; the aesthetically pleasing architecture amongst all those other concrete monstrosities and the history mirrored in the marble halls. These were the palpable pointers to an institution with the sort of soul that just wasn't evident at some of its more shallow competitors. It was a vague awareness of these vibes which drew me in from day one and it is why employees of the club, both on and off the pitch, so rarely choose to leave – that is with the exclusion of recent examples of certain senseless stars, with agents who've filled their heads with foolish 'grass is greener' foreign fantasies, where only in hindsight have they been able to truly appreciate what they left behind at the Arsenal.

Meanwhile I am stuck with the recurring nightmare, that up until the age of nine, I followed my father's example and was a fan of the football of the two North London teams. I can even recall being taken to derby encounters, with an Arsenal rosette pinned to one side of my little chest and a Spurs one on the other. Such eccentricities might be acceptable in a child, but couldn't continue into adulthood. Most of the boys in my school stood on one side or the other of this decisive North London divide. My precarious balancing act on the fence meant that I got it in the ear from everyone. Moreover my vacillating caused a split-personality disorder in the playground, as I was scything down my playmates, not sure whether I was Peter Storey, or Mike England.

Just think, I could have spent my entire 40 years on this earth as a sorry Spurs supporter, never knowing the euphoric feeling of following the best club in the country and the spine-tingling moment when one's team finally takes the title. For someone whose dithering nature leaves me prevaricating on many a morning over which paper to buy, I shall be eternally grateful for the decisiveness which eventually resulted in me setting aside any sympathies for Spurs, once and for all, in one defining moment on an unforgettable night in 1971. In the first week of June my old man took me to the European Cup final at Wembley. It was the first time I had seen fireworks on the terraces and I can still picture the smoke and the colours of the pink and blue flares of the Panathinaikos fans. I can also still sing (in Dutch!) the optimistic chant of the Ajax contingent that echoed around the Wembley concourse as they supped their lagers. I might have an eye for detail, but my cursed memory means much of my childhood is a muzzy blur. On this particular night there was such an amazing atmosphere that the minutiae have remained imprinted on my mind. Mind you, it was small consolation for missing out on the culmination of the Arsenal's first double a couple of weeks earlier. Considering all those subsequent trips to Wembley finals, it is a constant source of regret that we weren't present when the Arsenal finally limited Spurs' fans ability to laud it over us, by repeating the feats of their team of ten years earlier.

In fact, on the day I was sitting on the floor of our living room, all dressed up in my replica kit, along with all my other Arsenal accessories – hat, scarf, rosette and rattle – watching on TV as Charlie George put Liverpool to the sword with that sizzling strike. Wearing specs and having lost much of his famous lank locks, George may not be nearly so distinctive these days, but the fact that we still regularly see him schlepping all over the country with the rest of us supporters is why Charlie was and always will be 'our' darling. Every fan dreams of stepping off the terraces to score the winning goal in an FA Cup final. It might be a far-fetched fantasy for most, but in Charlie's feats, all of us were able to live out this dream vicariously. The famous picture of him celebrating his goal, laid out against a background of the luscious green turf, on a glorious May Cup final day, is one of the most memorable Arsenal images for Gooners of my age. Not being able to say 'I was there' still galls me but I could hardly complain of being a deprived child. Not when the Arsenal and my dutiful dad had conjured up what ranks as one of the greatest events of my entire childhood only five days earlier.

The fixture lists had thrown up a nice 'little' irony. The Arsenal's last league fixture on the Monday night before the Cup final was a derby duel at Tottenham.

If we were going to do the League and Cup Double first done by Spurs a decade earlier, we would have to win at White Hart Lane (or a goalless draw, but because of the peculiarities of the goal average system a score-draw would have handed Leeds the title). There was a Spurs-supporting lad who lived in our road whose dad was working that night, so Dad took the two of us to the game. Ian was my sister's age, three years older than me, and I am grateful for his more detailed recollections, when perhaps I was just too excited to take it all in. I hadn't seen him for years when he turned up at my father's funeral a couple of years back. Naturally, it wasn't long before we were reminiscing about this remarkable night. I remember arriving at the ground and seeing the queue for unreserved tickets stretching all the way around the corner into Tottenham High Road, but I was blown away by Ian's 'more front than Sainsbury's' story of how the bobby at the start of the queue had slipped us in. Apparently the old man told him that he'd just left his place to pick the kids up from school!

According to the old bill, there was 150,000 outside White Hart Lane, all wanting to get in. As a result there was a stampede when the gates finally opened and I can recall the sensation of being shepherded by my father, his huge arms around our shoulders, both to protect us from the crush and to propel us towards the turnstiles. In those days there seemed to be plenty of turnstile operators on the take and if there were no more tickets on sale, it wasn't uncommon to bung them a few quid to let you in. Such was the demand on this particular night that White Hart Lane was soon crammed to capacity and beyond. My father reckoned that official attendance figures of around 51,000 were farcical. He claimed that in reality there were always a few thousand more punters, as this was how most clubs stymied the tax-man, by syphoning off the cash for their stars' burgeoning bonuses and various other brown envelope-type bung activities.

Many Gooners have their own tales of the wonderful night we won the league at White Hart Lane, including those poor buggers who arrived to find the club had been forced to lock the gates an hour before kick-off. I suppose it was due to the way everyone rushed the turnstiles, but I have heard countless tales since of those who faced the torture of being stuck outside, even though they had tickets. Looking back, I realise how difficult it must have been for my dad, with two young kids amidst such a frantic crowd. It was only his determination that got us in. Otherwise I would never have seen a tantalising but typical '1–0 to the Arsenal' triumph (albeit many years before the 'Go West' tune) in which Ray Kennedy rose to head home the league-winning goal, with only three minutes to go, in the goal right in front of us. With it being less important to score but crucial not to concede, this was a task made for this Arsenal team. Having held on for three minutes that felt like a lifetime, all that tension ensured an incredible eruption at the final whistle.

I will always remember the celebrations that followed. As Tottenham fans trudged out, traumatised by their ultimate nightmare, the Arsenal fans completely took over the stadium. Funnily enough, amongst my magical memories of all the ensuing mayhem, I can't picture a trophy presentation. All I remember is that a high old time was had by all. We worked our way from behind the goal to the main stand with many other Gooners, while thousands more Arsenal fans invaded the pitch. In the bedlam, it was ages before they finally let the players escape to the sanctuary of the dressing room. As the fans on the pitch serenaded us in the main stand and we responded in kind, I continued to sing myself hoarse, long into an already late night.

It was when the crowd eventually began to disperse that my old man played his 'top-tastic' trump card. He'd been cultivating his connections at Spurs for many years and via some friendly badinage with the bod on the door, we often exited the ground from the public concourse of this stand, into the very private players' car park. As a consequence I have been left with an assortment of Spurs programmes from this era, amongst my sizable collection, and nearly all of them have at least one autograph on the front or back cover. I only wish I'd had the presence of mind to put a name beside all these illegible scribbles, or at least make a note somewhere. On the occasional nostalgic evening when I've dug out my programmes, I've spent hours trying to suss out these signatures, not sure if I'm looking at a meaningless, small potatoes moniker like DJ Pete Murray, or a big cheese like Bobby Moore.

My programme from that momentous match would have been special even without a single signature on it. Yet I ended up with several, after Dad collared players from both clubs as we sauntered around the car park. The perfect end to a perfect evening presented itself when my old man overheard Ray Kennedy looking for a lift to his parents' hotel. It wouldn't have mattered if it was miles out of his way, he wasn't going to pass up the opportunity to have the league-winning goal-scorer in his car. It was mind-boggling for the two of us, sitting in the backseat directly behind this footballing god. For the past 30 years I was under the impression that Kennedy told us it was his birthday to boot. Maybe he was speaking metaphorically, or about one of his folks, because when I came to checking my facts for this book, I was flabbergasted to find an inaccuracy in the story with which I've been boring the pants off so many, for so long.

Ray (we only ever met the once but after talking about him all this time, he feels like an intimate pal!) must have overheard me as I turned to my pal and said: 'They'll never believe us at school tomorrow!' He took both our programmes and signed mine: 'To Bernard whom I travelled home with after the game'. I don't wish to cast aspersions about Kennedy, but the use of 'whom' makes me think that my old man suggested what to write. Yet it doesn't detract from the fact that this programme takes pride of place amongst all my memorabilia.

Given the opportunity (and football fans don't take much encouragement to start swapping sentimental stories), most Gooners will point to Anfield '89 as their most memorable Arsenal moment, as portrayed in Nick Hornby's seminal story. Of all the incredible games I've gone to over the years, those quasi-religious roller-coaster rides through the full gamut of emotions, I will be eternally gutted that I can't include Anfield '89 on my Arsenal CV. It feels like a gaping hole in my own Gooner genealogy. When reminiscences turn to terrace tales from that particular night in any Arsenal gathering, I can usually be found wittering on about White Hart Lane in '71 by way of confirming my credentials.

In fact, I stopped attending the Arsenal and live matches altogether for almost the entire decade of the '80s. My interest waned in inverse proportion to the increase in football violence, as the possibility of getting stabbed on a Saturday afternoon was not my idea of entertainment. I may have been travelling home and away, to almost every Arsenal game for the last 12 years but my period of self-enforced absence has left me sensitive to accusations that I am a glory hunter. Or worse still, part of the nouveau breed of football fans who were attracted to the game in the boom that followed Gazza's Italia '90 World Cup waterworks. I rest my case with the argument that my renewed interest coincided with the latter days of George Graham's reign as manager, when travelling hundreds of miles every week to watch the midfield mediocrity of the likes of Hillier, McGoldrick, Jensen and Morrow was nothing short of masochism. Whether the football is abysmal, boring, or bloody marvellous, I have always loved the notion of spending 90 minutes with my vocal valves open, releasing a week's worth of road rage and all the other psychoses suffered by city dwellers. Once I realised times had changed somewhat and I was able to travel to most away matches – with the exception of derby games by and large – wearing Arsenal colours without fear of getting my head kicked in, the addiction soon took hold again.

What's more, having aroused an Arsenal interest in virtually all of Róna's family in Dublin, she initially took a 'can't beat 'em, join 'em' approach. She used to jest that at least it was one way of guaranteeing we spent time together. Yet any air of detachment soon gave way to a decided need for her own football fix. I first noticed it taking hold, when I'd go in the bedroom to watch footie on the telly, only to come back into the living room and catch her watching it as well, sacrificing her beloved soaps. It wasn't long before she was so hooked that, on the rare occasion I was prevented from going to a game, it was taken as read that she'd be going alone. However, I would never have risked taking Róna to away games in the bad old days. Whereas the changing times meant we could travel together, without having to worry that I might be putting her in danger, or that I was risking a kicking myself because Ró isn't a fast enough runner.

Many of the bellicose bovver-boys have been displaced by the prawn-cocktail corporate suits and a generally more civilised, middle-class crowd. It is a sad fact that this has been at the expense of the working-class fans who kept the game afloat for a century before the explosion in its popularity and the life-raft of television lolly (or the concrete shoes for those clubs whose credit line has recently been cut off!). More like going to the theatre, many of the new breed of football fan pay for their pricey tickets and sit back expecting to be entertained. Though they might be quick to complain out loud if not satisfied with the performance, they've become more spectator than supporter. There are few of us left who are happy to be part of the entertainment, in our attempts to assist our side in our traditional twelfth-man role. With all-seater stadia another accomplice, many of our grounds now have less atmosphere than the moon. I console myself with the thought that at least I am now able to share Ró's company wherever I go. Compared to many blokes who need to request permission for their sporting pleasures in order to skive off the weekly trip to Sainsbury's, I consider myself privileged. The fact that our Arsenal addiction comes at double the cost might be a serious financial strain, but you really cannot put a price on being able to share with someone you love all the ecstatic Arsenal moments we've been fortunate to experience these past ten years. Besides which, how much more enjoyable it is to have my missus to hug when celebrating goals, instead of trying to get my arms round the beer belly of the stranger beside me, who leaves his lovely odour of lager and fried onions for me to remember him by!

Finding an increasingly substantial sum for our two season tickets, a few weeks into every summer, is becoming a loathsome liability. We have often discussed moving to more affordable seats, in a more atmospheric part of the ground than our posh pitch. However with the West Upper being the stand I recall sitting in most frequently with my father, all those years ago, I have a sentimental attachment to the place. More importantly, we both absolutely adore being able to watch the Arsenal from our privileged position, close to the halfway line, a couple of rows from the front of the upper tier. Our seats have the benefit of being high enough to appreciate the tactical deployment of the troops, but close enough to translate the temperature on the pitch, from the sickening sound of some of the tear-jerking tackles. I am also in love with the illusion that our proximity to the proceedings actually allows me to have some influence on matters. I invariably berate the linesmen and the one lineswoman for any borderline decisions in the favour of our opponents. They may have been given a more exalted label but it certainly doesn't make them any more competent. Myself, I inherited the glorified new title of stage technician but I am still little more than a scenery *schlepper*! Then, when the official subsequently keeps his flag by his side, when one of ours is blatantly offside, I will often turn to Ró and take the credit, convinced the official is merely trying to avoid my cacophonous ear-bashing.

However, I am the epitome of self-restraint compared with the West Upper's worst offender. The raving lunatic a few rows behind us makes my ranting seem positively rational. There is a warning in every match day programme which states that the use of foul and abusive language will result in expulsion from the ground. This odd-bod must have a special dispensation for his dogmatic diatribes because the bloodcurdling invective he so often uses in his bilious, vessel-bursting volleys makes everyone in earshot blush. There was a game a few years back when old warhorse Des Walker had his head done in by this bloke's derogatory verbal diarrhoea. Now, Walker might have only had a vague notion where all this nasty noise was coming from, but there was no mistaking his intent when he eventually appeared to crack and clumped the ball in our direction. I swear he was trying to knock this blackguard's block off! On occasions, when he's gone beyond the pale and had a particularly putrid pop at an official (for example something concerning the catching of cancer) he has caused me to turn around; this crackpot comes across like a caricature, a rabid rage burning in his eyes, blue veins throbbing in his forehead and throat and spraying spittle at all those who happen to sit within the arc of his anger. I only hope that he has a wife, children and pets back home who are saved from regularly being knocked senseless because he's able to vent his spleen and any sinister traits by means of these terrace temper tantrums. Individually, no one appears too keen on tackling this nutter, but when he goes over the top nowadays hopefully he can't quite work out exactly who the wise asses are, when half a dozen if us break into a chant of: 'Arsenal loony, loony Arsenal'.

Good, bad or downright barmy, it is the regular characters who I've been sitting amongst for so many years that are the members of my Arsenal family: Ray, my neighbour, who's always ribbing me about being late; the Gucci Gooners in front, forever fretting that my doughty decibels might damage their eardrums (only at the Arsenal could one get a hard time for supporting your team by hollering too loudly!); the university student, a secretive smoker who seems to slag off all our players in the presence of his old man, his nerves shot without the calming influence of nicotine; the two old boys behind me who remind me of the old blokes on the balcony in the *Muppets*, the warm scent of cigar smoke wafting over from one of them during a hypothermic half-time break – I instinctively find myself feeling the back of my head for something horrible every time I hear the heaving rattle of his smoker's cough. Yet I don't imagine anyone is particularly delighted to be in my periphery, with the pleasure of passively smoking an entire pack of fags every game and more when I chain-smoke my way through some of the choppier moments of a match.

Whether it is urging the utmost from the Arsenal players, or abusing the officials and the opposition, I shout myself hoarse at most matches. It is my way of achieving the emotional release which often leaves me almost as exhausted as if I'd been out there playing for 90 minutes. As far as I am concerned, making my own small contribution to the atmosphere of the occasion is an integral part of the pleasure of live football. Sadly, despite my best efforts, those hair-raising moments when my voice is just one in a chorus of thousands, rising to a crescendo of tens of thousands all singing in unison, are all too few and far between in Highbury's modern incarnation. Especially in the most library-like seats in the stadium. Nevertheless, it just wouldn't feel right if we weren't surrounded by all our 'homeboys' and I am most comfortable in my Highbury home-from-home. Moreover I get my regular fix of full-blooded atmosphere by attending away games so religiously. It never fails to amaze me that the same folks who sit relatively quietly at Highbury most weeks will sing their hearts out for the lads when they find themselves in some small corner of a foreign field amidst a gang of like-minded, loyal Gooners, in their attempt to make their voices heard above those of the huge home crowd.

Over the last few years of Arsène Wenger's revolution, my team has evolved. 'Boring, boring Arsenal' have become one of the most entertaining sides in the country. It still takes a great deal of effort to follow them week in, week out, all over Britain and Europe. Yet for someone who grew up with the old-school Gunners, our exertions are without doubt worthwhile, because we are so often rewarded by witnessing football of the sort of calibre I couldn't possibly have dreamed of in the good old days. Over the years, compared to the success-starved supporters of many clubs, we have been fortunate to enjoy more than our fair share of seasons that have concluded with a cup or two. These days we often see many envious opposition fans marvelling open-mouthed at the feats of football on display, whereas previously they turned up, hoping to see their side mullah the mighty but monotonous Arsenal. Back then it was far more difficult to drag oneself out of bed at the crack of dawn on a Saturday, knowing you were facing the prospect of a painful journey of hundreds of miles, just to see a bore-draw up at somewhere like Bolton. I might not have struggled out of my pit suffering from the same sort of fervour I find I have now, but my commitment to the cause meant I was just as keen to be there, if not always by kick-off.

I have always had a healthy respect for the 'reap what you sow' ideals of karma and the clichéd principle of 'no pain, no gain'. Consequently in order to best appreciate the all too rare moments when your side scales the rarefied peaks of success, I am convinced that it is necessary to pay one's dues, by taking in plenty of troughs along the way. Fortunately the current team isn't troubled by too many troughs, but when I schlep all the way to Blackburn on a bleak Wednesday night to see a Worthless Cup collapse of an Arsenal second-11, it is because I know that when it eventually comes our way, the taste of success will be all the sweeter for my trouble.

Come to think of it, considering the dues we paid during all those years of George Graham's dour midfield dross (not to mention most of the Arsenal's mediocre midfield line-ups since the departure of Liam Brady), surely we deserve a dividend of at least a decade's worth of domination. Mind you, I dare not ponder the petrifying product of this improbable premise when applied to Spurs supporters (or those of most other clubs for that matter). Any poor Tottenham punter not old enough to be present in 1961 has endured a lifetime of pain, patiently awaiting their ascent to the peak of a Premiership prize. Perhaps they will have to resign themselves to a reward in heaven, because they certainly appear no closer to a title triumph here on earth!

There may be some Arsenal fans who are a little blasé about the high standards set by Wenger's sides, because they are unable to appreciate the feat of competing in the huge shadow cast by our northern rivals with their vastly superior resources. Meanwhile, most of us old-school Gooners regularly find ourselves sitting at Highbury, wondering if we've died and gone to heaven. After all, it wasn't so long ago that the Arsenal's aspirations in purchasing players from abroad were limited to unsuccessful attempts to sign John Collins from Celtic and the occasional bid for a sensible Scandinavian (since they were supposedly the only continental players capable of coping with the Premiership rough and tumble). It was only the arrival of a proven world beater in Bergkamp that finally confirmed the Arsenal's ability to compete with the titans of Italy and Spain for the signature of such stars at the peak of their careers. I couldn't believe this extraordinary exponent of everything that was brilliant about the 'beautiful game' was actually coming to the Arsenal and I will never forget his debut. I was far from being the only Gooner on Teesside that day, totally gobsmacked at the tantalising sight of Dennis Bergkamp actually trotting out in a red-and-white Arsenal shirt. Almost seven years later and I am still often tempted to pinch myself in order to confirm the reality of regularly witnessing Wenger's wonderful, cosmopolitan concoction, including perhaps the best midfielder on the planet, a smattering of his World Cup-winning colleagues and some of the most cultured players to come out of Sweden, Cameroon, Nigeria and Brazil.

Football fans need no excuse to exchange diverse opinions on the game. Previously, my pontificating was limited to a Gooner gabble around a pub table, or in a train carriage travelling to and from a match, until the Internet explosion. I was introduced to the marvel of the Arsenal mailing list, where I was astounded that I could opine on all things Arsenal to a couple of thousand Gooners scattered around the globe, by means of a single e-mail. I couldn't resist spouting off to such a large audience and whether I was inspired by the Arsenal's footballing feats, frustrated by the scarcity of homegrown talent from these shores and the resultant demise of the famous Arsenal spirit, depressed about the inevitable eventual last hurrah for our Home of Football, or excited about the new stadium project advancing apace, I suddenly found myself writing regular missives to the list, hindered only by my cack-handedness at the keyboard.

I was surprised to receive gratifying replies of encouragement from geographically challenged Gooners everywhere. Living little more than a Tony Adams' clearance away from Highbury (there may be little crowd noise these days, but we can hear the stadium announcer from our living room), compared to those who were stuck thousands of miles away from the love of their life, it was apparent that I brought them a flavour of the Arsenal experience, which they couldn't get from the sports reports of the regular media. Absence makes the heart grow fonder, but when it comes to the Arsenal, they become positively fanatic. My e-mails soon developed into a weekly diary which I have been e-mailing out for some years to the few hundred people who requested it. With the wall-to-wall football coverage of the media, it is possible to follow virtually every kick of the ball in the reams of coverage that appears after every match. As a consequence, I tend to avoid simply repeating details of the actual match. My writing therefore consists mostly of the sort of anecdotal tales involving the frustrations of funding my passion, the trials and tribulations on planes, trains and automobiles travelling to matches at home and abroad and the match-day superstitions and rituals familiar to most football fans.

My favourite aspect of the Internet is the network of Gooner pals I've developed all over the world, who I would have never met otherwise. When Arsenal played Dynamo Kiev, I met up with Vlad, the Ukrainian Gooner (as opposed to the Impaler!). On holiday in Kenya, we tracked down a family of Arsenal mailing-list mates in Mombasa (all the technology in the world is not much kop in Africa when the elements have done for the phone lines). I have received my favourite and extremely fresh Blue Mountain coffee from Jamaica and all sorts of gifts from countless grateful Gooners who I have been able to assist with match tickets when they've come over on a pilgrimage to The Home of Football. Not forgetting all the Irish Arsenal fans, the Green Gooners, I have come to know by means of their own mailing list (their e-mails are easily recognisable, as they are habitually discussing which pub to meet up in to watch the forthcoming match!).

The strangest side to meeting people who I have corresponded with on the Internet is that I am often at a great disadvantage. For while they might be relative strangers to me, they are often aware of all the intimate details of my life by means of my diary. On one occasion we met up with Lindsay, the teenage daughter of a lovely South Africa family. The family had come over a couple of summers prior, luckily just late enough to be able to accompany us to the first friendly of the season. Yet this time the daughter came over with her school and I had arranged a ticket for her first ever match at Highbury. Lindsay was so appreciative that she'd spent an inordinate amount of her own money on presents for us. However, along with various handmade African gifts, we were more than a little bemused when she presented us with some red boxer shorts for me and a red G-string for Róna. It turns out that Lindsay had been amused by my superstitious revelations about not changing my underwear during a winning run of games and she hoped her presents would prove lucky. Mind you, Ró doesn't subscribe to my belief that one's underclothes can affect the outcome of a football match and isn't in the habit of wearing G-strings, but even if she did, I certainly couldn't see her suffering the same one for several weeks (months if we are incredibly lucky) of a season!

Róna's brother is a broadcaster with the Irish radio station RTE. He first suggested my writing merited a wider audience and it is entirely thanks to Con that my diary has been published in *The Examiner* these past four seasons. As a consequence, there is often an Irish slant to my work. It is also thanks to the encouragement of my Internet readers that the following collection has come about. Most seasons I receive suggestions that my pieces would make a good read as a book, but although I have often thought about it, I have never actually got around to pulling my finger out. I have the Arsenal's astounding season to thank for making the decision for me. To keep each chapter in context I have added a preamble before each piece. If there is a peppercorn of the pleasure in these pages that our football has given me during the past year, then it will certainly make a good read.

1. Paying My Dues (a Tale of Pound Notes and Pain!)

It had been an extremely depressing end to the 2000–01 season. As far as the Championship was concerned, for the vast majority of Gooners the game was all but up as far back as February. After having delighted in a decade of defensive durability, courtesy of the colossuses of our fab back four, we knew the inevitable eventual demise of the dinosaurs Dixon, Bould, Adams and Winterburn would leave a gaping hole. Nonetheless, it still came as something of a shock to the system to see quite how much the Arsenal were struggling to fill their shoes. We suffered the humiliating performance of their hapless successors when we were well and truly trounced 6–1 at Old Trafford. Having conceded five goals in the first half, some around us were already slipping out of the ground at half-time, desperate to escape, as Man United went 16 points clear at the top of the table and The Theatre of Dreams became the scene of our worst nightmare.

For the more optimistic mathematicians among us, it took until mid-

ARSENAL ON THE DOUBLE

April, a month before the end of the season, for our title challenge to be conclusively terminated, on the day of a miserable 0–3 home defeat to Middlesbrough. We thought it couldn't get much worse when in the same week we crashed out of the quarter-finals of the Champions League. After beating Valencia 2–1 at home, we were left moaning up in the gods of a very steep Mestailla stadium.

Our season finally drew to its ignominious end with the FA Cup final in Cardiff. The *schadenfreude* gained from stuffing the forces of darkness from the wrong end of the Seven Sisters Road, in the semi-final at Old Trafford, was some consolation. Yet it was no panacea for the pain of Michael Owen's marvellous last-minute feats in the final.

However, as with fans of every football club, hope springs eternal at the start of every new season. With all teams starting from scratch, everyone looks to their pre-season friendlies in the hope of some sign that their pack has been shuffled to present a fantasy-filled new formula. There was much speculation over the veracity of Patrick Vieira's disappointing outbursts in the press during the summer, no doubt prompted by three seasons of playing the bridesmaid to Man United, Galatasary and Liverpool. His agent's Machiavellian machinations with Real Madrid left many of us fearing a repeat of the Nicolas Anelka saga. Securing Patrick's presence for at least another season would have been the best news of the summer, if it wasn't for the ultimate coup of capturing our North London rival's most influential player, Sol Campbell. Spurs supporters were seething at the fact that they had not only lost their captain to their deadly enemy, but that he'd departed on a free transfer. Exaggerated reports suggested that Campbell would cost the Arsenal an astronomic amount in wages, but the club didn't have to cough up a red cent to Spurs' depleted coffers. While we could appreciate their sense of outrage, wondering how we would have felt if Tony Adams had gone in the opposite direction, it wasn't going to stop us from teasing them until the cows came home.

In addition to Campbell, the arrival of Wenger's new signings Richard Wright, Francis Jeffers (seen as perhaps the solution to Thierry Henry's request for a 'fox in the box'), Junichi Inamoto and Gio Van Bronckhorst left us all eagerly anticipating the season's warm-up games.

In an age where the vast majority are only able to indoctrinate their offspring with the Arsenal religion via the television – due to the difficulty of obtaining tickets and the extremely prohibitive pricing – I always enjoy the friendly family atmosphere at places like Borehamwood and Barnet for pre-season games. It is wonderful to see the expressions of awe written across the faces of thousands of kids, in perhaps their only chance all season to see their heroes in the flesh. Amongst them was a substantial number of wide-eyed orientals, all desperate to catch a glimpse of Inamoto. With the rumours that his arrival had resulted in a contract to televise our reserve games live in Japan, many of us speculated on whether his signing had been a financial, rather than footballing decision.

Saturday, 11 August 2001

Can we put our demoralising FA Cup disappointment down to a presumptuous dunderhead at Highbury? I can't help but wonder if the timing of our season-ticket renewals was predetermined, in the hope that sadistic price increases would be swallowed up amidst the euphoria surrounding a silverware-laden sequel to our slipshod season. This presupposes that the club cares, but when our loyalty knows no bounds and even if it does, with a perpetual waiting list of wealthy mugs, why should they give a monkey's?

Time was when one could have cavorted out of Cardiff, with quarter of an hour to go, supremely confident in the Arsenal's ability to shut shop on a 1–0 lead, with another FA Cup safely ensconced in the cabinet. With a much coveted core of homegrown talent, trading on the sort of 'never-say-die' traits which used to be our own trademark, we were mugged by a bunch of opportunist Scousers. Black-and-white stripes would have been more appropriate for the side that slipped through our gaping back door with three minutes to go and stole two goals from the onion bag with the illuminated 'swag' sign.

Having heeded all the alarming travel warnings, even those of us with 'tardy' as our middle name had set out early enough to make kick-off in Cairo. So it was that we all arrived back from Cardiff to find the definitive example of adding insult to injury on our doorstep. Forewarned is supposed to be forearmed, but no matter how many years go by I never fail to be flummoxed, on this fateful day in May, by the discovery of the increasingly daunting cost of renewing our precious seats at Highbury.

This is not intended as a 'poor man/rich club' rant. When you consider what we were paying a few years back to watch the likes of Hillier, McGoldrick and Carter, the sumptuous skills on offer these days would appear value at twice the price. However, there is no denying the fact that backs of the sort of supporters who carried the sport for all those years before the advent of the TV billions are no longer broad enough to bear the batty financial burden of today. Considering that turnstile revenues are becoming just the icing on a media and merchandising cake, one would have thought that more clubs might have adopted the sort of affordable pricing policies seen at innovative clubs like Sunderland.

Sadly, the majority of other Premiership sides are pricing live football beyond the pockets of those fans who have traditionally turned up, expecting to be part of the afternoon's entertainment. Without their passion and fervour, our 'glorious game' is in danger of becoming a sterile shadow of its former self. It will no longer hold much attraction for those who, for the princely price of their ticket, expect their entertainment served up on a plate (prawn sarnies on the side!).

The Arsenal is at an important crossroads in the club's future. They are in the unaccustomed position of being dependent on our support for their visionary project because they need us to counter the highly organised and extremely vocal protests of a diverse hotchpotch of nay-saying NIMBYs and contemptible carpetbaggers of the sort who will latch on to any cause that enables them to espouse their Marxist mantras. So rare is it for the poor punters to have any pull that we should at the very least attempt to secure our own future in the 'brave new world' of the Highbury board, by forcing their agreement to a substantial proportion of 'affordable' seating and suitable concessions for kids, within the proposals for the new stadium.

While I have come to terms with the development of Ashburton Grove as a necessity if the club are to maintain and advance their position as a footballing power, I have to admit that as one of the fortunate few with a guaranteed seat at Highbury, I will not be too disappointed if the dissenters are successful in dragging the matter out through the European Courts (as long as the delay doesn't put the kibosh on the whole project). As we travel around Europe to all these wonderful modern sporting arenas, I grow increasingly sentimental about my seat at the Arsenal's ancient Home of Football.

Whether in this country, or elsewhere, there remain few top-class grounds where one is close enough to the action to be able to deduce the level of a players commitment by the crunch of a challenge, yet high enough above the pitch to have a feel for the tactics. Both Róna and I absolutely adore our seats at Highbury, considering ourselves privileged to have such a perfect view of the breathtaking ball skills of the world's best. There was a time when I would not have dared to dream that we'd be so up close and personal to the likes of Bergkamp, Henry and Vieira. In order to savour the experience for as long as possible, we will make whatever sacrifices are necessary.

Perhaps when it comes to the inevitable move to our new home, where I assume the majority of seats will be at such a distance from the players that binoculars will be required to read the expressions on their faces, we will opt for more affordable seating with the hoi polloi. 'Champagne tastes and beer money' was how my old man used to describe me and for once I appreciated this sentiment as I stared at the renewal notification. The £200 increase from last season on the cost of each seat meant that we had to find over £2,500 in less than a month. A couple of days later, as I sat poring over credit-card debts for last season's European extravagances, wondering if Róna's stockings would fit over my head, the phone rang.

At the other end of the line was a total stranger, who'd been given my number by a mutual acquaintance. He offered me seven weeks' work, for which the total remuneration amounted to exactly £30 more than the sum I desperately required. It felt like pure kismet and despite the fact that on reflection, twelve-hour days, six days a week meant that I would be working for a virtual pittance, it was too much of a coincidence for me to ignore. Thus I found myself sentenced to spending those gorgeous weeks of summer weather confined to a mini-bus in the capital's ceaseless congestion, from dawn until dusk. It was the most miserable job I have ever undertaken, as servant to supercilious stars of stage and screen and surly members of the crew, ferrying them back and forth from various locations. At best it felt like I was invisible to the ingrates on board and at worst they treated me like something nasty they had stepped in. I only endured through the motivation of my Arsenal SOS (save our seats) mission, by keeping my eye on the prize of the two little red books of vouchers, which would be my ultimate reward.

There were mornings when I leapt out of bed with the lark, so anxious was I to tease all my Tottenham pals with text messages about the treachery of their captain. Yet as the storm clouds gathered over the Vieira saga, all the portents of doom in the press left me heaving my aching bones out of my bunk, with a heavy heart. Without the prospect of Patrick plying his midfield craft I probably would have packed the job in! Superstitiously swinging past the majestic entrance to the marble halls at least twice a day, I would scan the streets for signs of some furtive footsteps, which might give a clue to some monumental signing.

I might enjoy watching Wimbledon, or the distraction of digesting another cricketing calamity, but in truth these are merely methadone for us football junkies, during the long months of June and July. In another remarkable coincidence, I was waiting impatiently for the final clap of the film-shoot clapperboard, as my purgatory came to a poignant end on the exact day of Arsenal's first friendly at Borehamwood. The words 'that's a wrap' were still ringing around the set as I hot-footed my way through North London. Forget rubbing shoulders with the stars at the wrap party, after my summer fast, I was positively salivating at the thought of this tasty appetiser, where I would party on down with debutants Jeffers and Van Bronckhorst.

The very next day it was down to the Highbury to hand over my hard-earned mullah to an extremely patient box-office pal, but sadly it was not the end of my suffering for the Arsenal cause. I have been struck down these past two weeks with excruciating sciatic pain down my left side. It seems that the heavy clutch on the mini-bus has left me with a slipped disc and I am not only doubtful for 90 minutes on a wooden seat at Barnet today, but will be fortunate to be fit for the eight-hour round trip to Boro next week. It is indeed ironic that someone as lazy as myself should be afflicted to the point where I can't sit down. My only solace during periods of relentless pain, between doses of painkillers, is that I must be paying my dues for some serious success this season. I wonder what the odds are on us doing the Double? If only I could make it down to the bookies!

2. Feast or Famine?

*Saturday, 18 August (Premiership): Middlesbrough (A) 4–0
Henry (43), Pires (87 pen.), Bergkamp (88, 90) 2nd*

What is the world coming to? The eventual demise of our Home of Football seems inevitable with the new Ashburton Grove stadium project advancing apace; no more *Match of the Day* since the BBC lost the Premier League contract and Des Lynam to ITV; the advent of pay-per-view football on Sky; and me unable to make it to our opening game of the season for the first time I can remember due to my back injury. Nevertheless, the omens were good, as the last time the Arsenal achieved such an emphatic opening-day victory was the Championship-winning season of 1997–98! Only Bolton bettered us with five goals at Leicester, which was a portent for the poor Foxes pitiful season ahead. Sadly, in a scene that would be repeated all too often in the months that followed, we ended up spending much of the second-half with only ten men, after Ray Parlour received a second yellow which ensured our red-card count was up and running. The score-line was a little flattering, with a flurry of goals in the last three minutes. In a largely unimpressive performance, at least Sol Campbell had a clean sheet to show for his Arsenal debut. Meanwhile, of those armchair fans who had not taken advantage of the reduced-price season ticket, I can't imagine there were too many prepared to pay Sky TV an exorbitant £8 per match to see Chelsea's cough start at St James' Park as they drew 1–1 with the Toons.

Monday, 20 August 2001

I finally came to terms with missing my first opening game of the season for donkey's years. On Friday my physiotherapist managed to frighten me into facing up to the seriousness of my slipped disc by recounting terrifying tales of hospital torture, which could be my fate if I am not more careful. As heartbroken as I was to have missed out on a magical first-day outing, at least as a result I should have the consolation of being able to hobble round to Highbury on Tuesday evening for our first home game.

On the first day of last season, we met up at King's Cross station with Amr, an Egyptian Gooner who, via the wonders of the Internet, had grasped the opportunity of a spare ticket for his first ever Premiership match. I distinctly recall the look of wonderment on his face in the heady atmosphere at the Stadium of Light, as the teams took to the field to the blast of fireworks, music and all the pomp of the opening-day party. Sadly, the rest of the afternoon proved to be an anticlimax and hard as we tried to put a brave face on it, the 1–0 defeat put a depressing dampener on all our hopes and expectations and made for a miserable journey back from Wearside.

It didn't stop me offering to sort out a ticket for Amr, when I heard he had managed to wangle a second trip over from Cairo, to coincide with another inaugural game in the North East. Some sort of cock-up at the club meant that our tickets didn't turn up in the post. I spent a frustrating Friday morning on the phone to Middlesbrough, tapping my way through another automated phone system – the bane of my life. All I ever want to do is speak to a human being, in this instance to confirm receipt of a fax from Arsenal. I would have been worried enough travelling all the way up to Teesside from London to discover that they hadn't heard a dickey-bird about issuing duplicate tickets. But after travelling thousands of miles to get to this game, the thought of my poor Egyptian pal encountering such problems alone, or perhaps being asked to prove he was me, left me positively petrified.

While I gave Amr detailed instructions that evening concerning the collection of the tickets, I retained some vain hope that I still might make the match and I suggested he call me again in the morning in case of a miraculous recovery during the night. In the past, blind loyalty and passion have seen me drag myself off to away matches on crutches with my leg in plaster and with pleurisy preventing me drawing breath. This should give you some idea of my current parlous predicament and when the phone rang on Saturday morning, it was all that I could do to painfully pull myself over to the receiver and inform Amr of the direction of those train connections to and from Boro which might prevent a debacle in Darlington. In the meantime I remained frustrated, flat on my back, hoping that I might at least hear the match on the radio.

ARSENAL ON THE DOUBLE

I can't tell you the relief I felt turning the radio on at three and hearing live coverage coming from the Riverside Stadium. Not being there was bad enough, but with all our hopes and aspirations for the season ahead riding on the outcome of this opening fixture, I am not sure if I could have borne the tension of listening to a different match. Worst of all are those mind-blowing moments when the sadistic presenters advise you that they will be going over to the only game that interests you, as soon as there's a break in the match they are commentating on. So you are aware an event of note has occurred, but you have to sit there and suffer, waiting to discover whether to don the sackcloth and ashes, or to run naked through the streets (if only I could!) in celebration. Being able to listen to a blow-by-blow account was a real bonus, especially considering the outcome. What's more, the commentary told a completely different tale to the all too brief highlights shown later that evening, on ITV's much maligned new footie flagship.

You would never have known it from the TV footage and the fact that three of the goals came in the last three minutes, but from what I heard on the radio and from those who were present, such was Arsenal's dominance for lengthy periods of this game the only way any of the Boro players would have got a touch would have been if they'd had a second ball to play with! As envious as I was of Amr being there, joining in with hearty Gooner celebrations that came across the airwaves loud and clear, there was a vicarious pleasure to knowing he was revelling in the real away-match experience. 'The best match I have ever been to!' was how he described an outing which more than made up for last season's disappointment and the fact that on his arrival in London the day before, he had been abused by some vindictive numbskulls as he walked down Oxford Street in his 'Campbell 23' replica shirt.

Talk about feast or famine, after being starved of real football for a couple of months, suddenly there is no escaping the wall-to-wall coverage of a live game almost every night. I succumbed to Sky's new season ticket on Sunday morning, at a cost of a further £60. I have no doubt it is just the tip of the iceberg of a pernicious pay-per-view purgatory that will eventually require footie fans to be taking out subscriptions left right and centre if they want to watch every game. As the TV companies attempt to extort some sort of return on their massive investment from the armchair fan, maybe, just maybe, they have plumbed the depths of the bottomless pit of football fans' loyalty. There is some startling evidence that perhaps the perennial Premiership boom is about to experience its first bust. Not only was there the surprising sight of 3,000 empty seats at the Riverside on Saturday, but Arsenal have also had a general sale of tickets for the first two home games, when previously one could have almost guaranteed that the limited capacity at Highbury would be sold out in an instant, to the hundred-odd thousand on the ticket-registration scheme.

Could we have possibly reached saturation point? Mind you, I will continue to stump up for the privilege of watching Ranieri's collection of individual star turns embarrassed by the combative team spirit of lesser opponents. Worth every penny in my book. Meanwhile, I shall be holding my breath in the hope that I will be fit enough to make use of my season ticket in the coming days, having slaved for seven weeks to pay for it, to the point of finding myself so incapacitated that I might not be able to sit on my seat for 90 minutes; now there's a definition of irony for you. However, all the pain will pale into insignificance (I hope), if Saturday's victory can become a springboard to a successful season.

3. Confessions of a Football Fundamentalist

Tuesday, 21 August (Premiership): Leeds (H) 1–2 Wiltord (32) 4th
Saturday, 25 August (Premiership): Leicester (H) 4–0 Ljungberg (17), Wiltord (28), Henry (77), Kanu (90) 3rd

It wasn't long before we had the wind knocked out of our sails, slumping to a defeat against Leeds in our first home game. Leeds hadn't won at Highbury since 1994 and their determination to break this run was evident from kick-off as they set about kicking anything that moved, receiving four bookings within 15 minutes. Seaman was still lining his wall up and Parlour had his back to the play as a quick-thinking Ian Harte stuck his free-kick in the net. We were back in the game three minutes later with Wiltord's equalizer. I can recall thinking it was alright when Viduka was left with one defender to beat and I looked up and saw the reassuring presence of Tony Adams. I and the rest of the stadium were shocked by the ease with which the Aussie went past our 'Mr Arsenal' to score Leeds' second. When shown a second yellow, Bowyer went nose-to-nose with ref Winter before storming off for an early bath. Mills soon followed him after one foul too many in his running battle with Ashley Cole. The Highbury crowd had delighted in Campbell's home debut early on with the additions to their repertoire of 'We got Campbell from the Lane' and 'Sol's a Gooner' but in all honesty Sol appeared overweight and a little too immobile for my liking. Despite plenty of pressure, we failed to take make the most of our numerical advantage over a nine-man Leeds and it ended up a depressing evening.

However we had little time to wallow in our defeat, with the distraction of the first-stage Champions League draw that pitched us against Panathinaikos, Real Mallorca and FC Schalke, followed by our first home triumph as we too tonked Leicester. It was an entertaining game, but a pity that the Foxes failed to turn up as the Arsenal were allowed to turn on the style by a side that already looked doomed to relegation. The only sour note on a sunny day was the sending off of Patrick Vieira after he and Dennis Wise were involved in a fairly innocuous handbags incident.

Monday, 27 August 2001

It grieves me to say that whilst my team might well be chasing the champions, I am still limping around after them. Harping on about it feels very boring, but sadly my slipped disc currently has such a stranglehold on my life that I can do little else. I could sense the mounting excitement in the Highbury manor as the eve of our first home game against Leeds approached, but I spent the day fretting over whether I would be fit enough for 90 minutes.

It might have taken longer than usual, but getting around to our seats in the West Upper was not a problem. It is sitting down that is literally such an agonising pain in the arse (and leg) that I ended up squirming my way through the first 45, unable to really savour the scintillating, fast-flowing, passing game that had most in rapture. An all too familiar failure to do damage during a period of such dominance caused some disquiet, but whether or not Wenger has found a cure for our failure to capitalize on all the chances we create it was evident to all that we are in for a season's worth of supreme entertainment.

If we had been sat behind the goal, where everyone is up and down like a jack-in-a-box as the game ebbs and flows, I might have found sufficient respite from sitting to last the whole game. Up in the West Upper the stewards are far too keen to countenance any lingering on one's feet. In order that I could concentrate on the game, I ended up hobbling home at half-time to spend the second-half in the only position I get any real comfort: flat on my back, with my head propped up sufficiently, to watch the coverage on the box in the company of Andy Gray. Mind you, between Leeds' spoiler tactics and the now almost annual bout of over-zealous refereeing, this opening-day party was well and truly pooped!

Blackburn's fight back against Man United the following night, in a fantastic game of football, came as some solace. However, as with United's 92nd-minute equaliser on Sunday at Villa Park, they managed to spoil my evening by turning defeat into a draw with another quick free-kick, resulting from Craig Short's sending off. Some would put it down to a 'never say die' spirit, but for my better half this is only further evidence that some nameless knight has sold his soul to the devil.

On the day of the Champions League draw in previous seasons I have been sitting at my computer for hours, on-line to two or three airlines at the same time. Usually there is only a short window of opportunity after the actual dates of the games being announced and before the conniving travel companies have conjured up the disappearance of all cheap seats on any convenient flights. So distracted was I last Thursday that I had to be disturbed from the sanctuary of a snooze to discover the results of the draw. There followed an anxious couple of hours, wondering if the fates would favour us with a trip to Mallorca and Athens, where the September sun would be in the sky and we could wear T-shirts and shorts, or whether we'd be lumbered with October outings in sweaters and socks.

If I'd been able, I would have danced a jig of joy, as the gods smiled down on us Gooners with the dates of both these away games. Despite being able to sit at my computer and surf the Internet for only a few minutes at a time (I am having to type this in short spells of suffering!), I managed to find cheap flights to Majorca. I only hope that I am not being too presumptuous about my back problem healing in time, but hopefully we will be frolicking in the sun for five days, between away games at Chelsea and Fulham. I would not have dreamt of missing either of these games, but I have decided to sacrifice Derby County away in order that we might pick up a last-minute package holiday to Greece, to coincide with our appointment with Panathinaikos.

Considering that we couldn't manage a holiday during the close season and a crowded fixture list made the prospect of a break all the more unlikely, it could not have worked out better if I had chosen the draw myself. Mind you, if the omnipotent one really wanted to show me a sign that we are his chosen people, the match that I am least likely to travel to, against Schalke in Germany, would have coincided with the Jewish New Year, instead of our home game against this side. As always this annual high holy-day/fixture clash will leave me with the dilemma of which particular temple to pray in.

Currently it would seem that this seven-day-a-week sport has become a religion that leaves no room for faith of any other kind. Friday found me attending to my devotions watching Liverpool in the Super Cup and this was the start to a weekend where, apart from the occasional short walk with our new puppy, I have been an absolute football fundamentalist. Come Saturday morning, I was so concerned that my slipped disc should disrupt our encounter with Leicester that I phoned the club to ask if I could stand in the disabled enclosure. Unfortunately, you cannot gain admittance without the obligatory wheelchair.

En route to the ground I met up with my Egyptian pal. Considering the eight players Amr had seen sent off – on his trip over for the first two games of last season and the two games thus far of his current visit – I should have had the presence of mind to place some money on at least a couple more red cards! At least I managed to last the 90 minutes, thankfully lingering by the bulkhead on our way out, and got to witness Kanu score our last-minute fourth goal. Subsequent to my exertions, I spent the evening flat on my back, sniggering, as Real Madrid's hundreds of millions of pounds' worth of individual players succumbed to Valencia's superior team spirit.

I continued to smirk come Sunday morning, on hearing of the surprising departure of Jaap Stam. Perhaps Fergie truly is favoured by darker forces. He must be if he thinks he can flog his best defender without affecting United's fortune. Or else he feels they are more capable of scoring a whole lot more goals than they are likely to concede, without a stable central-defensive partnership.

If one live Premiership game on a Sunday wasn't enough, we now have two. I guess we should have some pity, as there is now no respite for those poor weekend football widows. Yet not only has Sky's pay-per-view provided two tremendous games so far, the more points I see United drop, the better value Sky's season ticket appears! Although as far as football on TV is concerned, a quote from the Bard's *Twelfth Night* comes to mind: 'Give me excess of it, that surfeiting the appetite may sicken and so die.'

For the footie fanatic, we had the sacrament of Seville versus Barca for vespers, on Sunday evening – a comforting climax of Kluivert, Rivaldo et al. And as I write, Liverpool are about to kick-off at Bolton. Capable of doing little else, I guess I will just have to roll over, lie back and suffer.

4. New Season, New-look Team . . . Same Old Story?

Saturday, 8 September (Premiership): Chelsea (A) 1–1 Henry (17) 4th

After a week when Wenger got his knickers in a complete twist because the French connection were forced to fly all the way to Chile for a pointless friendly, we welcomed back our cosmopolitan contingent from all four corners of the globe. In reality, England had overcome the most ordinary German side seen in many a year. Yet on paper (specifically the tabloids) suddenly Sven was being lauded as our saviour. I suppose it was more than appropriate that Spunky played a pivotal part in the 1–5 mauling at the Olympic Stadium in Munich. After those 30 years of hurt, the red tops were roaring about the game as if it was the second coming!

Meanwhile the ignoramuses amongst the English press opined about 'the luck of the Irish' at Lansdowne Road. It was regrettable that all those flair players and the fun-seekers of the fabulous Orange Army would be absent from the World Cup as a result, but this fact was of little consequence in Dublin, where the craic was at 90 after they had done for the Dutch. I might be accused of bias, but in the context of a much tougher group and the comparative resources, this 1–0 to the Boys in Green was by far the greater achievement.

Following a blighted season spent warming a bench in Barcelona, Manu Petit reappeared on the Premiership stage as one of Ken Bates' ballerinas. There had been much speculation about him returning to Highbury, until we heard from Wenger to say that he was not for turning the clock back. While we all abhorred the idea of Petit appearing in the blue of Chelsea, the memories of his majestic performances in red and white remained so fresh that he didn't come in for the sort of stick from us Gooners that fickle football fans usually inflict on those players who have deserted their cause. Perhaps he would find some peace of mind amongst the prima donnas at Stamford Bridge, where he could turn it on with the rest of them when the mood took him.

There was a rare appearance for the centre-back partnership of Adams and Keown, as Sol was rested but the protagonists whose tempers have tainted recent contests between these two teams were noticeable by their absence. Dennis Wise had departed to Leicester, Vieira was suspended and with Dixon still out injured he wasn't able to renew biannual hostilities with Graham Le Saux. It was nevertheless a hotly contested derby and though the Arsenal's class told, they couldn't make it count where it mattered most. After Henry had put us in front early on, Hasselbaink had a goal ruled out for offside and then equalised from the spot, after Keown was adjudged to have brought Zola down in the box. There was more wrangling when, to our immense delight, the Chelsea goal-scorer was sent off for elbowing Keown with 20 minutes to go. Hasselbaink's suspension was eventually rescinded by a sitting of the FA's controversial video panel.

Elsewhere Newcastle heaped more misery on Steve McClaren by beating his Boro side 1–4 in the North East Derby at the Riverside. Ferguson rested some of his other internationals but Veron was on song, scoring his first goal at Old Trafford in United's 4–1 win over Everton. Yet it was Sam Allardyce who made a mockery of all the pre-season predictions. He swamped the Bolton midfield with five men at Elland Road, where they held on for a 0–0 draw to remain above their more illustrious rivals; Bolton were now two points clear at the top of the table.

Everyone at Highbury had read the earlier stories about Polish goalkeeper Jerzy Dudek's imminent arrival at the club, so we all had a wry smile about his disastrous debut at Anfield as Liverpool lost 1–3 to Villa. Steven Gerrard is one of my favourite non-Arsenal players but this match sticks in my memory for his disgustingly reckless challenge on Boateng, for which he was rightly red carded.

Monday, 10 September

I am looking forward to our forthcoming fixture at Fulham. For the sake of nostalgia, I almost went for the cheaper option of standing tickets, since the impending redevelopment of the Cottage means we might never again have the opportunity to stand at a Premiership football match. Blighted by my back problems, still unable to sit, I am beginning to regret that I didn't. With our flights to Palma already booked and with me still flat on my back, I began to panic last week that I might not be up to travelling. As a last resort and in the hope of a miraculous recovery by the weekend (if the boy Beckham can do it, why not me?), I checked in to hospital on Thursday afternoon for a cocktail epidural injection under general anaesthetic (and in case your thoughts mirror the corny wisecracks I have been forced to suffer, I shall respond in kind: it's a boy, 9 lbs, doing very nicely!).

Saturday's visit to Stamford Bridge became a dry run for Majorca. London derbies may be two a penny these days, but it is only our encounters with Spurs and Chelsea that inspire the sort of malevolent passions of a true derby game. It would take such a must-see match to make me want to recapture my misspent youth by venturing down into the dank depths of the London Underground. It may have meant that I wasn't forced to spend an hour or so suffering in a car seat, in traffic, but as always, there was a price to pay. It was the foreigners I felt most sorry for, as the train crept out of each station with every cubic centimetre increasingly crammed with Chelsea fans. The image of bewildered tourists trapped in a tube train by the blue-shirted beer bellys of some of the British Movement's more bellicose bovver boys hardly befits London at its best.

I have a terrible weakness for bringing back all sorts of tat as souvenirs from our football trips abroad. This stuff invariably ends up collecting dust in a corner reserved for an Everest-like mountain of memorabilia. I never dreamt I would find a use for my Milanese memento of our Super Cup encounter in the San Siro, seven years since, but there I was feeling something of a prat as we queued for the turnstile at the Bridge, cushion – in the colours of AC Milan – in hand, hoping it might enable me to sit for 90 minutes. I shouldn't have bothered!

For all its superficial, modern splendour, Stamford Bridge remains dilapitated mutton dressed up as lamb as far as away fans are concerned. On arrival, you can't help but admire the architectural vista of the Chelsea Village complex, but this soon gives way to the malodorous stench of burgers, beer and sweaty fans, in the craziest of tunnels, beneath the '70s nightmare construction of their East Stand. Before, during and immediately after, home and away fans are thrown together in the sort of proximity where I am surprised it does not 'go off' at every game. This East Stand was built before the word 'sightlines' had an entry in the dictionary of stadia construction. Arsenal fans are always lumbered with one of the lousiest views anywhere in the league. Though we are often penalized by price increases for what some clubs call a 'Category A' fixture, I felt well and truly fleeced having to fork out £35 at Chelsea.

Usually my shrieks of 'Siddown!' are amongst the most cacophonous complaints when stuck in the lower tier of these old-style terraces. It is frustrating, because if everyone remained seated we would all be able to see the entire game. Sadly the sheep instinct seems to take over and we end up like 3,000 jacks-in-a-box, depending on which end of the ground the ball is at. So often only the tallest and the quickest to react get to view the most crucial moments of the match. For once I remained firmly in the camp of those who refuse to remain seated, grateful for the fairly frequent relief from red-hot-poker pain in my backside (despite my cushion!). Yet I found the deplorable abuse of polite and amiable stewards by some of the more ignorant Arsenal fans quite embarrassing. It was only when they managed to keep us seated for more than a couple of minutes and I was forced to seek some respite, standing at the back, that I really began to appreciate their persistence at fighting this losing battle. Many of the poor sods who were unfortunate to find themselves in the back five rows would have seen more of the game if they had listened to it on the radio. Not only did they have a dreadful view of the pitch, between the heads of the thousands standing in front of them, but every time the ball went above head height, it was obscured by the concrete ceiling, so that one had to play 'Spot the Ball' to try and guesstimate where it would come down.

Talking of which, from our view of the two whole blocks of empty seats in the West Stand opposite and the lack of any signs of life in many of the million-pound corporate boxes, Chelsea's dandy highwayman is running out of victims. Perhaps they've all gone for the cheaper option of watching at home on Chelsea's TV channel? I am sure they could fill the empty seats, if only for appearances' sake, but then this would require a generous gesture on the part of Chelsea PLC.

With regard to the matter of this ball game's possible bursting bubble (give anything enough hot air!), it seems that Arsenal still had 100 tickets for Tuesday's match in Majorca, on sale Saturday morning. When I booked our flights, I was not only concerned that I might not be fit enough to travel, but I was also certain that we'd end up in a ballot, with at least a couple of thousand Gooners applying for a meagre allocation of 700 tickets. Instead of being ridiculously relieved to receive a call confirming our tickets were ready for collection, I should have been shrewd enough to make them an offer for the exorbitantly priced (by continental standards) £40 seats.

As far as I am concerned, Saturday's result was two points dropped, in exactly the same way we wasted points too casually early last season, hoping to catch up further in. From my rose-tinted perspective, all our fast-flowing, entertaining football was once again undone by the lack of 'fox-in-the-box' finishing. In this respect, none of us could understand the sense in leaving an in-form Francis Jeffers out of the squad completely. Also, Martin Keown did not really do us any favours when he assisted in Hasselbaink's sending off. Considering our best scoring chances came when hitting Chelsea on the break it did not help to have Zola left up alone, with nine others behind the ball. As for Manu Petit, he put in a stout and skilled performance in the September sunshine, but I have to wonder: how long will it be before he begins moaning about massive fixture pile-ups come the dark midwinter?

Hopefully by the time you read this, we will have cast all our cares away in the Majorcan sunshine, retaining plenty of optimism about our Champions League prospects. That is, fingers crossed I can last a couple of hours, strapped into the cramped confines of a charter-flight seat.

5. It's Not a Matter of Life and Death

Tuesday, 11 September (Champions League): Real Mallorca (A)
0–1
Saturday, 15 September (Premiership): Fulham (A) 3–1
Ljungberg (17), Henry (82), Bergkamp (90) 1st

The less said about our opening performance in the Champions League the better. Considering the game should never have gone ahead and since football is not played in a vacuum, I can only assume the players were as distracted as we were by the dreadful developing tragedy in

New York. We never looked like getting back into the game after Ashley Cole's dismissal and the resulting goal from the spot kick.

Obviously it didn't seem quite so important at the time, but the Arsenal soon got this defeat abroad out of their system with a victory at Craven Cottage. Between the toothpick chewing Tigana, Wenger and all the other Gallic flair on offer, it made for extremely entertaining fare in a very open game. After Fulham's £4.5 million signing, Malbranque, equalized, for a long time it looked as though all our efforts were only going to amount to a point, until we finally wrapped up all three late on. With Roy Keane receiving his ninth red card of his career as Manchester Utd sank to a 4–3 defeat at St James' Park, we were sitting pretty at the top on Saturday night, if only until Leeds beat Charlton at the Valley the following day.

Monday, 17 September 2001

So far this season I have succumbed to my weakness for splashing out a few quid at the match-day stalls around Highbury just the once. I was unable to resist the addition of a glimmering portrayal of Vieira dressed as a gladiator. I have managed to keep to my 'one in, one out' bargain with Ró, however, by disposing of a T-shirt tribute to the five-minute wonder that was Glenn Helder.

When we travel to football on foreign shores, sadly – like the player himself – the couple of favourite tops with the number 10 on the back usually remain at home in Highbury. With his fear of flying, there is little point to being a walking poster promoting the feats of Dennis Bergkamp to our adversaries abroad. My crisp, new sartorial representation of our Gallic gladiator might have made it into my suitcase last Sunday, for our trip to Majorca, but for specific reasons it has invariably been the same half-dozen tops that I have trundled across the continent these past eight years. There is the fashion item, in pleasant pastel shades, that can be worn without fear of attracting a beating from the baton of some overtly barbaric bobby, yet, with an inconspicuous red cannon embroidered on the chest, I am instantaneously recognisable to other Gooners as being of the faith. If I wore what to me is still a nasty nylon replica shirt, it is likely Róna and I wouldn't be able to meander to the stadium at our own pace, taking in the sights and sounds. We'd probably be herded with all the others in conspicuous colours – like sheep to the slaughter – separated from the locals by coppers whose disdainful attitude suggests they are determined to avoid contact for fear of catching CJD from those they consider unruly English animals.

Another favourite, for when the climate is not nearly so tense, is a bright red T-shirt which proudly proclaims my allegiance to one and all. However, it is the plagiarised version of Shankly's famous quote, printed across the front, that is often the reason I choose to wear it. It reads: 'Arsenal . . . It's not a matter of life and death . . . It's more important than that!' Worn with this whole message showing it is my way of expressing to others that I am the sort of nutter who would follow his team to hell and back (if we happened to draw Hades from the Champions League hat!). However with the last phrase hidden by the waistband of my trousers, I have occasionally worn this T-shirt as a somewhat futile gesture, a token of my disapprobation of the xenophobic Arsenal fans who travel abroad intent on insulting the locals and rubbing them up the wrong way with their misplaced patriotism.

We were standing at a bar opposite Majorca's vast cathedral in the capital of Palma, last Tuesday (completely horizontal or vertical remain the only comfortable positions I can manage), watching the world go by and the dispersal of coach-loads of Gooner day-trippers. While we satiated our sweet desire for sugar and caffeine with donuts and *café con leche*, the Arsenal fans outside were merrily plying themselves with their preferred poison. Intent on their customary boozy objective, it came as no surprise when the bar owner announced he had run out of the big glasses needed for their *cervezas grande*. I was praying that this copious *cerveza* consumption would not detract from the merriment and result in an all too familiar deterioration in the mood, when I received a text message about the collision at the World Trade Centre.

With CNN available on the television in our hotel room, we hurried back and spent the rest of the day aghast at the terrifying tragedy unfolding on the screen. We were watching an incomprehensible evil. If it had been a movie about a high-tech world where men armed with razor blades and cardboard cutters could wreak such devastation, it would have hardly been credible. These mad mullahs could have targeted any number of symbols of American life and had a similar psychological impact, without such wanton loss of innocent lives. As news of the tragedy gathered pace with each plane crash, my thoughts turned to the right-wing military muscle that had paved George W Bush's presidential victory. More lunatics, who might have been forcing Bush's hand towards the button of retaliation first and asking questions later. During the development of this desperate drama, it did occur to me that the end of the world might be extremely nigh.

Only a day prior, lying beside the rooftop pool of our hotel, with 80 degrees of bliss beating down on my slipped disc, I had found myself locked in an excruciating muscle spasm by foolish sun-induced thoughts of sex. It occured to me that if we only had three minutes to live, I'd be well and truly bolloxed. Despite the passing of the threat of an immediate apocalypse, with my thoughts of a fireman's report of those who had dived to their deaths from hundreds of floors up and the thousands buried under the resulting rubble, I was not alone in having absolutely no enthusiasm for the match. I certainly couldn't think of anything quite as crass as wearing that T-shirt. Whether it was right or wrong, to my mind it would have been a genuine act of solidarity if the matches that night had been cancelled, as opposed to the gesture of cancelling them the following day. Forget the fans – when have UEFA ever given a frig for our concerns. More likely it was their fealty to the TV stations that guided their tardy reaction.

I asked the barman at the hotel to write down in Spanish 'I have a bad back', in order that I might persuade the police at the game to allow me to stand. In spite of my best attempts to explain, the taxi driver shot some concerned looks at the dark-skinned passenger, lying prostrate in the back of his cab, as we travelled to Palma's brand new stadium. Apart from Ashley Cole's dismissal and the resulting goal, I remember nothing else from the game. I am never much kop at recalling our matches, but in this instance my brain has been completely occupied by the images of lower Manhattan. Suffice to say that, in the review of the match on a German TV channel, there wasn't a single Arsenal move deemed worthy of showing!

On the flight out to Majorca, the stewardesses had kindly let me stand, apart from during landing and taking off. Coming home on Friday, we were returning in a disturbingly different world. A world where, on arrival at the airport, it occurred to me that my middle-eastern colouring might not be advantageous (mercifully I have bright blue eyes). I could see some disconcerted faces as I stood at the front of the plane home. After take-off, in a slight confrontation with the stewardess, I explained that I could not sit, whilst knowing that they could hardly throw me off. The only noticeable instance of the shutting of the stable door after the horses have bolted, was that the door to the cockpit remained locked the entire journey.

We had arranged our trip specifically to be back in time for the match at Craven Cottage. Although this was the one game of the season where I might legitimately stand on one of the last terraces designed for this purpose remaining in top flight football, come Saturday, I couldn't rustle up the enthusiasm to put myself through the pain involved in just getting across London and back. In spite of my back trouble, we had travelled all the way to Majorca to watch the Arsenal play and yet now I was prepared to listen to the radio commentary of a match a few miles from home. If we have been transformed in the aftermath of last Tuesday's historic tragedy, perhaps now there is nothing that is quite as important as all that?

6. Disheartened by Highbury's Hilfiger Homeys

Wednesday, 19 September (Champions League): FC Schalke (H)
3–2 Ljungberg (33), Henry (35, 47 pen.)
Saturday, 22 September (Premiership): Bolton (H) 1–1 Jeffers
(74) 2nd

Thank heavens we bounced back from our nightmare start in the Champions League with a thrilling home victory against the Germans. The match lingers in the memory as a result of the incredible vocal support of the small band of Schalke fans, who put the home crowd to shame. Their team almost did as well as the fans and could have been three up in the first ten minutes. Fortunately we managed to score twice to settle our nerves after such a ragged start and when Henry scored our third after Vieira had been pulled down by their goalie, the Gooners behind the goal sang 'We're gonna win 5–1' – optimistically hoping for a repeat of England's outstanding score-line in Munich. It proved a little previous when Schalke pegged us back to 3–2 with 30 minutes left on the clock and, though we had plenty more chances, it was anything but a comfortable victory. Fans at Highbury caught their first glimpse of Inamoto, when he came on for the last 15 minutes.

As many pundits' favourites for relegation fodder, Bolton had put a few noses out of joint by hijacking top spot in the table. However, it was assumed that they would be handing us the league leadership by the time they departed Highbury. Yet no one bothered to tell Bolton. In the face of an all-out assault on their goal, they defended with extreme resolve, even after going down to ten men with an hour still to play. They finally succumbed when Jeffers came on as sub and scored his debut goal. Even then Bolton still could have pulled off a shock result with at least two other breakaways in addition to the one that eventually led to the equalizer. The Arsenal might have put on a show of class with some sexy football, but all too often our attacks would flounder on some unnecessary over-elaboration; all foreplay and no orgasm! It was left to Ricketts to show us how to finish with the most conclusive move of the day.

After limping off against Chelsea, Tony Adams' appearance against Bolton would be his last in the league for a long six months. It was the start of a plague of persistent injuries that seemed to strike down most members of our squad at one time or another, particularly the back line. Any European euphoria was short lived, as we proceeded to drop another two precious home points in the league. There was the consolation that most of our competitors were doing likewise, thus ensuring we stayed in contact at the top of the table.

Monday, 24 September 2001

If a football audience is supposed to represent a cross-section of the public as a whole, is it any wonder the world finds itself in its current precarious predicament? I was as gutted as any of the 30-odd thousand at Highbury on Saturday when, after having scored a goal which felt like it was never going to come, we let the ten valiant men of Bolton back into the game by conceding an equaliser. In fact, as our opponents repelled wave after wave of Arsenal attack in those frantic last few minutes, I was stomping back and forth between the exit and my pitch in the North Bank, whacking myself over the head in frustration with my match-day programme. Like the hordes of 'part-time supporters' already on their way out, trying to beat the traffic, I almost couldn't bear to watch the dying throes of two crucial dropped points. And yet I have seen enough last-gasp winners in my time that I would not dream of departing prior to the dulcet tones of the lady with the eating disorder (aside from the fact that our front door is only a five-minute walk away).

It was the chorus of general disapproval given to the participants in our afternoon's entertainment as they exited the field that I found so disappointing. I suppose it is the high level of expectation that gobbles up any generosity of spirit in the Highbury faithful. Some of our players might not have played to their full potential and could have been guilty of insufficient guile, but since there was no lack of effort on the majority's part, they did not deserve to be booed off the pitch. In times past and still at certain more hospitable homes of football, the incredibly resolute defending of our more humble opposition would have merited a gracious round of applause.

Limping home, at a pace prescribed by my eighth week of excruciating back pain, I figured I had far more reason to be pissed off with our performance than most of the pundits perambulating past me. Forgive me for boring you with the bane of my bad back, but it is hard not to feel bitter when I am lying on my front in order to type this piece.

I overheard a huddle of distinctly Essex-looking lads in their Hilfiger threads having a go at Thierry Henry and his decidedly 'fancy Dan' tactics, the same fickle fans who were hailing last week's goal hero. Others were laying into 'the horse', Oleg Luzhny, who defended more like a donkey. Everybody blamed our inability to batter down Bolton's wall. Not once did I hear a semblance of appreciation for the steadfast spirit shown by Sam Allardyce's side, the concrete that binds the bricks in this wall. Perhaps this is the prohibitive price of watching live football or the fear of failing to retain the place in the upper echelons of the Premiership that brings with it Champions League football? If recent events on this troubled planet have left any lasting impressions, it is their effect on my perspective. After an afternoon of healthy entertainment, in the fresh air, with no one hurt, or dying, I couldn't abide the gauche grumbling of these miserable Gooners.

I returned home in time to hear our manager state his preference for playing 11 v. 11 and how he blamed the lack of intelligence that resulted in his side chasing a second goal, to the detriment of the protection of their lead. Since the negligible ambition Bolton displayed with eleven on the field disappeared completely when they were reduced to ten, I have to agree that the ref did us no favours with the sending off. However, I can't help but wonder as to the astuteness of Arsène Wenger's reasoning. Professor Arsène may possess the acumen to be able to quote the Opta percentages of each of his players (and probably most of the Premiership) from memory, but he sometimes seems to have his head shoved so far into his statistics that he can't see the glaringly obvious.

Like many defensively minded teams visiting Highbury, Bolton managed to make it as hard as possible for us to play our way through the number of men they got behind the ball. Not for the first time, we ended up with four strikers on the field, with Wenger's battering-ram belief that eventually the weight of numbers would hold sway. To my mind it is simple. If we have spent most of the match unable to break through the defensive barrier, surely there must come a time to try and go around it? Since the departure of Overmars, the Arsenal have been bereft of a world-class winger. While none of Wenger's purchases appear to have addressed this problem, we have Pennant in our squad – a fearless young fledgling, who happens to be one of England's brightest prospects. Without even a player on the bench as an option, the mighty Arsenal are, in effect, a team of wingless wonders. I find it hard to believe that with all the millions the club has spent, building up such a talented armoury, the team can take to the field without a single player suitably qualified to supply them with ammunition.

Talking of money, with visitors over from Dublin for the first time this season, I was horrified to discover that the face value of tickets for seats in the West Upper have been increased to a frightening £50! As they had expressed their gratitude with a present of a bottle of whisky, I was truly embarrassed to take a ton off them for two tickets to a football match. Being on the halfway line, they are the top-priced seats and our Irish pals would have otherwise probably paid more to a tout, for a poorer pitch. Yet I imagine you can now get a seat at the Royal Opera House for less (where the footie might not be up to much, but the singing at Highbury sucks by comparison).

I opted for a poorer view of Saturday's game, since a sympathetic steward behind the goal allowed me to stand for the duration (I even managed a little lie down in the first-aid room at the break). Despite an awkward perspective of events at the opposite end of the pitch, it occurred to me that for almost a grand less each, every season, we could avail ourselves of all amenities of this modern stand. Having slipped out before the break, for something to wash down some painkillers, I was flabbergasted to find young kids already queuing at the in-house computer-game consoles, far keener on virtual footie than the real McCoy! But then who knows, we might soon find ourselves at a new 60,000-seater stadium altogether. If there is one thing I have noticed on the round-the-clock, subscription television coverage, it is an abundance of empty seats at stadia, home and abroad. If it is indeed the hiss of a bursting football bubble I begin to hear and the cyclical nature of things proves the gloom mongers' predictions of a world recession correct, then perhaps at least I can seek solace in the fact that our seats at Highbury might be safe for some years yet. The entertainment on offer is marvellous, it is some of the company I am not so certain about!

7. Two Goals Doth not a Season Make (Especially at Bleedin' Derby!)

Wednesday, 26 September (Champions League): Panathinaikos (A) 0–1
Saturday, 29 September (Premiership): Derby (A) 2–0 Henry (21, 63 pen) 1st

A second disastrous defeat in the Champions League out in Athens left me wondering if I'd been somewhat presumptuous to think that by not caning our credit cards to get to Greece, I might be able to tax the plastic for some of the tastier trips which might crop up in the second stage. The only result of the week was that at least I didn't end up coughing up even more TV subscription charges. There was a time when the world of commerce could count on the blind loyalty of football fans in order to fleece the wool off our backs. Despite the incessant advances of their advertising, perhaps it was a sign of the changing times that I was amongst the millions of discerning viewers who decided we could live without live coverage of every single Champions League match and the turgid diet of Nationwide football offered by the ill-fated ITV Digital.

However the month ended on an upbeat note, with a relatively easy victory up at Pride Park. Matthew Upson might have made a less than successful return to action in Europe after being sidelined for so long due to serious complications with his broken leg, but the injuries to Adams and Campbell ensured his long-awaited comeback in the league. David Seaman's troublesome shoulder finally resulted in Richard Wright making his full debut and with Francis Jeffers making only his second start of the season, Arsène was able to proudly proclaim his achievement in putting a team out with an average age of 24. Unfortunately Franny (our supposed 'fox in the box') limped off two minutes into the second half, to spend the remainder of the season in the treatment room, apart from rare appearances on the subs bench. His prolonged absence left many Gooners questioning the wisdom of paying Everton £8,000,000 for a youngster with a 'chronic' ankle problem. Another card-happy referee sent Martin Keown off with 30 minutes to go. The cocky chant of 'We've only got ten men' coming from the Arsenal end would become an all too familiar refrain!

Though I was devastated that my state of debilitation meant me missing the trip to Derby, at least there was some solace in being able to watch the score updates on TV. A total collapse at Tottenham saw them going from 3–0 up at half-time to losing 3–5 to Man United, apparently causing one potty Spurs punter to part with a £55,000 bet made at the break! Once again we only had Saturday evening to savour the heady heights of top spot, as Leeds leapfrogged us on Sunday.

Monday, 1 October 2001

After years of hardly missing more than the odd match every season, my unending enforced absence suddenly has me scared of turning into the sorry excuse for a supporter that is the armchair fan. Actually, a more precise description would be 'a lying flat on the lounge floor ligger', since I continue to be prevented from sitting, by the pain of my slipped disc. Considering the Arsenal's abysmal effort (or absolute lack thereof!) in Athens last week, one might have thought I would be grateful to have avoided our goal-shy gadabout in Greece. Yet facing up to being force-fed such flaccid football would have been far less of a fag in the hundred-degree heat of an Athenian autumn. We could at least have sought solace in this Champions League bonus of Greeks bearing the gift of an opportunity to sneak off for a fortnight stretched out in the Mediterranean sunshine.

Instead of being able to recharge our batteries, before bearing the brunt of a grey British winter, I spent two days before this game battling with my irrational bent to litter-up our living room with more wires and yet another black box to sit atop our TV. Even though we already have almost every available sport channel, both interactive and vegetative, faced with the frequent full-frontal assault of their fallacious advertising, I was just another feeble football-loving victim, dying to be fleeced! The slick telephone salesman at ITV Digital's call centre (the modern-day euphemism for an office chock full of banks of super-intelligent computers that can never cope with the fast-finger speeds of their pre-programmed employees) came awfully close to committing me to signing my life away, with their somewhat glib guarantee of 48-hour delivery, installed and in tune, in time for Wednesday night's whistle.

Thankfully, their sensitive software was not fooled by my fumbling attempt to invent a fictitious persona. Despite feigning surprise about a brief flirtation with this company in its former On Digital guise, at our address, I could hear the pennies of the poor salesman's commission drop as he dejectedly advised me of his on-screen demand for a deposit. He might have put the mockers on his sale and my match, but he couldn't possibly know that he might just have kept the Arsenal involved in European competition (hopefully with a little help from Thierry Henry et al.)!

It was two years back that I was the first (and probably only) person on our block to subscribe to On Digital. If we couldn't afford to make it to the odd match abroad, I didn't want to be forced down the pub, to watch exclusive live broadcasts. However, no sooner had their man turned up at our door, with our free digibox (they were struggling to give them away at the time!), than we were knocked out of this competition. The Arsenal fell through a trap door, which eventually led us all the way to the final of the far less prestigious UEFA cup. You'll forgive me if I gloss over our disastrous Danish encounter with Galatasary, save to say that because this tournament was broadcast live on terrestrial TV, our new digibox almost instantly became defunct. Naturally I cancelled our subscription and requested the return of their good-for-nothing gadget. The irony was that we spent nine months cursing this clutter, until the Arsenal qualified for the Champions League again and I became reluctant to relinquish it. Then came the knock at our door.

Considering our already parlous predicament in Europe's premier competition, it occurred to me that I could safely rely on sod's law to stick the knife in once more, the moment I re-subscribed. Moreover, at a cost of an additional £20 a month for the privilege, on top of already being milked 12 times a year by Murdoch's monkeys to the tune of more than £30, squeezed for our last drop with the irresistible extortion of their new £60 subscription for a season ticket (or the preposterous charge of £8 per view) and now bombarded daily by literature from Homechoice, proposing more pay-per-view perfidy with delayed broadcast of any match of our choice, even this football crazy camel's back cannot cope with so many, costly straws. Who knows, there may soon come a time when the prohibitive price of attending live matches will prove cheaper than stopping at home.

Although I had an invitation to spend last Wednesday night lying/standing on a nearby friend's already crowded living room floor, I ended up dragging our poor puppy around the streets for 80 minutes, as I listened on my tranny. My friends must have caught a fright at the face in their window, from where I managed to watch the last few minutes by feeding the pup a steady stream of placatory treats. I'd arrived at the death out of some superstitious sense that by watching, instead of listening, I could somehow affect events in Athens. I'm not sure which dumb animal was being kind to the other.

David Seaman was not alone in needing an MRI scan last week. Having gone through the gamut of alternative therapies, surgery seems to be my only hope of salvation, if only to be able to sit and enjoy a pain-free football match (what else is there?). So considering my condition and the general, gloomy Gooner mood, I rationalised on Friday that I couldn't face standing on a train to Derby and back, with the risk of being persecuted by a Pride Park steward, who couldn't appreciate my need to stand. Under normal circumstances the fact that I might have expected a dispirited bore-draw would not be a factor, as the travelling fan has to suffer the rough, to really appreciate the smooth.

And yet there is currently a perceptible air about the Arsenal camp, perhaps evident in certain players' lack of passion, that suggests a deal of disquiet all round. So when the phone rang during *Football Focus*, with reports of hail and the usual motorway hell on the M1, I was strangely content with having stopped at home. Obviously the moment Henry's free-kick hit the back of the net and the chants of my fellow fans could be heard on the radio, I was as sick as the proverbial parrot not to have been present. Just as one swallow does not make a summer, two goals against a debilitated Derby do not make a season. The Arsenal will have to sit atop the pile for a lot longer than 24 hours for me to be convinced this is a true reflection of the current climate at our club.

8. We Gotta Be in It to Win It

Saturday, 13 October (Premiership): Southampton (A) 2–0 Pires (5), Henry (73) 3rd
Wednesday, 16 October (Champions League): Panathinaikos (H) 2–1 Henry (23, 52)

England had assured their progress to the World Cup after Beckham's wonder-strike against Greece, while the Irish had beaten Cyprus 4–0 and were waiting to find out who they would face in the play-offs. The focus returned to domestic and Champions League matches.

Our first trip to St Mary's, Southampton's modern new stadium, was made easier by a home ground hoodoo which prevented the South Coast side from winning for nearly half the season. At last it would seem that stadia architects are paying proper attention, as the acoustics lent themselves to the sort of atmosphere that is all too often absent from many newly built grounds. I personally christened the new place by taking a pee during the break, which was a novelty in itself. Two toilets into a couple of thousand well-watered away fans just didn't go at the decrepit old Den. Nevertheless, The Saints fans weren't alone in missing their ramshackle old home. There are hardly any Premiership grounds left where the proximity to the pitch of the entire audience can make for the sort of intimidating and exciting occasions that have previously epitomised football in this country. Still, with every club obsessed with keeping up with the Joneses and the number of bums on seats, there's no room for sentiment as progress marches on at an inevitable pace.

Victories against the likes of Derby and Southampton would prove to be a bit of a false dawn, but two wins on the road and two clean sheets also put a spring in the step of us Gooners. Patrick Vieira was starting to show signs of getting back to his imperious best and Robert Pires was beginning to impose himself on games and influence their outcome. Perhaps Freddie was not on all four cylinders but he was firing up his engine and Thierry Henry was in a fine vein of scoring form with eleven goals to date. However any euphoria was tempered by our concerns about keeping hold of our manager. Fuelled by fallacious media mudslinging, Wenger's continued reluctance to confirm his contract renewal was a constant source of anxiety amongst us. Moreover, there are many in our squad whose attachment to the Arsenal is inextricably related to their relationship with Arsène. I couldn't help but wonder if Wenger's failure to call a halt to the unremitting barrage of questions by signing on the dotted line and nailing his colours to the Arsenal mast for the foreseeable future, was responsible for the apparent air of insecurity stalking our club and troubling our team spirit. I was mindful of a previous proclamation in which he'd referred to the potential problems in the dressing room during the last season of a manager's contract. It left me worried that Wenger's procrastination might be a ruse, an attempt to avoid these difficulties.

None of this was on my mind during a thrilling, albeit tension-ridden, midweek Champions League match that was a tale of two penalties, one save and 101 dives! On his home debut Richard Wright made a superb save from Basinas's spot kick and Henry slotted his home after Wiltord had been barged over in the box. The Greeks continued where they'd left off in Athens and performed their scandalous shenanigans. What I find most ridiculous about European regulations is that when teams are so committed to conning the officials and badgering them into booking their opponents, any resulting suspensions are so often disadvantageous to both sides. Usually it is another team in the group playing them next who benefits. Nevertheless, we were back on track in Europe and with Schalke 04 winning 0–4 in Mallorca, our prospects of progressing into the second stage were improving.

Monday, 15 October 2001

Hopefully, as you leaf through today's paper, you will not have been able to avoid banner headlines from the back pages, announcing that the Arsenal's European adventure is back on track, having given Panathinaikos a suitable pounding the previous night. Don't be mistaken for thinking that two wins on the trot against Derby and Southampton, little more than relegation fodder foes, have given rise to a rare bout of optimism (albeit that two clean sheets on the spin is the closest we have come to defensive consistency for some time!). It is just that the alternative doesn't bear thinking about.

Anything less than a victory against the Greeks could result in another calamitous Champions League campaign. We would be relying on unlikely results elsewhere in the faint hope that, like last season, we might scrape through to the second stage. Should we end up making such an early exit from Europe, eternal optimists among us might seek solace in the obvious plus point of being able to focus on the Premiership. Nevertheless, it is the prospect of the media's blanket coverage of Man United's customary progress and the reams of sanctimonious rubbish in the red-top rags, as they revel in the Arsenal's almost annual failure to live up to expectations that I cannot countenance. By contrast, I would be vaguely pleased with Celtic and Liverpool's continued involvement, as looks fairly likely. Although my joy would be jaundiced by the terrible thought of their tantalising midweek fixtures, in places like Turin, if we are left with the Worthless Cup, humbly entertaining the likes of Grimsby at Highbury.

Long-suffering supporters share the same steadfast stoicism for their involvement in the Champions League as they would for any other knockout tournament (and football in general). Each additional round is a bonus as far as the club's coffers are concerned and no matter how short or long the resultant roller-coaster ride, there is always next season. Sadly the same is no longer true for the participants. The sorry summer saga concerning Patrick Vieira has left a sense of insecurity around the club, with everyone dreading the possibility of a timer ticking down towards the implosion of the current squad. Frankly I cannot believe the man himself capable of such disloyalty, but whether the words that were rumoured actually came from his lips is not the point. It is the episode itself which could have left the question hanging in the minds of all our international stars. Is the Arsenal a team that is capable of fulfilling the players' greatest ambitions in club football? Or would they be better off stepping up from this stone, to side with the bottomless pockets of the established elite, who find dubious ways to permanently bend their ears with bountiful promises?

Bottom of their Champions League group, with 'nil point', Lazio are proof positive that money is no panacea, as far as winning medals is concerned. Yet should we end up exiting from hardly the most glamorous of groups, surely it will prove beyond even Wenger's most sensible statistical reasoning, to convince certain squad members that their best self-interests do not lie elsewhere. Personally I don't know how he had the front to counter the Harrods and Woolworth's analogy, used to compare the summer shopping baskets containing Veron and Van Nistelrooy and the bargain basement Jeffers and Van Bronckhorst. The first is fit for a team that expects to end up in the Glasgow final come May. While ours suggests a club whose current financial limitations leave them happy just to qualify for the tournament each season.

If the rumours are true, it would appear that David Dein has sold his long-term vision for the Arsenal to our manager. Hopefully the whole team will have gone into last night's game, buoyed by some confirmation that Wenger has put his signature where his mouth has been for months. Forget the rumours, the law of averages states that I've got to be correct one of these days and as Martin Keown has said, he hasn't exactly given the impression of 'someone about to jump ship'.

One would expect that a meticulous man like Wenger would need to dot every 'I' and cross every 'T' on any contract, let alone a four-year one. It is unlikely that the extremely virtuous Wenger would be capable of breaking his bond, be it verbal or written, and I assume he needed to be certain that the club shared his own ambitions.

Wenger might have decided that he is happy having carte blanche at the Arsenal, prepared to bide his time until a new stadium and the club's financial circumstances allow him to compete on a level playing field, with a team moulded in his image. But it would be preposterous of us to expect Patrick Vieira to do likewise. It would be criminal for a player of his calibre to see his career reach a climax without a cabinet overflowing with top-class trophies. I suppose you can't get much higher than a World Cup winner's medal, but could we really begrudge him leaving, if the Arsenal cannot offer him a genuine crack at top club honours? Most are sufficiently realistic to accept that this is probably his last season at Highbury. I only hope he goes out with a bang and not with a whimper. Half-hearted performances certainly wouldn't appear to be in this particular player's nature, but before Saturday there were those who had begun questioning whether he was simply biding his time till departure. Scurrilous rumours about a Spanish tutor won't have helped, but thankfully, at Southampton, he at last began to let his feet do the talking once again with trademark total midfield domination. Similarly, in the Champions League, I am sure all it will take is a few wins to bring the best out of Patrick and the wealth of potential talent in our current squad. But then, as the saying goes: 'You have to be in it, to win it!'

9. Still Paying My Dues ... But with a Pound of Flesh!

Saturday, 20 October (Premiership): Blackburn (H) 3–3 Pires (48), Bergkamp (53) Henry (78) 1st

We all had a good laugh at the expense of the Stamford Bridge Six – chinless wonders who didn't fancy the trip to Israel – when Chelsea were made to look real chumps by the tiny Tel Aviv side. Our smiles weren't so wide come the weekend, when we dropped points at home, as a result of the extremely impressive David Dunn's last-minute equaliser. Many would argue that it was no more than Blackburn deserved due to their spirited counter-attacking performance. The Arsenal might have beaten Brad Friedel three times, but we were guilty of failing to capitalise on our chances. This was to become a common complaint as the season wore on. Wenger explained that as the intuition and understanding between our squad developed, the team were beginning to attack with such pace, that they were bound to create plenty of openings around the goal. He thought there was no mystery, since mistakes and misses were always likely when playing the game at the speed of light.

We could hardly complain after such fabulously entertaining football. Moreover, Man United had dropped all three points to a late Michael Ricketts goal at home to Bolton. Then when Chelsea players attempted to redeem themselves in a scoreless draw against Leeds on Sunday, it made an extremely pleasant change for the Arsenal to remain top of the league come Monday morning. At least there were no goals to miss, while I messed around with the remote control, attempting to get my head round Sky TV's new interactive game. In my haste I hadn't noticed that I had actually paid to play. The thought of contributing even more to Rupert Murdoch's retirement fund ensured the novelty wore off quick smart. In fact I don't think I hit the revolutionary red button (with its ever-present annoying logo) again all season, apart from inadvertently, when playing a little rough with the remote in my more fervent moments of football-inspired frustration.

Monday, 22 October 2001

Well, actually it was more like a couple of ounces of grisly red goo than a pound of flesh that I found standing beside the hospital bed, in a clear plastic container. It was the herniated disc, which the surgeon must have left as a souvenir after having removed it from my back. He had told me it was enormous, but to my eyes, it was little to show for so much suffering.

It might seem a gory thing to want to keep, but somehow I can't bring myself to bin my own little body part. This back injury was a direct result of an attempt to earn the exorbitant amount needed to renew our season tickets. I therefore feel like taking this specimen of the corporeal cost of my support along with us to Highbury. Not only does it prove that I am red and white, both inside and out, but I would like to wave it in the faces of some of our players, as evidence of my bodily sacrifice. The least I expect in return is that they might sweat a little blood on the Arsenal's behalf!

ARSENAL ON THE DOUBLE

Gerard Houllier's heart scare has made the health risks of an all-consuming passion for football a topical subject. Yet no one appears to have given a thought to us poor impotent fans. The manager, at least, can have some impact on events on the pitch, with his instructions and crucial substitutions, while we are left screaming our heads off, proverbially peeing in the wind, in the vain hope of either giving our players the necessary encouragement, or a requisite coating off.

Traditionally the football stadium was a sanctuary, where you arrived on a Saturday, carrying the burden of a week's worth of frustration, and departed having dumped one's load, 90 minutes later, by means of hollering yourself hoarse. I am probably one of the most likely candidates, but peruse the punters in any football stadium and you will behold a variety of throbbing blue veins, threatening to burst their way out of the throats and foreheads of the faithful. With the volume of those who spend the entire proceedings venting their anger at players and officials alike, blood pressure at boiling point like some varicose Vesuvius, I find myself marvelling at the fact that few ever end up, like the lyric of the bovver-boy ballad, 'going home in a London ambulance'.

Even before his triple-bypass surgery, my uncle, who sits in the stand opposite us, was renowned for his regular habit of leaving his seat, the minute he became too wound up, or in moments of high excitement, to spend much of the match shooting the breeze with the sellers of salmonella sustenance, inside the stand. That he should spend such a fortune to watch sweet FA, is farcical enough. Yet for years now, even when he is sufficiently in control of his circulation to continue watching the contest on the pitch, whenever the Arsenal are in most need of a goal, he'll usually get a tap on the shoulder from one of the regulars. They have come to the conclusion that sending Herman outside is often just the required hocus-pocus for the Arsenal to hold sway on the pitch.

If there are those on the touchline and the terraces who are too involved in the game for their own good, it would appear that for far too big a majority of our modern-day stars, the exact opposite is true. Aside from any partiality on account of my Jewish genes, my face was a picture of pure jubilation at the poetic justice of Chelsea's Israeli adventure coming to such an ignominious end. A nail-bomb explosion outside a pub meant that there was more chance of their six suffragettes coming to some harm in West London last Thursday, than while sunning themselves in relative safety on a heavenly Mediterranean beach (which is how I imagined those who travelled to Tel Aviv might have spent their day, from the look of their lacklustre performance). That the bashful Blues turned it on come Sunday, with the exemplification of a staunch display up at Elland Road, only served to highlight their European howler. To my mind it was merely confirmation of certain squad members' casual commitment, to be turned on like a tap, when the mood takes them. Given the opportunity, there wouldn't be a single Irish player who would pull out of a precarious play-off trip to Iran.

Similarly if picked for their respective national sides, I doubt any of Chelsea's squad would refuse to travel to Israel. Obviously when it comes to their club, they are not nearly quite so concerned about their standing with the supporters, perhaps because it is an opinion they won't have to care about for more than a couple of seasons.

I shouldn't really comment on the quality of football on view in this live Sky broadcast, for I was far too busy wrestling with the remote control. To date, I haven't been too enamoured with the advent of the interactive revolution, but the amazing invention of 'Sky Play' is likely to be an irresistible innovation. It promises a future of many fun-filled Sunday afternoons, with fights breaking out over control of the precious remote in living rooms up and down the country. Perhaps it will be better suited to livening up more dour, mid-table clashes, as in this instance I was far too busy battling with the buttons to have the foggiest about events on the pitch. I was so concerned with collecting points, that I forgot to concentrate sufficiently to ensure that Leeds did not pip us to the Premiership top spot. As for Chelsea, if we have to worry about their results come the end of the season, then the Arsenal are in big trouble!

In recent times I have often bemoaned the fact that the increasingly cosmopolitan concoction of Wenger's Arsenal has seen our collective team spirit sliding down a slippery slope, to the point where I've had cause to wonder whether we're any better than all those mercenary big-time Charlies at Stamford Bridge. Events of the last few days have left us looking like a team full of British Bulldogs by comparison. Concentration, and a decided lack of that killer instinct, is currently my greatest concern. There is no doubting that Blackburn's point was hard earned last Saturday. The result stood as testament to Souness maturing into a capable manager and as further proof that Dunn is some prospect. However, similar lapses at the back against Mallorca and we are likely to find ourselves needing to outscore the Spaniards.

Far be it from me to argue with both Wenger and Ferguson, but when both sides are struggling to battle their way through the ten men that visitors to Highbury and Old Trafford tend to get behind the ball surely the simple answer is to go round them. Why then did neither team feature a recognised winger in Saturday's starting line-up? At least Smart Alex gave Giggs a run out in an attempt to rescue a result. While Arsène refuses to include, even in the squad, one of the country's brightest young prospects on the wing. Worse still are my worries that he is attempting to turn poor Jermaine Pennant into yet another striker. Currently we might be playing in Europe on a wing and a prayer, but I am sure I am not alone in praying for a winger!

RIP Bertie Mee
Reprinted from *The Gooner, 116,* 22 October 2001

With the death on 20th October 2001 of the man whose team was responsible for first floating my football boat, I decided to include my personal tribute written for *The Gooner* fanzine at the time.

For those Gooners with a sufficient number of grey hairs, a fitting tribute to mark the sudden passing of Bertie Mee could be summed up most succinctly in 11 words: Wilson, Rice, Mcnab, Storey, Mclintock, Simpson, Armstrong, Graham, Radford, Kennedy, George.

However, perhaps I should elucidate for the benefit of those poor young pups among us who did not have the privilege of gorging themselves on the glorious exploits of a side moulded in Bertie Mee's image. This team was a more staunch bunch of Gooners than you could ever hope to see, whose historic success was the foundation stone for establishing the modern Arsenal among football's elite. It is telling that the names of these particular players still trip off the tongue, more than 30 years later. Especially the tongue of someone who'd have to 'phone a friend', if his million quid depended on the naming of that same afternoon's goal-scorers.

A young whippersnapper of only ten years at the time, I might not have much of an image of Bertie Mee, the man, except as the figurehead for the football team responsible for my most cherished childhood memories. I was far from alone in this respect, as Mee was a most private man and even those in the game who knew him best would hardly claim to have been intimate pals. Perhaps it was my age at the time, or his absolute air of authority, for though I would not hesitate to write about the exploits of Arsène and George, it would seem somewhat impudent to refer to Bertie Mee OBE on a first name basis. As is often the case, it was ironic that he should end up beating his lifelong partner to St Peter's gates, having shut himself away for the last five of his 82 years to devote himself to his wife and her failing health. Otherwise the celebrations surrounding our second Double would have surely inspired a suitable commemorative occasion, where he might have had the benefit of appreciating quite to what extent the feats of his vintage Double side of '71 has shaped the Arsenal's existence and the indelible imprint left on all who shared the experience.

In Mee's parting from this mortal coil and this humble tribute, I seek some solace, as it presents a rare opportunity to dust off the history books and completely wallow in a cornucopia of my most wonderful Arsenal reminiscences, while digging for details to explain how it was that this apparently impersonal gent managed to have such a personal effect, on so many. What younger Gooner readers might not appreciate is that when Mee was handed the manager's job, Arsenal had spent 13 long years in a silverware-starved wilderness. And despite the relative league and cup rewards of Tom Whittaker's team in the early '50s, none of the incumbents who followed the great Herbert Chapman had managed to live up to such standards in the eyes of a demanding Highbury faithful. All eventually succumbed to Chapman's spectre, which continued to loom large in the marble halls, until Mee managed to exorcise the myth, if not the ghost itself (which many swear still haunts the Highbury hallways).

It might be hard to believe now, but we were living in the shadow of the satanic forces, from the wrong end of the Seven Sisters Road ever since Blanchflower and his glory boys achieved the impossible Double exactly a decade earlier in 1961. Many thought it was a feat that couldn't possibly be emulated, with the increasing pressures and fixture congestion of the modern game. It is hard to imagine the Hill-Woods and the rest of Highbury's old-Etonian board, swinging their way through the '60s, but the Arsenal saw its share of glamour during ex-England captain Billy Wright's four-year stewardship, although on the pitch Wright was presiding over a four-year flop.

Much of the media speculation about which big-name manager would replace Wright was lost amidst all the World Cup euphoria. Consequently Fleet Street was completely thrown when the Arsenal promoted their physiotherapist, many believing it to be merely a stop-gap appointment. After Mee's six years at the club as a trainer and then team physio, Denis Hill-Wood must have recognised something in Mee that made him worth taking, what many perceived as a potential risk. It proved to be an inspired choice. Although Mee only accepted the job on the basis that 'if it didn't work out after 12 months, he could revert to his previous position'. What I have come to respect most about Mee was, unlike many managers of the day, he never pretended to be a football maven. To the contrary, it was the fact that he recognised his limitations with tactics, teaching ball skills and training in general, which allowed him to form such great partnerships with, initially, Dave Sexton and then Don Howe. Both coaches were and still are recognised by a litany of this country's greatest-ever footballing talents as having an innate ability to pass on their consummate knowledge of the game and were happy to have such free rein on the training pitch. It would be totally remiss of me, in this tribute to Bertie Mee, if I failed to pay due respect to the role played by Gooner coaching guru, Don Howe, and his contribution in what was to become a perfect Double act!

It was another age compared to the multi-million-pound mayhem of today.

Nevertheless Bertie Mee's managership coincided with the tail-end of the '60s and early '70s. With the landmark lifting of the minimum wage, putting real spending power in the players' pockets, it was the first throes of the long hair and casual clothes period of the football player as pop icon. If you asked most Gooners to conjure up an image of the era, they would all choose Charlie George, lying prostrate on the Wembley Turf, having fulfilled every schoolboy's dream by stepping straight off the North Bank, with his long hair, flashy clothes and mercurial talent, to score the winner in an FA Cup final. However, our darling Charlie was the exception that proved the rule. For with his army background and as a maestro of man management, Mee immediately set about creating a side in which there were no real superstars. He managed to keep a lid on any egos that might have detracted from the fabulous team spirit in the dressing room.

At such an impressionable age, winning the league on Tottenham turf in the first part of Arsenal's Double was my childhood highlight. Only two seasons prior, Mee's side had won at White Hart Lane for the first time in eleven seasons! We all sang ourselves hoarse during the crazy celebrations on Tottenham's own turf. This highpoint in his career saw even Bertie Mee letting his hair down as he returned to the directors' box to acknowledge the crowd, having lost his club tie! This wonderful night culminated in that incredible conclusion, with Ray Kennedy the league-winning goal-scorer, actually confirming in writing in my programme that we gave him a lift home.

It was an amazing climax to a schoolboy romance that had begun a couple of years earlier. I used to believe it was playing in defence from a very early age which turned me into the sort of child who wasn't interested in pretending to be the playground Best, Hurst or Greaves. No, it was finding the likes of England left-back Terry Cooper on my *Soccer Stars* cards that brought a smile to my face. I have since come to the conclusion that it is part of my make-up that I get as much satisfaction from the prevention of a goal as the scoring of one. I became so enamoured with Mee's burgeoning bunch of winners, that when we made the League Cup final for the second successive year in '69, I simply could not accept the fact that we ended up being humiliated by Third Division Swindon. It was the only time I can recall lying in my exercise book, where we drew a picture every day at school, by creating my own acceptable conclusion to this match in my imagination. Bob Wilson and his team-mates found the shame of this result similarly unacceptable. Wilson believes the phoenix of the Double side arose from these ashes, as they were a team who were 'determined that it would never happen again'. They craved success with an even greater intensity as a result.

Some of you might recognise in Mee's aloofness from his players and his strict disciplinarian attitudes, some of the traits of George Graham's reign, lessons which he picked up from his mentor. As a direct result, neither Mee nor Graham, two of Highbury's greatest-ever managers, will be remembered with the sort of affection that other fans have for the likes of Shankly, Paisley and Busby. Yet in an age now when success means everything, we should appreciate their achievements more than ever.

We revelled all the way through some of those never-to-be-repeated replay encounters, en route to five finals in five years, finally shutting up Spurs fans for ever (one can but hope!), by eclipsing their sides achievements.

Sadly, after losing to Leeds in the Centenary FA Cup final of '72, Bertie Mee's career headed downhill. Some blamed him for breaking up the Double side too early, or for failing to add to it and Mee was permanently put upon to defend Arsenal's failure to play entertaining football. He continued to nurture some fabulous talent from the Arsenal production line, including the likes of Liam Brady, but in an effort apparently to try and imitate the total football of Ajax, we ended up with our fair share of totally unsuitable lummoxes like Jeff Blockley. Eventually, two years after his old adversary Bill Nicholson retired, Bertie Mee decided to call time at Highbury. Brady describes how Mee gave a morale-boosting speech of Churchillian proportions before he announced, in tears, to a stunned press conference that he would retire at the end of the season (1975–76). Apart from the rare flash of temper, it was perhaps the first public emotional display from this polite and reserved man.

What a relief that we managed to escape relegation in one of our worst ever league finishes. It would have been criminal for the career of such a wonderful caretaker of everything that the Arsenal stands for to end with the ignominy of our only ever relegation. Like most others, I can only recall the many highs.

RIP Bertie Mee.

10. Tinker Taker Two Points Away?

Wednesday, 24 October (Champions League): Real Mallorca (H) 3–1 Pires (61), Bergkamp (63), Henry (90)
Saturday, 27 October (Premiership): Sunderland (A) 1–1 Kanu (40) 3rd

Going into the penultimate game of the first stage of the Champions League, we needed to beat Mallorca by more than the one goal that they beat us by in Palma. Otherwise we'd end up needing a result against

Schalke 04 in the last game in Germany. Again we played some brilliant football for an hour but with no end product. When we were finally rewarded with the two goals we required, we didn't have long to gloat before the Spaniards pegged one back and I was chewing my nails again, wondering if it was going to be another déjà vu European disaster. When Pires had a goal disallowed moments after the three minutes of injury time were indicated, it was the signal for the part-timers to start streaming out. As the roller-coaster peaked again seconds before the end of another enthralling ride, with an Henry goal that made the next match superfluous, not for the first time I tried to equate how beating the rush could possibly be worth missing the climax of this contest. Although it is a bit rich of me to rail at those who regularly leave before the final whistle – my tardy tendencies have seen me miss the odd moment of rejoicing at the start of a game, before I've even reached the front door!

It was Man United's turn on Saturday. In their early kick-off at Old Trafford, Solskjaer scored yet another last-minute goal to rescue a point against Leeds. For once I wasn't so gutted about another last-gasp United goal, because with Leeds topping the table, it was in our interest for both teams to drop two points.

I was doing my best to get the gen on this gripping encounter from my tranny with a carriage full of Gooners hanging on my every word as our train headed for Wearside. Despite our lack of success at the Stadium of Light, it remains my favourite of all the newly built stadia. Our matches against Peter Reid's sides are invariably combative affairs which make for a great atmosphere. Sunderland are also one of the few clubs with a more sensible pricing policy which results in the sort of mixed audience who haven't lost the use of their lungs.

With only one win in seven, the Wearsiders set out not to lose, with Phillips alone up front and Reid's customary approach of making up for any deficit in ability by kicking us up in the air. Most of us were particularly peeved because we thought we could play our way around such negative tactics, if only Arsène had picked his best team. No one could understand his reasons for more squad rotation. Not only could we afford to rest the whole team for the meaningless match in Germany three days later, but also our French contingent were soon off on a relaxing break from the relentless rigours of club football for a farcical international friendly in Australia. Our day out up the North East really went downhill at 1–1 after 70 minutes, when Vieira fluffed a penalty that he should never have elected to take. Yet it was uphill all the way home on a journey that seemed so much longer due to our dismal failure to leapfrog Leeds at the top by capitalising on the earlier result of our rivals.

Monday, 29 October 2001

I have never set much store by statistics and if ever I needed proof positive of the proliferation of piffle provided by the goggle-eyed statisticians at Opta, I was presented with it in a Premiership preview on the box on Friday. With old adversaries, Fergie and Wenger, both unable to resist stoking the fires of the Henry v. Van Nistelrooy debate, this became a hot topic of conversation around Highbury last week.

Most Gooners will gladly go down on our knees in gratitude for the privilege of watching one of the world's greatest talents ply his trade in the red and white of the Arsenal. Since some of Henry's striking instincts might have been dulled by spending much of his career on the wing, to my mind it is evident and most commendable that a player of his calibre appears to have been working his socks off to improve those areas of his game which have previously been subject to criticism. Certain star strikers, with egos to match their wage packets, come across with an attitude that suggests their goal-scoring prowess grants them a divine right to leave menial tasks, like tracking back and heading, to more mundane members of their team. I have to respect the sort of modesty which is reflected in Henry's willingness to augment his all-round game.

Yet I could find few Gooners to disagree with my opinion that, by comparison, Van Nistelrooy is by far the more complete centre forward and I was flabbergasted to find this contradicted in absolutely every Opta statistic used to compare the two on Friday's TV show. I even checked out the Opta web site, in case we'd been shown a skewed selection, but both in Europe and the league, in all 24 categories used to rate players, Van the man only came out on top in one: the percentage of passes completed in the opposition's half! Perhaps the Dutchman has the excuse that he has only recently returned from a career-threatening injury, into a new team, with whom he has still to develop a decent rapport and whose unusually fragile form hasn't exactly provided him with an endless array of Opta indexing-type opportunities. Nevertheless, if I ponder on the penalty-box potential of a line-leading striker, in terms of aerial ability, the strength to hold off a defender, fearlessly throwing oneself in where the boots are flying, to scuff a ball in with any part of your body and all those qualities associated with a traditional centre forward, I can't see how there can be any argument.

On his day, there isn't a defence in the world that can hold sway over the irrepressible Henry for the entire 90 minutes, as evidenced by the fact that after just over two seasons at Highbury, he has recently eclipsed Ian Wright as our all-time record goal-scorer in Europe. However, possibly a more pertinent pointer is the fact that Wrightie scored his goals in 19 games, where Henry has participated in 30 European matches. I wouldn't mind betting that with the relative improvement in squad strength in recent times, Thierry has managed to squander a significantly higher number of goal-scoring opportunities than were offered up to Ian in his time.

Personally I am far more patient than many of the fickle fans that surround us in the posh seats. So long as we hit the target and our opponents are forced to pull off a save of some sort, I will rarely complain. I get so wound up by some of the regular whingers, in the knowledge that we certainly aren't going to benefit from berating our players out loud. Some can buckle under the pressure, preferring to pass the ball, instead of taking any further responsibility, for fear of the fans getting on their back. I guess the exorbitant prices we have to pay and perhaps some envy over the preposterous size of the players' pay packets, make many fans feel that they have a perfect right to verbalise their feelings. While I can often be heard sarcastically muttering under my breath, speculating perhaps on how many millions we paid to watch a particularly profligate player fluff his shot, I am of the opinion that, as supporters, the least we can do is support, or otherwise keep schtum. As a result, the nearest I get to perforating nearby punters' eardrums is when I attempt to reassure the culprit of the most recent cock-up, as a counterbalance to those perverse punters who wouldn't dream of getting behind their team with slightest word of encouragement, but who seem to get some satisfaction from permanently picking on a particular player.

Mind you, while Henry was far from being the sole sitter-missing sinner against Mallorca last Wednesday, in the pressure cooker situation of the second-half, I was struggling to contain my frustration. His touch had evaded him all evening and he appeared to take on his particularly distinctive, definitively Gallic, depressed demeanour: standing out on the wings, within the confines of the limited width pitch, in the widest of open spaces, head flopping and shoulder shrugging with every pass forward which failed to come within a couple of feet of his person. As a team playing in Europe we haven't clicked all season (with Saturday's draw at Sunderland reflecting a similar story in the league). The couple of minutes spell that included the individual magic which took us 2–0 up was not really a true reflection of a match, where a fairly limited Mallorca side had worked extremely hard to maintain the scoreless draw they required. Having not managed a clean sheet so far during this European campaign, we knew we were in for an extremely long half-hour before the final whistle, which would either confirm qualification, or a probable multi-million-pound mishap, with any number of complicated consequences for the club's future.

In the light of what transpired, I'd have to go way back to recall a game in which I spent so much of the match with my heart in my mouth. None of us could understand the substitution of a highly energised Bergkamp, perhaps more motivated than others, because his phobia so often prevents him having any influence on European proceedings (I definitely can't remember the last time he scored with his head!). Why did Wenger feel the need to alter the dynamics of a winning team? When Mallorca scored three minutes after, there was a murmur of 'told you so' tut-tuttings and an electric atmosphere went completely flat, as though the Spaniards had sucked all the wind out of our Champions League sails in an instant.

I knew exactly how the Black Cats fans felt on Saturday, with their last-minute winner ruled offside, as we were similarly up out of our seats three days prior, when Pires hit the back of the net. With the amount of incredibly near misses in those last few minutes, this really felt like our last roll of the dice. There I was thinking that with our fate no longer in our hands, but with the faintest of chances of still qualifying, I would have to travel to Germany this week. Thierry was limping along the halfway line, holding his thigh, perhaps pretending to the Spanish. Without a shot on target all night, I certainly had given up on him, but thank heavens Henry had not given up the ghost. As he received the ball in the dying seconds, with their goalie off his line, I was convinced he had blown it as the keeper had time to recover. It felt like an eternity before he shot. One of those occasions when, instead of hitting it instinctively, it seemed like he had waited far too long, with so much time to think of how much rested on this one shot, that he was bound to fluff it. Even as the ball left his foot, I was sure it was going wide. All due credit to Thierry for his perfect portrayal of coolness under such extreme pressure.

Moreover he saved me from an arduous overland coach journey to Schalke this week, which certainly wouldn't have been what the doctor would have ordered for my still delicate derriere. Despite my recovering back and a blasted cold, the euphoria of Wednesday night convinced me that I was capable of travelling almost the length of the country to Wearside on Saturday. As the Trans-Pennine choo-choo chugged from Newcastle to Sunderland at a painfully slow pace, I fiddled desperately with the reception on the radio, trying to keep abreast of the Old Trafford score-line. We all alighted with great Gooner grins, having eventually established a final score that gave us an opportunity to gain ground on both our major competitors. I was therefore quite disappointed to arrive at the Stadium of Light, a ground the Arsenal have yet to win on, to discover Wenger had somewhat arrogantly left three of our best players on the bench. It seemed like an 'anything you can do' statement to Man United, especially when I read the rather conceited quote from Wenger, in the Sunday press: 'I heard it was easy to come to the Stadium of Light, after Man United won here.'

In a side struggling for some consistency, it feels like much of our disjointed play is due to Wenger's constant tinkering with his team. In his shoes, I would have tried to build on Wednesday's triumph by starting with the same line-up. If he felt there were players who might benefit from a break, he could have taken them off, if and when they had secured the three points which might prove so crucial when we get down to the wire. Moreover, I struggle to understand how it is possible that our pedantic *Professeur*, who in all other aspects manages from the major to the last minutiae, can let his team take to the field without a designated penalty taker. I can't really blame the rush of blood that saw Vieira grab the ball, as we'd had plenty of other chances before Patrick's schoolboy error, but I think that the gutless display of those better suited to take the spot kick, in passively playing along with Paddy's panto penalty, is perhaps an indication of a more worrying malaise.

11. The Worm's A'Turning Well Before Winter

Tuesday, 30 October (Champions League): Schalke 04 (A) 1–3 Wiltord (71)
Sunday, 4 November (Premiership): Charlton (H) 2–4 Henry (7, 60) 5th
Monday, 5 November (Worthington Cup): Manchester Utd (H) 4–0 Wiltord (15, 31 pen., 45), Kanu (66 pen.)

I felt sorry for the 1,000-strong, hardy band of Gooners who schlepped all the way to Germany for the match against Schalke 04 to see such a sorry display. Nevertheless the Gunners made it into Friday's draw for the second stage. The nature of the Champions League beast is that the further you go in the competition, the bigger the football fish to be fried. If the Arsenal were going to get into the quarter-finals for the second year running, we would have to battle our way out of an extremely daunting group including Deportivo, Juventus and Bayer Leverkusen.

Feeling particularly smug, I proceeded to tell anyone who would listen about the cheap trip to Turin I'd managed to book, when terrace talk on the Sunday turned to forthcoming outings to our three obdurate European opponents. We weren't alone in lacking focus on the task at hand, as a lack of concentration on the pitch cost us another three crucial home points. Funnily enough, there was an ad campaign on the box around this time, in which Charlton's Jason Euell was shown charging out of Highbury. Sadly he remained in the ground on Sunday to play an important part in a famous victory for Charlton, their first at our place since 1955, in a match that was meant to be a formality for us.

This was evident when those amongst our fickle faithful who remained at the final whistle expressed their displeasure in no uncertain terms. By rights all these ungrateful Gooners should have stood and applauded such a stalwart defensive performance by our opponents. Euell strutted out of Highbury and back to South London with his side having successfully knocked the Arsenal out of our supercilious stride by means of four painful sucker punches. As depressed as I was at dropping points in our second defeat in seven days, I hardly felt entitled to complain. It might have been a rotten result, but the sumptuous skills on show ensured perfect entertainment for the purists. With a record 25 shots on goal to Charlton's nine, if it hadn't been for an all too familiar profligacy in front of the net and some decidedly dodgy defensive errors, we could have won by a cricket score. At least then we might have conquered the curse that we've succumbed to these past few seasons, when our form has taken a nosedive every November.

There was some consolation in having seen Man United lose to Liverpool in the televised coverage from Anfield that morning. The Scousers finished United off in fine style, causing Ferguson to fret publicly for the first time that his stars might have lost their hunger. With this being Liverpool's fourth consecutive victory over United, we wondered if we should be less concerned about United and Houllier's health problems and more worried about his Liver Boys. Perhaps Fergie would punish his miscreants by making them play again a mere 24 hours later in the Worthington Cup? In the most scandalous fixture foul-up yet, the postponed third-round clash between the Arsenal and United had been rearranged for the following day.

Sylvain Wiltord signed off with a hat-trick against Man United before flying off to Australia with his French colleagues for their foolishly arranged friendly. It was marvellous to mullah Man United, especially since we were still having nightmares about last season's humiliating 1–6 defeat at Old Trafford. Yet this result couldn't really count as revenge. Dwight Yorke and Phil Neville were United's only recognised first-team players and they fielded at least one player that none of us had ever heard of. Personally I would have preferred Wenger to have been similarly adventurous and let us run the rule over a few more of our young prospects. Although I am not sure the other 30,000 paying punters would have been quite so happy to have coughed up their hard-earned cash to watch the sort of football they can see for free at our reserve and youth team games. Either Wenger included a liberal sprinkling of our stars out of deference to all us die-hards who turned up the day after our derby defeat against Charlton, or he felt we needed to win. Whereas Fergie's approach suggested the Worthington Cup was a needless distraction.

Unlike the attitude of many towards the Worthless trophy, I enjoy this competition. The intense pressure for a result in almost every other match in all other competitions means that these cup encounters are often the only occasion when Wenger dares to give our youngsters an opportunity to prove themselves. Moreover, with the exception of the equivalent round in the FA Cup, or an increasingly rare run of a lowly giant killer, it is the only chance I get these days of ticking off another outpost of lower league opposition on my list of clubs I have visited. Mind you, I was quite grateful for a home draw against Grimsby in the fourth round. Don't get me wrong, doubtless I would have gone as always and probably enjoyed my outing. A visit from a glamour club attracts plenty of once-a-season stragglers to lower league opponents. Even so there is usually an intimate family vibe at these grounds which makes me somewhat envious. Through my rose-tinted sentimental specs, such stadiums rarely have a glory-hunting corporate suit in sight and everyone is that bit more familiar with one another, as most have supported the club from birth, turning up every week without any realistic hope of the seductive inducement of success. What's more, a visit from the venerable Arsenal might be the high point of their season and as their cup final so you are often guaranteed a great atmosphere. The 'being there' is always brilliant, but just occasionally the 'getting there' is not such an attractive proposition with the thought of travelling hundreds of miles to watch a team made up of peripheral players.

Apart from Wiltord, who only played for 20 minutes against Charlton, Richard Wright and Van Bronckhorst were the other two involved in both matches on Sunday and Monday. It demonstrated how much Wenger has improved our strength in depth. However, having become an increasingly cosmopolitan hotchpotch, it also meant that we had many more players disappearing all over the world, with another break in the domestic calendar for international matches.

Monday, 5 November 2001

A constant theme in the straws being clutched, after Sunday's depressing derby debacle, is the hope that the Arsenal might react to this calamitous result in the same way as they did some years back. Since the 1997–98 season, the month of November has been making an annual appearance as our nemesis. It was a frank and forthright team meeting, subsequent to a similarly embarrassing episode against Blackburn, that has gone down in Highbury folklore as being the basis for all that followed, in a delicious Double delight which was the fulfilment of every Gooner fantasy. As we've suffered watching the silverware slip through our fingers every season since, various nightmare November cock-ups, like this inexplicable catastrophe against Charlton, have left us on our knees, praying for a repetition of this rebirth.

Having won only one of our five home games in the league, conceding seven goals in the last two matches and with both Leeds and Liverpool looking far more credible title challengers, Arsenal appear further away than ever from having a prayer of the Premiership's big prize. In 1997–98 we had a new manager, a new team and a totally new style of football. Not to mention a captain who took it upon himself to call that famous team meeting.

Whereas now we have a world-weary manager, whose reluctance to put pen to paper and commit his future to the club can't exactly be encouraging his charges. They are a collection of highly talented individuals, but with only two British players in Sunday's line-up there is a decided absence of the vital home-grown backbone, evident in each of the starting elevens of our competitors. Moreover, with Tony Adams absent through injury for the foreseeable future, our captain's armband is being worn by a player who was only ever going to lead our team by example and only three months prior wasn't exactly setting the best of these, when apparently he wanted out ASAP. Just as each catalytic element combined initially to create the magical chemistry of the Double side, we are now left with a catastrophic concoction that is responsible for our current malaise.

Whether fact, or fiction, Vieira's tawdry summer temper tantrums appear increasingly justified. The media constantly compare the purchasing power of the established elite with European Cup wannabees like ourselves. It is hard even for the most loyal amongst us to disagree with the bargain-basement look of our two summer buys, compared with the millions blown by clubs in the top bracket. Morever, can we honestly expect Vieira to motivate his team-mates, chasing Champions League qualification, let alone the title, when participation in next season's tournament might well result in them facing Patrick on opposite sides of the pitch.

The Aufschalke Arena in Gelsenkirchen was described by many well travelled Gooners as the best stadium they'd ever visited, although the closing of their clever roof before kick-off meant that I missed out on the first ever competitive European fixture indoors. But boy was I glad not to have been present, to watch us being carved up by the Krauts.

As I bury my head in the back of a cornflakes pack on a depressing Monday morning, in order to avoid the newspaper headlines screaming out our title surrender, I dare not even contemplate our progress in Europe. If the humble

South Londoners can make such a laughing stock of our defence, I dread to think what monkeys Deportivo might make of them. What upsets me most is that I cannot imagine the majority of our current squad feeling anywhere near as shattered about Sunday's fiasco as the fans. We had an Australian Gooner, an Internet pal, over for her first ever match at Highbury. Having persuaded her the previous week that she had to experience the atmosphere at an away match, I had felt a bit of a fraud forcing her to break her budget and schlep all the way to Sunderland, only for a disappointing draw in which Wenger had not even deigned to dish up three of our best players. Since they were not required against Schalke, it wasn't like they needed the rest.

And then having forked out the relative fortune of 150 Aussie dollars for her ticket at Highbury, there was a moment during the week when I feared that she'd turn up on Sunday, after a journey of so many thousands of miles, only to find that all her French favourites had already flown in exactly the opposite direction. It was a battle to put a brave face on matters, 2–1 down at half-time. At least she would get to see two Thierry Henry goals. Yet by the time Charlton scored their fourth, I was so bitterly disappointed on her behalf that I couldn't even turn to face her without feeling on the verge of tears for her troubles.

She's off on her own European tour for the next two weeks, but I am determined that she shouldn't return home feeling like some kind of Jonah who can never come back again. So I will try and persuade her to change her return flight, in order that she might travel with us to Ipswich, where I would hope the law of averages might fall in her favour. Of course it could compound matters, if our defence should continue to display the lack of leadership and concentration which is at the crux of their inconsistency and our forwards should fail to find the shooting boots that should have buried a fair few more than just two of the 25 shots on Sunday!

The worm has turned very quickly as far as the manager is concerned. Only four points off the top and still involved in Europe, yet the Sunday-night radio talk shows were teeming with turncoats. With whom would they replace Wenger, is my response to these impromptu experts. My support remains unwavering, yet I am finding it harder and harder to contest the competent arguments of an increasing number of malcontents, who are convinced that Alex and Arsène both have begun to lose the plot. Monday's Worthless Cup encounter between the two teams could prove interesting, from the point of view of which team has the most promising reserve side. I fully expect a result which will reflect United's greater strength in depth. However, on current form, both sides might well end up chasing a new champion come May.

If there were few positives to be drawn from the international commitments of the Arsenal's senior players, the opposite was true for our kids. I received one of the best 40th birthday presents on Sunday afternoon from a lad named Justin

Hoyte. By chance I happened to turn the telly over, just in time for the second-half of England U19s' contest with Hungary. The Arsenal right-back and the youngest player in the side charged up the pitch to perform a one-two on the edge of the penalty area, which resulted in a goal from the perfect example of a bicycle kick. Unfortunately Jerome Thomas, another very promising homegrown Highbury youth, wasn't involved due to an injury. Also one of his contemporaries and perhaps the brightest star in the Arsenal firmament, Jermaine Pennant, earned rave reviews playing for the U21s two days prior. Depressed by the general demeanour of our first team and their dispirited defeats, it is the thought of Jermaine, Justin and Jerome that has me hoping for a future that might yet turn out to be red, white and bright.

12. Sol's Homecoming Hullabaloo

Saturday, 17 November (Premiership): Tottenham (A) 1–1 Pires (81) 5th

With their team permitting them little pleasure for so many years, Tottenham fans are often far more interested in events down the road at Highbury, hoping they might get some solace from a rare failure by their rivals. As a result, the North London Derby is a much bigger occasion for them, often the climax in another slipshod season and they didn't come any bigger than this one. Some Spurs fans had been plotting for weeks in advance, trying to organize various visual protests to prove to their former captain how vexed they all were. As far as they were concerned Sol Campbell had committed the ultimate act of betrayal and they weren't going to let him off lightly. In the end, from where we sat at White Hart Lane, their puffed-up protests all looked a bit shambolic, as the majority of bewildered Spurs fans looked like they didn't know whether to wave their white balloons emblazoned with the word 'Judas', turn their backs to the pitch, or simply boo. However, my Spurs pal later told me that he'd rarely heard anything like the vitriolic barrage of abuse aimed at Sol the entire match.

Although the colossal summer coup in capturing the signature of Tottenham's most influential player was a constant source of boastful pride amongst us Gooners, Campbell had begun the season unfit and seriously overweight. To date we had seen little sign of the confident leader who'd marshalled the troops at Tottenham. Campbell had been playing like a nervous cog in an Arsenal defence prone to lapses in concentration. The resulting costly goals that we had conceded so far left none of us particularly convinced about him. In fact Spurs fans had been consoling themselves and teasing us that we'd signed the wrong player, since Ledley King had filled Sol's shoes quite admirably up to that point, putting in far more assured performances than we had seen from Campbell.

This derby at White Hart Lane proved to be the turning point. By daring to face his detractors that day, Sol was able to use the verbal victimisation as his motivation. With the consummate example of a commanding performance, Campbell's conversion was complete and for the first time we were able to chant 'Sol's a Gooner' with absolute conviction. Considering Sol's crucial contribution in what transpired during the rest of this season, I am almost certain that any subsequent success was in no small part due to the Spurs supporters' deplorable conduct that day and, believe me, I haven't stopped expressing my sincere gratitude to all those I know ever since.

Having fallen to fifth in the table, our lowest position all season, we required more than a draw. Consequently Spurs' last-second sucker punch caught us squarely in the solar plexus. Yet on reflection there was something about the nature of our spirited, staunch performance which gave us an inkling that the Arsenal were on the up. Man United might have won (but then everyone was taking a turn at tonking a decidedly lacklustre Leicester), but at least Leeds succumbed to their first defeat of the season at Sunderland and the Scousers dropped points to Blackburn. Any pain I might have felt was nothing compared to Hasim Rahman's headache much later that night, when Lennox Lewis well and truly recaptured the heavyweight crown in the fourth round, with perhaps the biggest knockout punch of his career.

Monday, 12 November 2001

The way the Premiership is panning out, it could prove to be the most interesting Championship chase for many a moon. Admittedly it is unlikely that we will ever return to the unpredictable era, when any top-flight team could challenge for the title. Yet compared to the relative heavy going of the one-horse race of recent times, the weekend's results reflect a fixture list in which there are far fewer foregone conclusions. Despite Sky's best attempts to sterilise their spearhead sport, in their quest for some return on all the spondulicks spent, with scrambled start times and a turgid almost daily diet, they might at last have a spectacle on their hands.

This will be a novel experience for the neutral, but I am hardly amongst their number. Otherwise I would have been looking forward to Saturday's North London Derby, on the basis that it provided an interesting contest between a resurgent Spurs and our perennially underachieving Arsenal. However most Gooners view the Derby with about as much enthusiasm as one would have for a tooth-plucking dental appointment. Much was made of the malevolent mood of Sol Campbell's initiation at White Hart Lane. The bilious bad blood, born out of the Spurs fans' perception of his act of betrayal, meant that Campbell was a conduit through which they could vent the bitterness which had been brewing for all those seasons, suffering in the shadow of our haul of silverware.

It was Sol's first public taste of the splenetic ire of Spurs fans, while we suffer the same sense of trepidation over the short trip to Tottenham every time. To each set of supporters, the other side is scum and though there are plenty of fans in both camps who are more than worthy of this moniker, Spurs seems to attract a larger proportion of this undesirable element. The tension in the air at Tottenham and the aggravation getting in and out of the ground always makes me afraid for Róna's safety. If it wasn't for my desire to be there to support my team in the face of all that animosity, I would be sorely tempted to take the easy option and watch the beam-back on the screens at Highbury. I have wonderful memories of being taken to these encounters by my old man, as a child. Yet I would not dream of exposing a youngster to the intimidation the Arsenal fans experience these days. It is sad that modern-day kids are missing out on the magical attraction of the intense Derby-day atmosphere, without the aggro.

Moments after the euphoria of going one–nil up with ten minutes to go had waned slightly, my thoughts turned to escaping White Hart Lane. Trouble outside the ground after last season's match resulted in thousands of Gooners getting corralled by the police for an hour after the final whistle. Instead of the Spurs fans dispersing, they had reason to remain and bait the enemy, until eventually (in their wisdom!) the old bill decided to frog march everyone down the High Road, whether they wanted to go in that direction or not. I could never leave before the final whistle, but in my attempt to avoid such petrifying pandemonium, I should assume some blame for Spurs' equaliser (along with Richard Wright!). Róna reckoned that in the act of leaving our seats in the very back row of the upper tier, to effect our rapid exit, we caused the karmic disruption that sealed our fate. The instant we started to skedaddle, the Arsenal succumbed to yet another last-gasp goal. I am the last person to argue with such superstition. Earlier in the game I suggested that we swap seats at the break, for fear of a bonk on the head from any bacchanalian celebrations of the Gooner beside Róna. Yet after our goal had led such a charmed first 45, I didn't dare do anything to offend the fates.

I was so pessimistic about our prospects prior to the game that I would have gladly settled for the draw, so I couldn't really complain about the result. Although it would have been a far more enjoyable experience if we had equalized in the dying moments and salvaged a single point, instead of blowing two! There was no time to consider this calamity. As I zipped up my coat past the collar, to cover up any foolhardy sign of my fealty and avoid waving any red and white rags to the Neanderthal bulls waiting outside, my mind was already in 'escape enemy territory' mode.

We're so familiar with being the Derby favourites that it was weird leaving White Hart Lane happy to have avoided weeks of humiliation by my Spurs pals. The cyclical nature of all things might lead them to believe that their time as top dog is long overdue. I cling to the hope that it is merely a temporary state of affairs. Considering the potential distraction of the whole Sol sideshow and the fact that Man United apart, none of our competitors managed to profit from our misfortune, perhaps I should welcome a difficult Derby point that keeps us in touch at the top. As we cantered back to the privately owned car park, it certainly wasn't so much my concern for two points dropped, as the daylight robbery of paying double the price of previous seasons to leave our vehicle. The economic downturn can't have hit the pockets of the Spurs punters, who not only fill this car park at a tenner a pop, but are also prepared to pay £15 for the privilege of a pitch by the exit. It is hard to comprehend the fact that there are Spurs supporters who pay more to park their vehicle during the season than the cost of many fans' season tickets!

At least Spurs last-minute goal meant that I didn't lose my seat on the sofa later that night, having arranged to watch the big-fight in the cinema-like circumstances of my closest Spurs mate's lounge. While the draw meant we were both able to bear each other's company, he took plenty of stick for the 'part-time' support that saw him nipping off long before the final whistle and having to listen to what might be one of his season's high points on the car radio. Moreover I was tickled to hear that the Arsenal team coach broke down last week and they were kindly offered the use of their neighbours vehicle on Saturday. How ironic that Spurs morons smashed up their own team's transport. We've bigger fish to fry this week, with two massive games that will be a telling indicator of which way the Arsenal is heading.

13. Gooner Grit . . . At Long Last

Wednesday, 21 November (Champions League): Deportivo La Coruna(A) 0–2
Sunday, 25 November (Premiership): Manchester Utd (H) 3–1
Ljungberg (48), Henry (80, 85) 3rd

In contrast to our domestic form, where we hadn't lost away from home, our away form in the Champions League was abysmal – five successive defeats. So I don't know what possessed me to want to go to Spain for our match against La Liga leaders Deportivo, as we were on a hiding to nothing. However it was an equally daunting task a couple of years ago, when we were drawn against them in the UEFA Cup, having fallen through the trapdoor into this tournament from the Champions League. Perhaps it was these memories that made up my mind, as we demolished them 5–1 at Highbury in one of Arsenal's most impressive European performances. Despite losing in La Coruna 1–2, I can remember being extremely jealous of all those who returned from a costly trip we couldn't afford at the time, with tales of a kick-about on La Coruna's beach in 80-degree sunshine. I guess I was determined to get there this time. I hate missing out on any Arsenal match, especially when we are likely to lose, as my absence ensures I am left feeling personally responsible for a defeat.

Sunday's victory over Man United would have been a highpoint in the season for everyone at Highbury, but it will have meant that little bit more for the 400-odd die-hard Gooners who plumbed the depressing depths of our defeat against Deportivo. There was some speculation about Richard Wright's injury being genuine. We wondered whether Wenger had simply substituted him at half-time in Spain, in a rare moment of wrath resulting from his gullible goalkeeping for both Deportivo's first-half goals. Yet one goalie's gammy knee proved to be another's good fortune, as Stuart Taylor came on and at least kept a clean sheet after the break. Our home-grown goalie grasped his opportunity to make his mark with both hands, stepping from relative obscurity into the limelight of European and league debuts.

Three days from getting the key to the door he must have been struggling to keep his feet on the ground. He took his place in goal before a packed North Bank for perhaps the biggest game of the season. I can't imagine he could have wished for a better 21st birthday present. The ongoing injury problems of Seaman and Wright resulted in a ten-game run for Taylor in which he performed so admirably that no record of this season would be right without a footnote that credited his considerable contribution. However, the wonderful victory against United will be remembered, above all, for Fabian Barthez's blunders.

I should have known to have a bet on Scholes for first goal-scorer, when the last thing I heard on the box before leaving for the game was that he had never scored at Highbury. Better still, according to my neighbour in the West Upper, I could have got odds of 28/1 on United leading at half-time and Arsenal winning by the final whistle. Still, United's 1–0 lead at the break was far from a true reflection of what had transpired on the pitch in the first half. The final shot tally of 18 to 4 in our favour was testament to our total domination in this match and if it wasn't for our players' now customary profligacy, combined with Barthez's competency, we might have recorded a result which would have really revenged our 1–6 trouncing at Old Trafford last term. His superb saves were soon forgotten, when Barthez totally gifted us two goals – and as a result all three points – in the last ten minutes. It was a rare pleasure to hear the whole stadium join in as we mercilessly teased the man by singing 'Give it to Barthez'. I almost felt sorry for him until he responded in kind with a two-fingered salute.

As the United players trudged off in the teeming rain with their heads hung low in shame, we lingered awhile to savour the goals again on Highbury's giant screens and to discover that Liverpool had retained top spot by beating Sunderland.

Monday, 26 November 2001

'Barthez is a Gooner' was the jubilant chant reverberating around the ground, as 35,000 beaming Arsenal fans hokey-kokeyed their way out of Highbury on Sunday. It feels like an eternity since we last experienced this sort of euphoria. But then home fans have had to endure two draws and a defeat against unfancied Bolton, Blackburn and Charlton in the Premiership, during the dolorous three months since our last Highbury high. We may have been singing in the summer sunshine after our four-goal felling of a feeble Leicester side, but it hardly stood comparison to our unadulterated delight, dancing deliriously in Sunday's winter drizzle.

What a tonic, after travelling some 2,500 miles to experience our timid defeat to Deportivo. These lordly lionhearts bore little resemblance to the losing side in La Coruna. That only 380 loyal lunatics suffered the short sojourn in the seaside town on the northwestern tip of the Spanish mainland suggests I was far from alone in suspecting we'd see sod all success from this second-stage Champions League opener. After all our fruitless European forays I was so willing to accept a draw that it wasn't the defeat that was depressing, but the gutless un-Arsenal-like way in which they let themselves and us Gooners down.

The Arsenal defended their deflowering by Deportivo with less regard for their reputation than the residents of the house of ill-repute which was apparently besieged by our boys in their bacchanalian bonhomie the night before the game. That's the Gooners on the overnight trip, as Wenger wouldn't include such extracurricular activities in the team's itinerary (plenty of broccoli, no bonking!) – although at least this would have been some excuse for their footballing fiasco. Amongst us foolhardy fans there was a determination not to let our limited expectations get in the way of a good jolly. With the consumption of copious amounts of liquor constituting a crucial ingredient, many of the day trippers gravitated towards the Guinness on offer at an Irish pub. Like Chinese take-aways, there seems to have been one of these in every town I have ever visited. On Arsenal outings, one can guarantee they will be full of Gooners.

While some attempted to catch up on the alcoholic headstart of the earlier arrivals, I tucked into my tortilla and various indeterminate tapas, ordered by means of my multi-lingual, point-and-mime method. My pessimistic mood lifted somewhat, seeing TV pictures of Henry training the previous evening which suggested he might play some part in proceedings. The newspaper headline, 'Henry es la gran duda del Arsenal' had me wondering if our funky French striker had forced our Spanish foe to be struck by the fear of God – until it was pointed out that this meant he was 'a big doubt' as opposed to 'the great dude'! The press also poured scorn on the fact that three coaches were required to ferry the team, their flunkeys and half a hospital to their hotel. Either they made miraculous recoveries, or didn't feel such a dire need for excuses, as Richard Wright apart, it was amazing how little we've heard since about the injuries that five of our squad were carrying in Spain.

The Riazor Stadium is at one end of the bay around which La Coruna is situated. En route to the game I joined the Depor fans walking the length of the beachside promenade. I always notice a preponderance of spruce elderly ladies amongst Spanish supporters. In fact their fans in general appear far more family oriented and tastefully attired (even their recidivists are more respectable than our designer-labelled larrikins). In this convivial atmosphere, I tarried to take in the twinkling lights of La Coruna by night and the row of multi-coloured inflated stick men, bending in the stiff sea breeze, as they boogied to the tune of pop music blasting out from sea-front speakers. With man-made music in one ear and nature's own accompaniment of the waves washing over the beach assuaging the other, I realised this might be the highlight of my night.

Thankfully the coppers did not confiscate my cancer sticks as an offensive weapon. With a carrier bag full of cartons of Camel, I had calculated that I would at least profit financially from this equivalent of football purgatory. Whereas according to the bevvied-up body language of stocious Gooners staggering around the terraces, many would have nothing more than a hangover to nurse the next day. Later, at the airport, I overheard this sleepy comment: 'I'm never coming on another European trip. I was so blathered, I slept right through the match.' Little did he appreciate quite how lucky he was!

Personally I believe Le Prof should shoulder some of the blame. He blew it by bigging up our opponents, as the team who 'can achieve anything . . . one of, if not the, best in Europe.' This was the noose around Arsenal's neck which left them in no doubt that Depor could kick the chair away. However, he more than made up for this 'faux pas' with the 'savoir-faire' used to finesse the Fleet Street hacks on Friday. The constant furore over his failure to commit to a new contract had left an air of insecurity hanging around Highbury's marble halls, like a bad smell. Arsène's earnest affirmation that his future lies at Arsenal was a perfectly timed ace.

One of the advantages of living five minutes away from Highbury is being able to watch the build up to Sunday's match on the box. We saw the smug smile on David Dein, as he assured the United suit that Wenger wasn't going anywhere. Arsène's statement that he wouldn't be seduced away by five times his current salary told his team and the world that the Arsenal is a club worth fighting for. He inspired the required response from his troops, especially with the reintroduction of Ray Parlour. Parlour might not be everybody's idea of the perfect solution to our problems, but he certainly is no powder puff. It is his sort of mettle that has been missing of late. Vieira was imperious, but Parlour was my Man of the Match for his willingness to get stuck in right from the whistle. He set a spirited standard which forced others to follow suit.

Although the Arsenal are still short of the vocal captain who could command some cohesion, it was United who played like 11 disparate individuals. I am still not sure if we were marvellous, or they were so mediocre. Before his balls-up, Barthez was probably United's best player and without his aid, once again we would have been left ruing our inability to capitalise on countless chances. This contest might not be the title decider of previous seasons, but it could prove no less significant. It remains to be seen whether we can repeat this raising of our game, using Sunday's subjugation of United as a springboard for a successful season.

14. Muddied but Unbowed

Tuesday, 27 November (Worthington Cup): Grimsby (H) 2–0 Edu
(4), Wiltord (74)
Saturday, 1 December (Premiership): Ipswich Town (A) 2–0
Ljungberg (5) Henry (56 pen) 2nd

Only about half the number of fans turned up at Highbury for the Worthless Cup game against Grimsby as had come to see us play United in the previous round. When Wenger first started using this tournament as a proving ground for our youngsters and fringe members of the first-team squad, these matches were included in our season tickets. However, the club received complaints from those who felt cheated by the absence of most of their favourite stars and the lesser-known line-ups. It didn't stop them from going to the matches and many were just chancing their arm by claiming a refund after the event. The club soon wised up. For the past few seasons we have all been forced to buy our tickets from the box office, where they have a notice in each of the windows with a warning about the possibility of weaker teams, so there can be no comeback.

The unsold seats at these Worthless Cup games ensure a rare treat for lots of deprived (if only of live football) kids. We often take this opportunity to see a match at Highbury from another perspective, joining in the terrace banter behind the goal in the Clock End. It makes a change to be part of a chorus, instead of putting on my usual solo performance in the West Upper (or I should say a duet, as it would be remiss of me to suggest that my missus doesn't also make the effort). There are lots of youngsters present, perhaps for their one Highbury high of the season, as their parents can't obtain tickets for all the other sell-out games, or can't afford such an expensive outing for themselves and their offspring. I find myself wondering whether they might be disappointed having been so excited about seeing live football and their favourites in the flesh, only to discover half the heroes they were hoping to see have been given the night off.

Mind you, there are plenty of other kids who are far too blown away with just being present at Highbury to care less who is actually playing. Whether it is a charitable act, or just an investment in the Arsenal's future, I am not sure. Whatever the motive, it is wonderful that the club allocates a proportion of unsold seats to the local Islington schools on these unusual occasions. For one reason or another Ró was unable to go to a subsequent game and so she suggested I should encourage the ardour of an Arsenal-mad son of a single-parent pal of hers, by taking him to the match in her stead. I consider it a privilege to pass on my enthusiasm and spend 90 minutes in the company of an enraptured child. It pains me that I should be so puerile, but I have to admit to being slightly miffed because the youngster wasn't quite as ebullient as I expected. This was already his third trip to Highbury having been lucky in the ballot at his school for free tickets to both cup games.

With a World Cup draw which appeared to leave Ireland with better prospects of progressing than England (who had to escape a 'group of death' to go any further), it had been an eventful week in football terms. Liverpool fans were livid to see Kop-favourite Fowler sold to Leeds for £11 million. Fowler's training-ground tiffs couldn't have helped with Houllier's health problems and his arrival at Elland Road didn't immediately benefit David O'Leary, as his increasingly cash-strapped club could only manage a 0–0 draw at Fulham. Having announced his retirement, Fergie might have put the mockers on Man Utd's season. They followed up their hopeless showing at Highbury, by going down 0–3 to Chelsea at Old Trafford. Another infamous media spat meant the entire press corp were being given the cold shoulder by Fergie. Yet it would have taken a brave hack to point out the irony that the first letter of each team that had triumphed over Utd so far – Bolton, Liverpool, Arsenal, Newcastle and Chelsea – spelt the name of the ageing centre-back purchased to replace Staam!

Monday, 3 December 2001

Despite securing all three points, I was a little disappointed by Saturday's defeat at Portman Road of the team currently propping up the table. After heaping praise upon the purring engine at the hub of our heartwarming humbling of the not so mighty Mancunians, I was hoping to witness a repeat which might prove evidence of our marked improvement. In the event Arsenal were left hardly having to put pedal to the metal, pootling along in second gear for the majority of the match, after extinguishing much of the East Anglian enthusiasm with the mazy movement that lead to Freddie Ljungberg's fifth-minute opener. Not that I care to criticise a clean sheet, on top of a two-goal away-day triumph, but a slightly stiffer examination by our opponents might have resulted in the required reassurance. An indication that we hadn't merely managed to raise our game the previous week, as a one-off, in honour of Fergie's extremely enigmatic United.

I usually enjoy an annual saunter to Suffolk and the south coast. In this respect I would be delighted to see both Ipswich and Southampton avoid the dreaded drop. Give most Gooners such a jiffy of a journey any day, relative to the motorway monotony or infernal train rides of some of the alternative nightmare northern outings. Any day, apparently, apart from Saturday!

With Róna gifted swollen glands by some loathsome lurgy, I set out for Liverpool Street alone, with only a few quid and a spare match ticket in my sky rocket. After the cost of the tube and a carrier bag full of red-top comics, wrapped carefully in some more respectable reading matter, I was left with nothing more than 60p and a conscience-troubling credit card. Late as ever, I arrived with seconds to spare before the one o'clock train departed. As I wandered through the carriages searching for the mates I'd arranged to meet, I received a phone call which revealed a complete role reversal. I had counted on being able to ponce a few quid from Nell or his pals, until I found a recipient for Róna's ticket, but for once it wasn't me who was tardy, as they were stuck on the tube at Whitechapel.

Fortunately my train was already rolling, as I was tempted to wait instead of travelling alone. Being so skint, after months off work because of my blasted back problems, if I had the bottle, I also might have been tempted to bunk the journey in the little boys' room. Then again, with the embarrassing events at Old Trafford being broadcast live, it was bad enough getting some sort of reception on my radio in the carriage, let alone trying to tune in in the kazi! There were surprisingly few Gooners on the train, as I guess many must have travelled earlier to gawp at yet another United disaster.

When I strolled back through the train for a second time I finally found a friendly face, from whom I could purloin the price of a cup of tea. So by the time we arrived in Ipswich about an hour before kick-off, I was desperate to off-load Róna's ticket. It must be my aversion to the turpitude of ticket touts that makes the words 'anyone need a ticket' stick so completely in my craw. I so abhor the thought of being mistaken for one of their number that I have often ended up giving away a spare ticket (in more affluent times!). Despite an abundance of Gooners desperately seeking seats on Saturday, I would have still been standing there if it wasn't for a gregarious fanzine flogger who found me a buyer (face-value, naturally).

It was only when the goal went in after five minutes that it occurred to me to find out if Nell had missed it. They were still stuck on a train, in the middle of nowhere. I counted my blessings, as I heard how they'd missed the 13.15 departure, been on the wrong platform for the 13.30 and eventually boarded one that had broken down. As I kept Nell abreast of proceedings on the pitch, his text message replies told of their increasingly parlous predicament. There were ten minutes left on the clock when he phoned to tell me they'd given up the ghost. Having been forced to abandon the train, with the engine on fire, all the passengers were being ferried to Colchester, in one car, three at a time! Nell suggested that with no trains running as a result, I might need to find an alternative means of getting home. Instead of savouring our success, I spent the remainder of the match screaming above the celebratory chants down the phone to friends in the crowd in a vain attempt to cadge a lift back to London.

Trudging towards the train station, I managed to glean some depressing details from a geezer about the laughing stock (as opposed to rolling stock!) of the misnomer that is Great Eastern Railways. According to him, they could only organize a couple of coaches to cope with the thousands of fans trying to get home. Perhaps it was the thought of joining the throng of supporters resigned to standing outside the station, awaiting rescue by our moribund rail network, which caused my non-conformist neurosis. In La Coruna airport some days prior, I was bleating like a sheep, when without an independent thought amongst us, we all marched to the wrong gate and back. So this time I marched off on my own, thinking I could be safely ensconced in the living room with an episode of *Casualty*, having hitched my way home, while the others were still shivering in Suffolk.

Having failed to ask for directions, I plodded up a never-ending hill in typical pig-headed fashion. My vague conviction that the crowd ahead was leading me in the right direction disappeared with them, step by step, as they dispersed down side streets and into cars parked on the grass verge. Without a sign of a single Gooner in any of the passing cars, I suddenly envisioned myself stranded in a leafy suburb of Ipswich. At long last I espied an Arsenal sticker on a van parked on the verge. I whimsically wondered out loud whether they would fancy ferrying me back to London. 'Sure, but the van's stuck in the mud,' was the forlorn response of one of the two rotund Gooners standing stoically in front of their stranded vehicle.

No matter that I might be minus one recently removed, herniated disc, I jumped at the chance and into the mud and put my dodgy back into pushing the van. Assisted by his weighty mate, we rolled the van onto the road in a matter of minutes. Mercifully I soon found myself homeward bound, squashed in a Steve sandwich, between my two new, similarly named, Arsenal supporting pals.

As for Nell, he and his mates arrived home about an hour before me, but at least for all our travelling tribulations, I didn't have to wait for the *Premiership* programme for an inkling of what transpired in the match. By the way, in case you weren't aware, we won 2–0! Although by the time you read this, the trauma of our trip to Ipswich will have been a mere trifle compared to the tension of Tuesday night's titanic contest with Juventus!

15. It May be a Library to Some But it's Home to Me

Tuesday, 4 December (Champions League): Juventus (H) 3–1
Ljungberg (21, 88), Henry (27)
Sunday 9 December (Premiership): Aston Villa (H) 3–2 Wiltord
(47), Henry (72, 90) 2nd

By far the Arsenal's greatest week of the season so far began with a brilliant result against Juve. The frequency of midweek Champions League matches has ensured we've all become a little blasé about the big European nights which used to make our hair stand on end. After opening the second stage with a defeat everyone appreciated the importance of this occasion. The Champions League was about to shut down and we needed to be on terms when it started up again in February, with back-to-back games against Bayer Leverkusen. So for once the atmosphere was suitably electrifying. Personally I believe there was no coincidence in the correlation between three successive victories and a consistent line-up in each game (after policy and necessity had resulted in so much early-season tinkering with the team). It shouldn't detract from the fabulous first-half display that we took the lead courtesy of a howler by Buffon, the most expensive goalie on the globe, when he spilled Cole's powerful shot for Freddie to fire home.

Moreover, the fact that Juve managed to get back into the game as a result of Stuart Taylor's unfortunate own goal should take nothing away from a terrific performance, which cemented our confidence in his ability to do the job at the highest level. Our silky skills in the first-half were complemented by our resilience in the second. It was a result that provided the proof we desperately required of a pedigree which enables us to dine with the rest of the elite at the cash-rich trough that is the European top table. The prima facie evidence which would have flashed across TV screens on the continent came in Dennis Bergkamp's cameo performance coming on as sub for the last 20 minutes. We were already foaming at the mouth when Freddie executed an exquisite lob for our third goal because Dennis had us all gobsmacked with a few seconds of football that will live on in our memories forever. He mercilessly teased a Juve defender with the very best excerpts from a book of tricks, which in Bergkamp's case must be of biblical proportions, before the final ignominy of flicking it over his head into Freddie's path.

Such was my state of euphoria that I was almost pleased for Paul Merson when he scored Villa's first goal on Sunday. It might have felt like an act of betrayal of his roots, but how could I possibly be angry with the man responsible for so many magical memories. It was evident that Merson was enjoying his football again and positively revelling in his return to Highbury, but I am sorry Paul, when you assisted Stone with Villa's second, that was tantamount to taking the piss!

It was also obvious that Fergie had lost the Premiership plot. It seemed as though he had swallowed hook, line and sinker, the romantic rubbish in the media and had been focused solely on bringing the curtain down on his glorious career with a Champions League finale in Glasgow. Having dissed West Ham, by resting a bunch of players, including Beckham, from their starting line-up, United were doomed to another home defeat delivered by the head of the eye-catching Jermaine Defoe. It was only December, so nobody was fooled by such fakery but United had slipped so far off the Premiership pace that Alex was already conceding the title. It made a pleasant change from their custom of having the Championship all sewn up by Christmas!

At half-time against Villa many were worried that the Arsenal were about to do likewise. It looked like we were going to end the day six points away from the Scousers at the top, after they'd beaten Boro on Saturday. I spent half-time telling all and sundry that I would willingly settle for a draw and even when Wiltord restored some belief two minutes after the break, it seemed to be the most we could hope for. I hadn't counted on one of the greatest comebacks of this, or any other season, as Thierry Henry made believers of us all, with his 21st goal of the season two minutes into injury time. The only black mark (well yellow actually) on what turned out to be a beautiful day, was a fifth booking for Patrick Vieira which would leave him suspended for our pre-Christmas confrontation with Liverpool.

Monday, 10 December 2001

'2–0 in the Library' sang the Villa fans, celebrating somewhat prematurely before half-time on Sunday. Indeed the only sounds coming from the not so supportive home crowd were the occasional cries, castigating the usual culprits. After a feeble first-half performance, it was hard to believe this was the same Arsenal side which had played Juve off the park five days earlier. Nevertheless I simply detest the way the more demanding amongst our fickle faithful find it so much easier to get on the backs of some players, instead of getting behind them. Most London clubs have traditionally attracted more capricious crowds and I can remember a time when I was extremely envious of the dogged devotion of the Northern fans who revelled in their 12th-man role, through thick and thin.

In times past, the premier objective of any away side was to stifle the home team for the first ten minutes and silence the crowd, to the point where they no longer provided any inspiration. Whether it is our expectations which have increased in direct proportion to the exorbitant expense of our sport, or that this cost has contributed towards crowds composed of far more white collars, the stands all over the country are no longer full of the blue collars who once backed their team come what may. These days, if they are not sitting back waiting for the team to produce the sort of entertainment that merits their support, the fans are baying for the blood of some poor overpaid, under-performing player.

I take a perverse pride in saving my most stentorian support for each week's victim of the worst tirades of the West Upper whingers around us. Otherwise I'd be forever berating these backseat Beckenbauers, demanding if they can do better! They booed the players off the pitch at half-time on Sunday. How dare the blackguards blacken the name of Dennis Bergkamp, the Dutchman they'd been drooling over only days earlier, with the wizardry of his 11-touch footballing equivalent of a multi-orgasm. The maestro's artistry left anyone that witnessed it openmouthed in absolute awe.

How quickly they go from hero to zero. Even Ray Parlour, whose indomitable desire has made such a difference in recent weeks, returned predictably to being public enemy number one. It was hard not to harbour a grudge with those Highbury hypocrites, taking part in a tumultuous standing ovation come the final whistle. Ray and his compadres strained every sinew, successfully treading that fine line between success and failure for the following 45 minutes. Despite the Arsenal's very best efforts, without an equalising goal and a glorious injury-time winner, they would have parted the pitch to another poisonous panning, instead of the plaudits.

Amongst ref Wiley's many dodgy decisions, with a possible penalty ignored (albeit Henry was hardly likely to earn one, having starred in a video highlighting his best dives) and with a perfectly good goal ruled offside, it felt like fate was conspiring against us. And yet, as they say, we made our own luck, with a 'never say die' attitude not seen since '98. I am a clean-sheet aficionado, but it was almost worth the double dose of defensive frailty to see a second-half revival. It was a sign to many Gooners that we might just have what it takes to stay the course this season. Tentative Championship chants echoed around the cavernous North Bank as we exited the stadium. These might have been tempered by Vieira's yellow card violation, which takes our vital Senegalese cog out of the seasonal six-pointer equation up at Anfield.

Some weeks back I suggested that Wenger's signature on a contract might be timed for maximum effect on our flagging Champions League foray. With Wenger finally confirming his future as he did last week, if I was of a cynical nature I might believe it was all part of a concerted plan to finagle the frying of a big-building fish. We were celebrating last week's humbling of the haughty Italians over a bowl of pasta when I buttonholed vice-chairman Dein, hoping to glean how confident he was of a council decision in favour of the building of the new stadium. Dein gave little away, except for a response that referred to our 'cup final' this week (and he wasn't talking about Tuesday's Worthless Cup game in Blackburn!). The past three weeks have seen tremendous triumphs over United and Juve, culminating with Sunday's resurrection, Wenger signing on the dotted line, players pledging their future to the club, not to mention Henry's blatant attempt to curry favour with the council (dedicating Tuesday's goal with his 'I love Islington Council' T-shirt!). It all couldn't possibly have been better timed to coincide with the last big public relations push and the reams of press coverage, to raise the club's profile to the rafters for Monday's landmark planning application meeting.

A Gooner gathering has been organised to lobby councillors. With many having limited lobbying experience, will we be attempting to hold sway over the lucid arguments of the protesters by resorting to our repertoire of Gooner chants? Yet as on previous occasions, I feel obliged to attend along with other Highbury residents, to prevent the militant protesters hijacking the meeting. The club have bent over backwards in their attempts to appease the counter arguments of a motley assortment, ranging from the extremes of the Socialist Workers Party, to right-wing 'anywhere else but my back yard' yuppies. I ended walking out of the last meeting, fed up with hearing them shout down anyone who spoke on behalf of the project. One couldn't help but wonder who were the concerned householders and who were the football hooligans! One woman became so stressed that she passed out in the aisle and had to be carried outside. I had to bite my tongue as she came to and began ranting about the health hazards of having a rubbish dump on her doorstep.

In fact the club plan to replace the rubbish dump that currently exists in Ashburton Grove by building a modern waste transfer unit beside this lady's run-down council estate. One of the reasons I believe the council will decide in favour of the new stadium is that the Arsenal have promised to spend millions building all sorts of social amenities, instead of the local-government funds that would be required to help regenerate a depressing dilapidated area. A project of this magnitude couldn't possibly take place without treading on some toes, but the benefits far outweigh the negatives for the club, its supporters and the prosperity of Islington and its residents. I guess we will find out tonight if a majority of Islington councillors are Gooners at heart, or believe they can curry favour with local voters by ensuring Highbury's end is nigh and the club is a goner from their borough.

Home from Home?
Reprinted from *The Gooner*, *118*, 10 December 2001

From a historical perspective in terms of securing the Arsenal's future this was indeed a pivotal few days. Arsène Wenger finally put pen to paper on the contract he had promised to sign some weeks back and on the Monday night, planning permission for all three parts of the Arsenal's massive Ashburton Grove project was granted. In the end the vote was passed by a large majority in the Union Chapel in Islington, before a packed audience of interested parties. It was wonderful news considering how hard the club and the Independent Arsenal Supporters Association had worked to ensure the new stadium will eventually become a reality. Yet I couldn't escape a certain sense of sadness as this was the decision that would guarantee a harrowing day a couple of years hence, when we enter Highbury's portals for the last time.

Driving home from work, I became aware of the proliferation of yellow estate agent's boards that had suddenly sprung up on every building along the length of one side of Drayton Park. Further evidence (along with the ever so slightly insincere slogan on Henry's vest!) that the club's PR department had gone into overdrive. Writ large on these were the weighty red words: 'Acquired For Development by Arsenal FC'. That is apart from the single stubborn businessman who's sign read: 'We Are Not For Sale. Business As Usual'. He couldn't have stated more clearly where his allegiances lay if he'd added 'Come On You Spurs'. Although I wouldn't have liked to speculate about the longevity of his glass shop front if he did!

Following my daily route, I turned right into Aubert Park, up the hill and then left, naturally, into Avenell Road. I kid myself it is quicker than continuing on to Blackstock Road. Truth be known, despite my almost twice-daily dose, I can't get enough of the only Home of Football I've

known. These signs finally impressed upon me the poignant fact that our
new stadium project is primed for lift-off.

When the move to the new stadium was first mooted a couple of years back, my
arguments against it were probably as vociferous as any of those voiced by the
NIMBY protesters. Unlike them, I adore having our Highbury home in my backyard.
Knowing many who have to go to such lengths to get to games from all four corners
of the globe, let alone the UK, it is an absolute blessing to be able to bowl out the
door just before kick-off, having watched the pre-match build up on the box.
Moreover, from our near perfect pitch almost on the halfway line, a couple of rows
from the front of the West Upper, I always feel privileged with such an amazing view
of some of the most talented players on the planet. Following the Arse around
Europe and the rest of the country, it is evident that few remaining football grounds
offer such a priceless perspective of a seat high enough to be able to ascertain the
tactics, yet close enough to feel the crunch of an Ashley Cole challenge.

Most of the modern concrete monstrosities are completely soulless structures by
comparison to the divine art-deco aspects and the heritage at Highbury's vibrant
heart. Sure the architects amongst us might slaver over stadia like the San Siro.
70,000 fawning Italians seated amongst the flamboyant flares and humungous flags
is enough to send a frisson down anyone's spine. Yet to my mind the majority of
these grounds are just a shell, inhabited for 90 minutes each week; the rest of the
time they are depressingly drab and desolate places. Whereas no matter what time
of day, or day of the week I pass by Highbury, it is invariably a hive of activity. Often,
early in the morning, I will see a queue forming at the box office and wind down
the car window to enquire which game is about to go on sale. I know I am really
late for work if I see Gooners collecting on the steps for the 11 a.m. guided tour.
During school holidays, most afternoons there will be parents picking their little
darlings up from courses at the community centre. Even at its quietest, you will
always find tourists having their pictures taken and the cash registers of the club
shop playing their costly tune to the constant stream of customers.

If I'm in a melancholy mood, or after a hard day's graft, usually I am
guaranteed respite from the gloom of a grey winter's evening when I catch a
glimpse of a forthcoming fixtures notice. On this particular night, as I swung
round the corner into Avenell Road and my favourite view of our fabulous
football ground filled my vista, I was suddenly overwhelmed by the dreaded
reality of finally having to face Highbury's inevitable last stand in the not so
distant future. I accept that I'm a sentimental and selfish old sod, with the season
tickets which mean I don't have to give a monkey's for all those who have spent
an eternity on the waiting list, or who toil away ad infinitum on the Ticket-bastard
phone lines. After months of persuasive argument, I have eventually come to
terms with the sound economic sense that necessitates a 60,000-seater stadium for

the club to continue to exist amongst Europe's elite. And as these projects go, ours does indeed appear to be a peach.

However even if Ashburton Grove turns out to be the most amazing edifice ever built and although I am overjoyed that it will only involve a few hundred yards further for us to walk, the move will mark a momentous occasion, in as much as watching the Arsenal play will never again be quite the same. I understand Arsène has made it his business to have some say in every detail of the new stadium, no matter how trifling. Apparently he appreciates the home team advantage of having the crowd right on top of the pitch. Nevertheless I will be pleasantly surprised if I can maintain the misguided belief that I am capable of influencing proceedings, as I do at present. I remain convinced of my capacity to harangue flag-happy officials (both when they are correct and when they've just cocked up another costly decision), to the point where they might occasionally favour the Arsenal just for a quiet life!

Perhaps my fears are unfounded. They might have a method of configuring all those seats, so that none of us need binoculars to know that Ray Parlour's roots need doing! And by bringing Herbert Chapman's bust and the brass name plate, along with all the other historic arse-facts, to install in a re-creation of the marble halls, they could just carry it off (even Herbert's ghost might manage such a short hop?). However, even if they manage to replicate the material aspects, it is our emotional attachment that can not be monkeyed with.

My dear departed dad's ashes might not be fertilizing the hallowed turf with those of hundreds of others (although his fag ash might have made a decent mulch) but they might as well be. It was about 35 years back that I first shuffled through the same turnstiles we've been using ever since, hidden between the old man's legs by the folds of his winter overcoat. The West Upper is therefore an integral part of my memories of him and obviously of many of our most magical footballing moments.

Whether I am friendly with, dislike, or indifferent to those same faces who've sat around us for many years, they are part of the fabric of my football experience. It is these and other more intangible factors which are likely to make the move such a complete and utter wrench. Doubtless after a few years watching matches amidst the luxury of our state-of-the-art new stadium, not missing the second-half while queueing for the karsey or a cuppa, I will find myself wondering how we put up with Highbury's ancient facilities for so long (North Bank apart). Still it won't matter how many toppings I am offered on my pizza, we'll have to be there for many years, building up Ashburton Grove's own bank of reminiscences, before the new ground even begins to replace the huge Highbury void left in my heart.

16. All I Want for Christmas is an *A-to-Z*

Wednesday, 12 December (Worthington Cup quarter-final): (A)
* Blackburn Rovers 0–4*
Saturday, 15 December (Premiership): West Ham United (A) 1–1
* Cole (39) 2nd*

Tragically, after the head gasket went for a second time my trusty Gooner mobile was headed for Jag heaven. The last time the car let us down was en route to our traumatic 1–6 humiliation at Old Trafford last season. So I was relieved that at least this time it didn't occur as an ominous omen on the way to a match. However a replacement had to be found and these were the circumstances that led to me travelling alone to Blackburn, on a tortuous train journey via Castleford, to purchase a replacement Jag, for which I had bid the princely sum of £800 on an Internet auction site. While the car drove like a dream, the football was something of a fiasco as a team consisting largely of Arsenal hopefuls, including a rare start for the anonymous Inamoto, did their future prospects little good in an embarrassing defensive display against Blackburn. It was only the Worthless Cup but it was disappointing to go out of the tournament just two games away from a Cardiff final. What's more, it certainly wasn't a performance that would promote the all-important winning habit.

Come Saturday, apart from the few of us who bothered schlepping all the way to the North, the Worthington Cup didn't count. Most were expecting West Ham to be the formality of our fifth win in a row, but by the time we left Upton Park we were grateful to have extended our unbeaten away record. Not for the first time and certainly not for the last, Wenger's infallible belief in the ability of this team to outscore any opponents was demonstrated in his adventurous selection of Henry, Bergkamp and Wiltord up front. Three strikers away from home! There was a time when we Gooners would count ourselves lucky to see one.

Beckham was busy with Xmas shopping in London, while his team beat McClaren's Boro 0–1 as the pupil duly deferred to his teacher. The top teams were taking turns at inconsistency. By Sunday we were only three points from the leaders, after Liverpool suffered a 0–4 bashing at Stamford Bridge. It was Bobby Robson's dark horses (or more appropriately zebras) that were moving up on the rails. By beating Blackburn at home Newcastle were level with us on points.

Monday, 17 December 2001

I've been driving the same route to Upton Park for the last ten years, but somehow on Saturday I missed a turn and found myself lost in the least salubrious part of East London. The incongruous strains of Prokofiev's 'Dance of the Kings' from *Romeo and Juliet* blasting out from the radio's live broadcast signalled the rapid approach of kick-off time, but it was a relief to know that I had a match commentary to keep me abreast of any action. Sadly I'd have little chance of recouping the £32 cost of the spare ticket in my pocket once the game had started. Instead of following my nose into further trouble, I stopped to ask directions. After being blanked by four passers-by, it began to dawn on me that perhaps it wasn't my cockney accent that they couldn't comprehend, but English. Eventually I found someone who pointed me towards Green Street, the bustling shopping thoroughfare on which West Ham's ground is situated. I was relieved to know I was heading in the right direction, but it was painfully slow progress, inch by inch in the worst Christmas traffic. On a Saturday before Christmas such congestion should have come as no surprise, if it wasn't for the fact that that 90 per cent of these shoppers appeared to be Asian.

At last West Ham's spanking new West stand loomed into view, but I still had to find a pitch where I wouldn't spend the whole game worrying about a £40 parking ticket. I had already missed ten minutes of the match by the time I scurried to our stand, so it came as a bit of a blow to be informed by a steward that I now had a ten-minute hike around a council estate at one end of the ground to reach the new entrance.

Limited by my bad back to a brisk walk, there was hardly a soul to be seen by the time I rounded the corner towards the turnstile. With the Hammers having dominated this derby duel until then, according to the radio, it sounded like my side needed my support (or were they courteously awaiting my arrival?). My only options were either to enter the ground, with the spare ticket as an expensive extra bit of leg room, hand it to the stewards at the door in the vague hope that a suitable recipient might materialise, or offer it to the sullen-looking kid, spied lagging a few yards behind. His expression suggested he thought I was bonkers, as he rightly hesitated before taking this gift horse from a complete stranger. As I heard the clunkety-click of the turnstile right behind me, I was grateful that he didn't look it in the mouth.

It wasn't until this somewhat bewildered-looking boy sat down beside me that I realized he couldn't have been more than 12. It suddenly occurred to me that he might have someone at home worrying about his whereabouts. Despite his understandable disquiet, I managed to ascertain that he had been on his way to get some grub from the chipper and that as I had expected of a local lad, he supported our opponents. I am sure he had sufficient street smarts to know the score, but thankfully a few minutes before Kanoute sent the home crowd into rapture with West Ham's opener, I'd had the presence of mind to suggest that he'd best not jump out of his seat with this event. It is crazy what this world is coming to, but I felt so awkward that I went through half my pack of fruit Polos before offering the lad one, for fear he might think I had ulterior motives.

The Arsenal may have come back into the game in the second-half, following Ashley Cole's equaliser before the break, but sadly my overall impression was that they did not display sufficient desire to deserve anything more than a draw. After the impressive mettle seen in recent matches, it was disappointing to see players like Pires bottling out of putting his precious limbs anywhere near the sort of full-blooded challenges which have to be won in these heated London derbies. Our recent improvement had coincided with the return to the first team of a raring to go Ray Parlour and to my mind his absence through injury was responsible for our overall lack of grit in this game. However, it would be an injustice to the Hammers to suggest they were all iron and steel, as Messrs Cole, Carrick and Di Canio produced some stylish football. Joe Cole showed zero respect to one of the world's greatest midfielders and we were regaled with his full repertoire of tricks, which teased us into some thunderous tackles. Although, as a disciple of Di Canio, he hasn't quite mastered the art of diving, despite exhibiting an embarrassing number of far too theatrical, swallow-like falls.

West Ham more than deserved their point and but for a couple of goal-line clearances, could have kept all three. However, considering the rest of the weekend's results, it will be a gutter to get to the end of the season and find that only Bergkamp hitting the crossbar stands between us and the Championship. It is so tight at the top, that I reckon every missed opportunity might be regarded in this manner. Out of the corner of my eye, I am sure I caught the youngster singing along with us at some point. You never know, I might have made a convert (well the boy Beckham grew up in the same environs supporting United). Even if not, it was well worth it, just to see the look of wonderment on his face, being in such close proximity to his heroes.

I predicted a draw as I walked out the door earlier that afternoon, so I could hardly complain. It is our continued lack of commitment in less important matches which causes most concern. I assume we'll be more fired up for our visit to Anfield, but with Vieira suspended, Owen returning and the Scousers smarting from Sunday's spanking, I'll be pleasantly dumbfounded should we defy an

Anfield hoodoo which leaves us desperately clinging to ancient 'one minute' memories from '89. Still we might get a taste of the rarefied air at the top prior, if Newcastle continue their lengthy losing streak in London. Although, if I was a betting man, it wouldn't be a bad time to begin backing them to break it. Let's hope we can avoid the law of averages and the Toons can conjure up one more capital cock-up!

17. Mortally Wounded by the Slings and Arrows of Outrageous Fortune?

Tuesday, 18 December (Premiership): Newcastle United (H) 1–3
Pires (20) 3rd

This was to be a crucial seven-day period with the Arsenal playing the two teams either side of us at the top of a finely balanced table. With our abysmal record at Anfield, most Gooners would have expected three points and gladly settled for four from the two fixtures, but few assumed we'd achieve them in the way we did. I imagine many Gooners will have forgotten a first 45 minutes of some of the most sensational football we have ever seen, since the events that followed left us all trying to put this match out of our minds. The Toons were so totally overrun that it was unbelievable to think that this was the team who would overtake us into top spot. Then again, if the Arsenal were so capable of wiping the floor with the team that was statistically the best in the land at that time, we should be able to win the league hands down.

You might have heard the huge guffaw from Gooners everywhere some weeks later, when referee Graham Poll was selected as England's one representative amongst the officials chosen for the World Cup. Thankfully it would be even longer before Thierry Henry would be called to the FA (a conspiracy according to Fergie!) to face the disrepute charge resulting from his verbal assault on Poll at the end of the game. Seizing every opportunity to spread their scandalous stories about the Arsenal's disciplinary problems, the media made such a mountain out of what was really a relative molehill, that Henry might have been banned for months if he had been dealt with immediately. According to Titi's comments at a later date, there was more than a little irony in the incident, as he was haranguing Poll because he believed it to be the second time in a matter of months that this ref was culpable in an Arsenal catastrophe. Whereas, in fact, this was a matter of mistaken identity, as it was Dunn, not Poll who had failed to spot Henchoz's handball, in a calamity that might have cost us the Cup final.

It can be frustrating filing my diary on a Monday, when events so often overtake it before it appears in the *Examiner*'s sport supplement on a Wednesday. Graham Poll left me feeling so livid that instead of lying awake, praying for divine retribution, I decided to sit up into the wee hours, venting my anger at the keyboard, perhaps offering some comfort to a couple of thousand other angry fans on the Arsenal mailing list on the Internet.

Tuesday, 16 December 2001

I have always felt that the longer Newcastle's London hoodoo lasted, the more the law of averages swung in favour of them finally cracking it. To the extent that if I was a betting man, I would have began putting money on them (although I doubt I'd be able to bring myself to bet against the Arsenal). Moreover, with such a prolific goal-scorer as Alan Shearer never having failed to score at Highbury his entire career, I guess such a prolific striker was long overdue a goal.

Being far too long in the tooth to be flummoxed by the slings and arrows of outrageous fortune, no matter how disappointing, I would have dealt with tonight's defeat in all good grace, if it wasn't for another party playing such an incredibly frustrating role in the outcome of this fixture.

Let's face it, after 30 minutes of dazzling, dominant football from the Arsenal, they should really have floored the visiting side with far more than a single goal. If we hadn't been so profligate with the panoply of perfect goal-scoring opportunities, without doubt it would have been all over bar the shouting by the break. And boy was there some shouting!

So imperious were the Gunners during that early period, that I turned to my long-suffering neighbour to suggest that it was hard to believe we were playing the third-placed team for the right to top the pile (long-suffering because if I haven't made him deaf in one ear prior, he certainly must be suffering some symptoms after enduring some doughty decibels tonight). Even Bobby Robson freely admitted that on the evidence of the first half an hour, there is a gulf in class between these two sides.

It was annoying enough to witness a proliferation of officious punishments at Upton Park on Saturday. In the heat of a London derby, where one would expect tackles to come flying in for all of the 90, with the fervour of such frantic affairs, there wasn't one challenge of sufficient malicious intent to merit a single booking, let alone seven!

I dashed home tonight in time to catch the post-match interviews. Despite the reporter's persistence, Wenger was far too wily to be drawn on referee Poll's penal performance, avoiding adding insult to injury by lumbering himself with the large fine which might have resulted if he had spoken his mind. Though undoubtedly as full of frustration as every Gooner, the only inkling of his feelings on camera came with the wry smile that accompanied his final response: 'I don't speak about the referees, never . . . especially not this one!'

I have to admit that Alan Shearer was quite gracious in victory and said that the match was spoilt by the red cards. He was also quite correct in his assertion that the refs have a difficult job. I am sure that the majority of fans in their place would be far more fallible than most of football's officials. They're under increasingly intense pressure from the crowd, the all-pervasive TV cameras and their peers who sit in judgment on them each week.

I may regularly rant and rave at their every mistake (on the rare occasion that they're right, it doesn't stop me screaming) and pillory the official policy that sees refs punished, should they show the slightest sign of practising common sense, instead of the customary card-happy handouts. Yet at the end of the day it comes with the territory of the true supporter to stoically take the rough with the smooth, hoping against hope that fortune does indeed even itself out over a season.

However, whilst I walked away on Saturday disappointed but not too downhearted, tonight, after rabidly foaming at the mouth for the entire second-half I left Highbury dumbstruck by the downright injustice of it all. We've seen far too many matches spoilt by over-zealous officials and, with children starving in Afghanistan, it is not the most consequential crime. Nevertheless, in my attempts to secure more than £2,500 to pay for our season tickets, it was almost worth the sacrifice of my slipped disc for the privilege of watching live 30 minutes of 'total football' tonight from our perfect pitch in the posh seats. I certainly did not suffer four months of excruciating agony in return for the relative purgatory of Graham Poll taking centre stage for the remainder of the evening.

I get angry enough forfeiting 40-odd quid for each Highbury occasion, only for referees to book players all match long, to the point where we are left discussing their incompetence, instead of the beautiful game. It is wrong that their penchant for putting players in their place by showing who's boss, should so often leave us deprived of so many sensationally skilled stars through silly suspensions. It is the for the pleasure of watching these players, our heroes, that I fork out far more than I can sensibly afford, a few months in advance of each season, in good faith. I don't bargain for the duty-bound zealots, who appear determined to have maximum impact on every match.

What galls me most about Graham Poll is that unlike other refs, who at least appear respectfully remorseful that the current rigid rule-bound policy forces their hand in many instances, Poll appears by contrast to actually revel in his storm-trooper role, undoubtedly taking pleasure in casting himself as the pantomime villain. Most refs judge their best performances to be those in which they've been inconspicuous. Poll, however, appears to actually enjoy casting himself as the leading man.

After Parlour's sending off, the Clock End began serenading Poll at the start of the second half. Before the end of the game even the sedentary snobs of the West Upper were sufficiently angered to sing along with the ribald rhyme of 'Oh Graham Poll, you're a f*cking arsehole!' Coming from the stiff-upper-lip school of officiating, the majority of refs try to give the impression that they are impervious to intimidation from the fans. Whereas Poll had a smile on his face like the Cheshire cat who had got the cream. After winding up the 22 players who probably earn more in a year than he will in a lifetime, his expression suggested a smug satisfaction at having managed to get the goat of 35,000 Gooners. At 1–0 up but down to 10 men, Wenger might have been better off relying on the grit of Grimandi than the ball skills of Van Bronckhorst for a second-half substitution. What's more, Gilles might not have gone missing, as Gio did, when O'Brien headed home a near-post equalizer.

Poll might have redressed the ten-men-a-side balance by sending Bellamy off, but he was only compounding his cock-ups. I could not believe it when I got home to discover that Bellamy's faintest use of his forearm had merited a straight red in Poll's book! When Shearer finally broke his Highbury duck with the penalty at the death, it was par for this catastrophic course, to hear via the radio commentary, that Campbell's challenge had been timed to perfection.

It is the ultimate irony that the referee who tried to rule with a modicum of discretion, instead of instantly dismissing players as directed, was condemned to be relegated to the Nationwide. Whereas even if both Parlour and Bellamy's red cards are rescinded and the penalty proved wrong, the most Poll will have to put up with is probably a ticking off in a referee's private post-mortem. Even if Parlour's red card is miraculously quashed, it will be of little consolation if come May, we are three points away from the Championship and this game was the point when Poll put the mockers on our entire season.

Instead of going on to Anfield on Sunday, top of the league above Liverpool, high on the sort of football that was being played until Ray's dismissal, we will be heading north without Vieira (suspended yet again, despite hardly committing a crime of note all season), with a heavy-hearted hangover, possibly with Henry facing charges from the FA (or even criminal!), with the loss of our crucial leading goal-scorer hanging over our heads like the sword of Damocles.

The pompous pundits preached about how the Arsenal must learn to take such losses on the chin. Without doubt Henry's violent verbal barrage was downright foolhardy. Yet even as we stood there praying for someone to successfully pull him aside before his temper tantrum cost him a ten-game suspension, he was merely expressing the frustrations of every other Gooner. In this case we all had good cause to be sore losers. No matter how much of a numbskull this raving lunatic was in giving the red-top tabloids an excuse for a witch hunt, I couldn't help but admire our frontman for his verbal assault. Unlike some of his more mercenary contemporaries Thierry's passionate outburst reflected the same intense desire for the Arsenal's success as courses through the veins of those of us on the terraces. It was proof positive that Thierry is red and white right down to the core.

Newcastle had sent out a press release listing their 27-game losing streak in London. Despite an inkling, I still fancied three points tonight, followed by a result at Anfield similar to all those we've experienced these past nine years. A miserable Xmas could ensue, as a consequence of our meeting with Graham Poll (Freudian slip, sorry Newcastle!). Or just maybe tonight's game and any resulting repercussions might inspire a backs-to-the-wall, Fortress-Highbury response. Perhaps it will prove to be a defining moment, to test our mettle and to discover if we really have the taste for a decent Championship chase.

I began writing tonight, as my only means of venting my exasperation. So if I am allowed one Christmas wish, I know it should be world peace, but I wouldn't half love to condemn Poll to the karmic payback of a return in his next life as a Gooner, forced to spend eternity grinding his teeth on the terraces at all his own dreadful decisions!

18. Profiting from Paying Our Dues

Sunday, 23 December (Premiership): Liverpool (A) 2–1 Henry (45 pen.), Ljungberg (53) 2nd

Wenger would point to the triumph of ten men at Anfield, our first win there in nine years, as the inspiration for all that followed. Far be it for me to disagree with Le Prof, but I also think that it was the sense of injustice that we brought to this game from the floodlit robbery a few days earlier which was an extremely important contributing factor.

Of the 40 red cards received during Wenger's reign Van

Bronckhorst's was probably the most ridiculous, as he made absolutely no attempt to appeal for a decision when he went down after half an hour of this breathtaking clash. Instead of 'only' we were left singing 'We've always got ten men', utterly dejected at the thought of the game going the same way as the Newcastle match. Yet where Poll had managed to ruin a mesmeric Arsenal performance, when our heads dropped as a result, in this instance there was no fear of them feeling emasculated after Durkin had done his worst. In fact the exact opposite was true, as it only seemed to harden the resolve of the ten men. To the point where we were left absolutely dumbfounded at the sight of the habitually languid Kanu rolling his metaphoric sleeves up and getting down and dirty, displaying anything but indifference for his newly acquired defensive duties.

'Chim chiminey, chim chim cheroo, who needs Anelka when we've got Kanu?' made a return on the Gooner hit parade. Not just because of the surprisingly industrious efforts of our Nigerian striker, but also to wind up the Scousers. It was rumoured that the Arsenal had first dibs, but it came as a complete surprise when Liverpool announced their Christmas present to themselves was the free transfer of Anelka. Arsène obviously wouldn't take the troublesome Frenchman back, but there was much debate amongst us on the subject. According to Houllier/ Thompson Anelka was expected to knuckle down, because he was desperate for a stage on which to perform, so that he could retain his place in the French side in time for the World Cup. Although in light of what took place in Japan, in retrospect he probably considers himself fortunate that he was eventually ignored.

With Vieira's enforced absence we had been worried that there would be nobody to stop Steven Gerrard gobbling up all the middle ground. We had the fabulous fleet-footedness of 'Le Bob' Pires to thank for putting the youngster firmly in his place (as an impressive talent still learning his trade, but on an off day!). The ginger gherkin could have made life easier for us if he'd produced a second red card when Dudek took Freddie's legs away in the area. Myself, I was far too happy when Henry slotted home the resultant penalty to even notice that the inconsistent little git hadn't even produced a yellow. However, who knows, Durkin might even have done us an inadvertent favour. A victory at Anfield against one of our closest rivals would have been mammoth no matter what the circumstances, but it was the accomplishment of this ten-man 'team' performance that was the building block for the climax of our beautiful game to come.

From the inexperienced Taylor to Henry, including the early bather

Van Bronckhorst, they were all such heroes on the day that it would be wrong to single out the performance of any one of them. Yet since there always has to be a Man of the Match award, I don't think there were many to disagree with the choice of 'the Romford Pelé', Ray Parlour.

We might have clarified our championship credentials at Anfield but for the moment we had to be satisfied with second spot, since Newcastle had confirmed the fact that they were no flash in the pan by beating Leeds 3–4 at Elland Road. As for United, since Fergie had publicly conceded the title (without breaking his press ban) his team had responded with three straight Premiership wins, scoring 12 goals with only one against. A buoyant Gordon Strachan brought his Southampton side to Old Trafford on the back of three wins out of their last four games, only for his team to spend this Saturday afternoon chasing shadows as they were slaughtered 6–1.

Monday, 24 December 2001

After 30 years watching this wonderful game of ours, I still never fail to be amazed by its incredible capacity to confound. If you had asked me seven days ago, I would have predicted three points from our home game against Newcastle, followed by yet another profitless plod to Anfield, where a short sojourn at the summit of the table would have been all too swiftly curtailed by the Scousers. Yet if there is one thing I should have learnt by now, it is that the Arsenal never do things the easy way.

Hopefully the cost of Graham Poll's ridiculous refereeing won't prove too catastrophic. Perversely, the outrage felt over the dubious decisions of Poll and his pal Durkin on Sunday might just prove to be the catalyst, sparking the sort of 'strength through adversity' feelings that are currently coursing throughout our club. This same sense of injustice has often provided the backbone to all the Arsenal's best seasons.

It was evident at Anfield, when a couple of thousand Gooners found themselves in the grip of a cursed Groundhog Day loop, dumbstruck in our dismay at the sight of another senseless sending off. Up to that point, despite our poor prospects without the vanguard of the suspended Vieira pulling the strings in midfield, we had been full of Christmas cheer. Although much of it was more spirits than spiritual, as we persistently teased an apoplectic Phil Thompson to 'sit down Pinocchio!'

Being afraid that Liverpool were bound to score with 11 men on the pitch, I would have taken the draw there and then. A victory was almost unimaginable. I will not try to excuse the inexcusable, especially where that tubby little tyrant

Durkin is concerned, but I believe when he reacted initially to the Dutchman falling down in the box, he didn't realise he had already booked Van Bronckhorst. As I prophesied to Róna the next rumpus in the area would result in a penalty. Similar to the Bellamy sending off a few nights earlier, I was certain Durkin would try and even things out somehow. It might have been a blatant penalty, but in other circumstances, at the Kop end, I wouldn't have been surprised if the ref ruled against us.

Thankfully our feelings of devastation at going down to ten men didn't last. There we were, with our tails up at half-time, wondering if we could hold out, a man down, for another 45. Personally I wished we could go home, not only avoiding the traffic, but the agonising tension to come. The drive had taken some Gooners nearly six hours and with all the hope engendered by our half-time advantage, the return journey would have seemed twice as long after a second-half surrender. If this was to be avoided, I felt we had to score again, as our current defence doesn't appear capable of keeping a clean-sheet. From the Arsenal of old, down to ten men, we could count on the bulwark of a 'backs to the wall', 'they shall not pass', 'do or die' (along with countless other clichés) type commitment from all present. However the current side oozes far too much flair and not sufficient steel in certain quarters to grind out a '1–0 to the Arsenal'.

On the bench, I am sure Wenger must have been tearing his hair out, at 2–1 up, while we continued to tear forward recklessly, leaving gaping holes at the back. Although as far as I am concerned our chances of victory are greatly improved when we take the game to our opponents. Only by keeping the opposition sufficiently threatened by our attacks can we prevent them pouring forward and taking advantage of the momentary lapses in concentration that we are so liable to in defence.

I only hope Arsène isn't prone to heart problems like Gerard Houllier, since the sort of supremely fraught football which results is enough to blow anybody's aneurism. It certainly left me spending much of the second-half with my head buried in Róna's shoulder, hardly able to watch every time Liverpool approached our area. There are few (fit!) remaining members of the old guard, like Keown and Parlour, who are prepared to risk life and limb by putting some part of their person between the attacking Liverpool players and the nervous young novice between the sticks. Aside from the likes of Ashley Cole, amongst the majority of our current crop (and footballers in general), loyalty to the club doesn't run deep enough for them to play exclusively blinkered by the cause, with absolutely no regard for their own safety and the fitness that safeguards their future livelihood. With our limitless loyalty it is something supporters have been forced to come to terms with.

Even though we can no longer count on an Arsenal player blocking every single goal-bound shot, on Sunday fate seemed to favour our goal with its own force-field. It not only prevented Michael Owen (was he playing?) from scoring his 100th goal for the Scousers, but ensured every second-half strike deviated towards a Kop full of increasingly depressed faces. After nine years of Anfield angst, Róna reassured me that it was going to be our day. Nevertheless, it wasn't until a 19th-minute wayward bullet from Berger that I finally felt the force was with us.

To the uninitiated, it is hard to convey the climactic euphoria of such an 'against all odds' conquest. To appreciate it fully, one has to have schlepped to Spain to be defeated by Deportivo, or to Blackburn for the second string to slump 0–4 in an insignificant cup sortie. Such hardships are the dues we endure, in order to truly savour the unadulterated high of Sunday's celebrations. That sense of oneness with those players who came over at the final whistle to share a few moments of mutual respect and in whose expressions of delight you see your own ecstasy reflected.

As we returned to the car, surrounded by sorry-looking Scousers, I attempted to assuage them all with the reminder that it had been a long time coming. Whether it was my voice, hoarse from cajoling the troops into presenting us with this comeliest of Christmas presents, or my cockney accent they couldn't comprehend, but my crumbs of comfort didn't seem to cut much ice. I had clambered out of the pit at the crack of dawn to avoid the torment of the traffic, but fuelled on the adrenaline of reinvigorated aspirations, there were no signs of flagging on the long drive home.

19. Will the Shelf Sag Under the Weight of all those Cards or Our Championship Battle Buckle?

Wednesday, 26 December (Premiership): Chelsea (H) 2–1
  Campbell (49), Wiltord (71) 1st
Saturday, 29 December (Premiership): Middlesborough (H) 2–1
  Pires (55), Cole (80) 1st

Derby encounters between us and Chelsea are rarely uneventful occasions, but after the high drama of the last two games, we were due something a little more humdrum. I've said it before and doubtless I will continue until I am blue in the face. If we could tackle them in their ivory TV tower, I'd want to hang, draw and quarter the person ultimately responsible for early kick-offs. Suffering from the usual excesses of Christmas over-indulgence, it didn't feel as though any of us were too happy about turning up at Highbury for a noon kick-off on Boxing Day, least of all the players. They are forever complaining about the exhausting demands of a crowded Christmas fixture list, but you can usually guarantee our gratitude for any excuse to get out of the house and escape yet more mince pies and another family contretemps with distant cousins.

We would all probably have been raring to go at three in the afternoon, but as the two teams trotted out at this early hour, they were greeted with an atmosphere which was as icy as the weather. It was so cold that even the tough little nuts like Ashley Cole had resorted to the namby-pamby comfort of gloves (with the exception of complete nutters like Keown). If I didn't know better until Wiltord's eventual winner I would have said that the two teams had come to an amicable arrangement in the tunnel. Although 'amicable' wasn't an appropriate adjective to describe the way Le Saux barrelled into a kneeling Patrick Vieira. Le Saux is a strange sort. A placid person who all too often becomes Satan's own spawn the moment he dons his boots. Instead of received his marching orders, he managed to escape Scot free from the resulting 'handbags'-type mêlée. Although so did Vieira when Hasselbaink's face hit his elbow ('onest, guv!). Patrick didn't escape the all-pervasive Sky TV cameras and with the media delighting in any opportunity to wallow in one of Paddy's misdemeanours, this was bound to be the incident which ended up in front of the faceless video review panel.

On a more positive note, this match will be most remembered for Sol Campbell's debut goal. It was the sort we had been waiting for him to score all season, as he met a Pires corner with a towering back-post header. From the celebrations of our normally inscrutable Sol, it would appear that he too quite enjoyed his 'Gooner gone mad' moment. Chelsea managed to stifle Pires and Ljungberg – the source of all our most inspirational football these past couple of weeks – and we were much relieved when Wiltord finally came up with a winner. We had to make the most of our 'We Are Top of the League' celebrations as we were only there for three hours; when the whistle blew at St James' Park, the Toons had tonked Boro 3–0.

Elsewhere Robbie Fowler began repaying some of his hefty transfer fee with a hat-trick at Bolton, Anelka got reacquainted with British football when he came on as a sub in Liverpool's 1–2 win at Villa Park and United continued their resurgence in a comfortable 0–2 victory at Goodison Park.

The most important aspect of our victories over both Chelsea and Boro was the six points. We appeared to have discovered the trait of all true champions. In the same way as we got frustrated watching Man United over the last couple of seasons, as they kept coming away with the points after poor performances, at last we were also managing to beat opponents when not playing anywhere near our best. No one has enjoyed the football we've played of late more than me, but the Holy Grail of being able to grind our way to a result was the key to success we've been searching for these past three seasons.

Sol Campbell took the season of goodwill a bit too far, when he presented Noel Whelan with a gift-wrapped goal courtesy of a woefully casual back pass. By taking an early lead McClaren was able to alter his adventurous tactics and, like the vast majority of visitors to Highbury with less ambition, he left one man up front, with the remainder getting behind the ball and inviting us to break them down. All too often in the past our narrow Highbury pitch has made this task much easier for the opposition and despite dominating possession, we are far too used to the frustrating failure of our battering ram against their brick wall.

However, we seem to have developed the sort of supreme faith in our ability which enables us to play with total patience, certain of the fact that eventually one of our number will display the necessary guile to garner a goal, or two. In the past we could rest assured that one would be enough, but until such time as our back line develops the sort of rock-solid relationship we could once rely on for regular clean sheets, unfortunately we can be all too confident of the calamitous consequences of the odd defensive cock-up. We will continue to out-score our opponents so long as we maintain our rich vein of form, with goal contributions coming from all areas of the pitch. However, unless we eventually become clean-sheet connoisseurs once again, we Gooners are guaranteed plenty of time on the edge of our seats.

On Saturday no one at Highbury was too bothered about the route we took to three-point heaven, because come quarter to five we were sitting pretty at the top of the table. It was a southern conspiracy, as Chelsea did us another favour with a victory at St James' Park and Liverpool were held to a 1–1 draw at West Ham. The relentless repositioning at the top continued as Leeds went above them into third by winning at Southampton and the weekend ended with United only two victories away from top spot after their 2–3 triumph at Tigana's Fulham. Thanks to their recent victories against all our rivals Chelsea were just behind in sixth.

Talking of resolutions, no matter that it was only a goal difference of four, the Arsenal started the New Year as they intended to continue, leaving all our rivals with a view of our rear.

Monday, 31 December 2001

There I was berating Alen Boksic on Saturday morning for failing to turn out for Boro because he was 'poorly' and here I am bed-ridden, no doubt struck down by a similar bug. I'm wondering if I'll be fit enough for Tuesday's trip to Leicester. Sitting here, struggling to express myself, in a feverish sweat, I can't help but wonder if it is fate's friendly way of informing me that I shouldn't be so quick to judge. Having not seen their side score in nine hours of football, as a Boro fan I would expect nothing less than pneumonia to sideline this overpaid not so hot-shot, while he nicks more than 60 grand a week from the club's cash-strapped coffers. The Croatian hitman would struggle to convince that it was anything more than a bulging bank balance which brought him from the Lazio limelight, to the mediocrity of Middlesborough. Nevertheless, it isn't Boksic in particular I'm condemning. It is the proliferation in general of narcissistic, feckless fortune hunters, whose lack of loyalty to the cause has permeated the upper echelons of our glamorous game.

There was a time when a squad was where young men sat out their national service. It was nothing to do with a sport in which the same 11 players saw out a frantic five-fixture Christmas season, where no less than a broken limb would be cause to limp out of any confrontation. Whereas these days the majority of players consider themselves and their fitness such precious commodities, that the slightest semblance of a strain is sufficient to excuse them from even the most crucial contest. The clubs and coaches are as much to blame for mollycoddling these prima donnas. Mind you, such is player power these days that to some extent clubs are forced to pander to their every whim. Although a club can be so overly protective of their delicate property, prolonging the return to fitness of a particular player that the first time they send him out in a competitive game on a freezing cold afternoon the player ends up straining something the moment he stretches his legs.

Perhaps the players are ensuring the longevity of their careers by being far more clued up than their colleagues of yesteryear, many of whom ended up clapped out and in some cases crippled as a result of cruel cortisone injections. Although occasionally I find it hard not to begrudge some bench-warming malingerers and their exorbitant earnings, when we supporters with our unwavering loyalty would at least expect them to attempt to do their bit in vital battles. And it is not just Johnny foreigner suffering from the relatively modern phenomenon of so many tweaked knees and strained hamstrings. Those home-grown players who once had loyalty running through the very marrow of their bones, and who would lie about their fitness in order to play their part, are now few and far between.

Above all, what bothers me most about this malaise is the obvious lack of bottle in certain stars. Nothing upsets me more than to see an Arsenal player jump 3 ft in the air in anticipation of a tackle, happy to concede possession so long as he avoids injury. Or to see players making a half-arsed challenge for an aerial ball, when 30,000 spectators become patently aware of a player who isn't prepared to put his head in where it hurts. To my mind the absence of valour in such shrinking violets is not only a dereliction of their duty, but also, from everything I ever learnt, it is an apprehensive attempt for the ball which is most likely to be the cause of injury.

I shouldn't single out any particular pansies, as traditionally, by and large, one could draw a line somewhere across the midfield of most teams, between the mettlesome mules at the back and those whose main role was to mesmerise the spectator. Moreover, even the most sentimental amongst us supporters are going to have to come to terms with the fact that we can no longer expect the vast majority of players to live up to our own steadfast devotion; many have the mercenary mentality whereby each club is merely their place of employ until they move on.

For some Gooners on Saturday, Robert Pires was their Man of the Match (as he has been many times this season), if only for his luscious long-range shot which arced its way into the top corner with perfect precision, for our equaliser. I know Pires is a mild-mannered man, who had reservations on his arrival about the rigours of the game in this country. However there have been occasions recently when he has been sufficiently motivated by the macho midfield endeavours of partners like Parlour, to combine his dazzling fancy-Dan skills with the sort of defensive donkey work necessary when the Arsenal have been up against it. And yet far too often I find myself frustrated by Pires's reluctance to throw what little weight he has into regaining possession and the redoubtable Ashley Cole often ends up with a blot on his scutcheon for the want of some sturdy support down his flank.

Naturally there will be those who will argue that players like Pires offer far too much finesse going forward and just jockeying the opposition in possession is more than sufficient. After all, we wouldn't want them pulling a muscle putting their foot in. However, any team can only carry so many meek when chasing the ball and while the Arsenal currently look wonderful when controlling the game, it is our inability to keep a clean sheet that I find most concerning. This is not only due to the occasional frailty of a defence that is only beginning to find its feet as a unit, but also due to the fact that they often lack the protection of a midfield, where every player is prepared to roll their sleeves up, no matter the weather or whether it's a glamorous encounter.

With 20 minutes remaining on Saturday, as the Arsenal attempted to swamp Boro's stalwart defence and find some means of breaking the stalemate so that we might proudly bestride the table's summit for the rest of this year, our first sub appeared on the touchline. I didn't appreciate Pires's anxiety to leave the field and the undoubted look of disappointment on his face, as it dawned on him that his job wasn't done and it was Ljungberg going off for a warm up in the dressing room.

By contrast there is more talent in Pires's big toe than in both Gilles Grimandi's French feet. Wenger's favourite utility player is perhaps one of the least-likely squad members to end up as some kind of Cup final hero. Even so he ranks high up in my book of all important Gooner allegiance, for the way in which he point blank refused to be removed late on during a Worthless Cup game. He might score few goals with such feats of fidelity, but it is this sort of team spirit which is the cement that bonds a championship-winning side.

It will indeed be ironic if the unlimited loyalty which resulted in Thierry Henry losing his head with Graham Poll results in a lengthy title-busting ban. While his delirious demonstration cannot be condoned, I have to admit there was a heart-warming side to his hot-headed tantrum. I don't want to jump on any officiating bias bandwagon, suffice to say that I can't comprehend how we merit more than double the amount of cards (not Christmas, but red and yellow!) doled out to Man United not to mention those sides which are far more deserving of a dirty label. At the end of the day, in the face of all the critical suspensions that might result, it will be the strength of this mettle mixture which decides whether the Arsenal are merely a mite more consistent than the likes of Chelsea, or have the staying power for the Premiership prize.

20. Ruing a Lack of Third-round Rough and Tumble

Saturday, 5 January (FA Cup third-round): Watford (A) 4–2
Henry (7), Ljungberg (9), Kanu (62), Bergkamp (84)

Few of us complained when a 5.30 p.m. kick-off at Filbert Street allowed us a New Year's Day lie-in. It was strange that the match was called off early in the afternoon, due to a frozen pitch, considering the games that took place a couple of hours earlier in more northern climes. I don't know of any fans who actually forked out a fantastic £8 per match, compared to the more reasonably priced season ticket. Yet I doubt football's paymasters at Sky TV were particularly happy about the resultant pay-per-view complications.

As a result there was another reshuffle at the top with Leeds overtaking us by beating West Ham and Liverpool going off the boil, dropping two points at home to Bolton. Chelsea's resolve didn't last past 3 p.m., as Ranieri's team were back to their inconsistent best, beaten at home by Southampton. So when Man United beat Newcastle 3–1 the following day in Sky's big live presentation from Old Trafford, the new year shake up left a group of five clubs with serious Championship pretensions.

I am sure our lads must have benefited from the breather as they were straining at the leash come Saturday. The third round of the FA Cup is always a great weekend. After the minnows have spent months battling their way through the muddy pitches of the preliminary rounds, the fortunate few get a chance for some much needed exposure and perhaps the opportunity to pit their wits against the big boys, Meanwhile managers of struggling top-flight teams get the chance of a cup run to invigorate their club's season and in some cases, save their own hides.

Live on Sky once again, our noon kick-off at Vicarage Road meant we were first into the hat for the fourth round. At two goals up after only ten minutes, many Gooners believed we were already motoring, hopefully on route to another Millennium Stadium final. It seems they weren't alone, as the team immediately took their foot off the pedal and Watford pegged one back. Yet the Hornets managed to pose little more threat apart from their last-minute consolation prize, or we might have ended up ruing so many missed chances before Bergkamp came off the bench towards the end to make matters more comfortable. I can't imagine how the Watford players must have felt after doing their best to contain us to a respectable 1–3 score-line. Just as they begin to feel a little leg weary, they look up to see the likes of Bergkamp and Wiltord coming on, full of beans, to replace Henry and Kanu! It must have been more than a little demoralising and emphasised the gulf in class between the two sides.

Not for the first time, fortune favoured Man Utd when the pitch invasions at Villa Park were completely overshadowed by the crowd trouble at Cardiff, as Leeds made the biggest splash of the round, sinking 0–2 to the Welsh side owned by the publicity-seeking Sam Hamman.

Monday, 7 January 2002

We were still debating over dog-sitting duties on New Year's Day, when the postponement of the match was announced on the TV. It was about the first time we've profited from my penchant for tardiness, as the majority of Gooners were halfway down the motorway to Leicester, which is where we would have been if by some miracle we had been on schedule. I should have quit while I was ahead and made early rising a New Year's resolution. On Saturday I arrived in Watford in good time, but spent so long looking for somewhere legal to leave the car that I was just walking up Vicarage Road when our first goal went in. Fortunately the action on the pitch caught my eye as I entered the ground and I lingered by the disabled enclosure for a moment. Otherwise I might have missed the second as well. I would have been gutted to miss both, for although there was plenty of pretty football to come, in fact by the time I finally took my seat, the game was over as a contest.

For many of the 4,000-odd Arsenal fans present, Vicarage Road is more of a home game than Highbury. With such an early kick-off, at least the short journey left us with a lie-in. Unlike last season when the FA Cup 3rd round presented us with about the longest possible trip in the league, with a trek to Carlisle. Still, part of the beauty of the bottom-rung of this glorious competition for the big boys is a one-off opportunity to visit weird and wonderful pastures new – a once-in-a-lifetime chance to linger in an about-to-be-condemned wooden terrace, filled with fair-weather locals who turn out once a season, in the hope of seeing some pampered Premiership prima donnas taken down a peg or ten. I have been tickled in the past by the thought of some of our more pompous footballing princes, hopping about on the cold floor of a dingy dressing room at a club where the facilities are dictated by the debt owed on last month's leccy bill, and then having to come out and ply their trade in parlous conditions on a pitch that bears no resemblance to the pristine surface at Highbury.

Invariably the chaotic pace dictated by the underdogs, in what is basically their cup final, and the calamitous conditions, leave little room for class to tell, as the Premiership royalty is forced to play down to the level of the relative paupers, in some good old-fashioned tournament rough and tumble. Yet it was the battling spirit forged in places like Carlisle which permitted us to prevail all the way to Cardiff last season. So in some respects drawing Watford from the hat (or the FA's new-fangled plastic contraption!) was a bit of a disappointment. Being a friendly, family-oriented club compared to the (supposed) slick corporate machine of the Arsenal, I've no doubt many a young Gooner regularly attends their games, because either they can't afford, or can't obtain a ticket at Highbury. With the teams training on neighbouring pitches and with the opposition ranks comprising Islington-born, ex-Arsenal apprentice Paulo Vernazza, along with the other familiar phizogs of Marcus Gayle and Vialli, this match appeared to take on an almost testimonial-like tameness.

Admittedly it could have been the two goals in the first ten minutes, like taking candy from Vialli's babies, which could have left Watford too traumatized to throw their toys out of the pram. Nonetheless, far be it from me to complain for once about an absence of bookings, but in this case it is a reflection of the lack of fervour which feeds the romance of this famous competition that the ref produced only one yellow card the entire 90. It could be that Vialli had drawn the devils he knew a little too well and being all too aware of how dangerous we are, he failed to inspire the sort of belief and commitment seen in Sunday's remarkable cup upsets. What I do know is that such games turn on goals and if Watford had raised the Vicarage Road roof by scoring first, it could have been a whole different story. As it was they showed us far too much respect and were duly punished in what turned into nothing short of a belated turkey shoot.

'Can we play you every week?' cried the triumphant Gooners, as we dared to dream prematurely of another May Day party in Cardiff. Yet the only reason I'd want to play Watford every week is because of a bountiful belly-filling feed up at my mum's, whose house happens to be en route home. With a crowded fixture list full of crucial games about to come thick and fast, I guess I should be happy for our relatively easy route into the fourth round and an all too rare opportunity for the lads to cruise through 80 minutes on auto-pilot, compared to the unrelenting tide of injury-time thrillers they've toiled over in recent weeks. Yet sitting completely stuffed on my ma's sofa waiting for the three o'clock start to all the other cup thrills and spills (little did I know I had a further 24 hours to wait), my appetite might have been satiated, but I still had this gnawing Gooner hunger.

It wasn't just our almost customary profligacy in the opposition penalty area which saved Watford from the sort of score-line seen when the Saracens appear on the same pitch. No, a goal for every four shots squandered is not bad by the Arsenal's current superfluous standards and four is the most we've seen hit the back of the net in all competitions this season. It was that I felt cheated of the rumbustious third-round affair we've come to expect from the greatest knockout competition in football. But then there's no pleasing some people. Last week all I wanted was a boring '1–0 to the Arsenal', after all the nail-biting drama of our festive duels.

If we'd been starved of excitement at Watford, there was a surfeit of it on Sunday. After Villa's dismal failure to remove another potential May Day party pooper, where once again Van Nistelrooy won the day for United, we had the fourth-round draw. As bland as these events are, not knowing our number left me sweating over every announcement, ticking off the trips I didn't fancy until only the Arsenal and Liverpool were left. Considering our inconsistent home form, the draw might not have done us any favours. It leaves us with two visits from the Scousers, separated by a trip to Leeds! A significant effect of the Leicester game's postponement is that it means the influential Ray Parlour will be suspended for our next encounter.

Beating them three times this season still won't make up for the misery of Michael Owen's match-stealing last few moments back in May. I am banking on this for the necessary resolve to prevent Liverpool getting a look-in. As we steel ourselves to sustain a solid challenge for the title, in the most exciting competition for many years, every game takes on an importance of almost unbearable proportions. However it is strange to think that our whole season could be finely balanced on our form against this one fairly formidable side. If anyone knows Houllier's heart doctor, would they mind bunging him a few quid to keep Gerard in his bed until the month's out!

21. Knick-knack Paddywhack Gives the Bozos a Bone

Sunday, 13 January (Premiership): Liverpool (H) 1–1 Ljungberg (62) 4th

It was a bad week for football in general, as the recriminations from crowd trouble in Cardiff continued to reverberate across the back pages of the press. The coins and a bottle thrown by both Spurs and Chelsea fans in the first leg of their Worthless Cup clash only helped to fan the flames of the media fire.

At least the focus on this furore had the effect of diverting some heat from Highbury and Henry's contretemps with Poll. When asked why the club had failed to respond to the FA's charges, Wenger showed his appreciation of the nuances of life in Britain by suggesting that the Christmas post might be to blame! Losing the club's top goal-scorer to a lengthy suspension would be a disaster at any time, let alone when he was in such fine fettle. So the club were bound to do everything in their power to delay Henry's appearance as long as possible. Who knows how much of a help it was to have a vice-chairman who spreads himself over both sides of the FA and Arsenal divide; Ferguson, though, sure couldn't resist crying 'conspiracy' when the matter remained unresolved months later.

It turned out to be a bad week for the Arsenal, in particular when the Scousers came to Highbury and gave us a taste of our own old medicine. Riise's equalizer resulted from one of only two attempts on goal in the entire 90 minutes and so it was our turn to serenade them with the 'boring, boring' chant which used to follow us everywhere. Dropping a further two points at home undid all our industry up at Anfield and in the light of events elsewhere, neither team did themselves a favour in this bore-draw.

With Man United winning at Southampton and Newcastle beating a depleted Leeds side, we dropped to fourth and everybody shuddered as a resurgent Man U suddenly resurfaced at the top for the first time this season. Unlike many of us, Arsène managed to maintain a supremely optimistic mood. His attitude was apt in the circumstances as it was so tight at the top that we were only two points behind the leaders with a game in hand. The Scousers had no such saving grace, sitting below us in fifth and it was strange to think that little over a month before it had been them who were eleven points ahead of United with a game in hand. In typical turncoat fashion, all the mistakes Fergie had made around Christmas were now being lauded as masterstrokes from the mind of this footballing maestro! It was a similar story at the bookies where they must have been regretting the generous odds of 7/2 offered on United after their sixth defeat of the season a month back; they were now odds on favourites.

In a season so far where top spot in the table appeared to be changing hands more often than ever before, most of us were coming to the conclusion that the Arsenal could only achieve success if we were able to maintain a consistency which was superior to that of our inconsistent rivals.

Monday, 14 January 2002

In spite of Vinnie Jones's lairy *Lock Stock*-style presentation, I was so engrossed in Channel 4's *Top 100 Sporting Moments*, that I completely forgot *The Premiership* programme on Saturday night. By the time I turned over, Chelsea's lack of championship credentials were on view in their draw at Bolton. Miffed to have missed the match of the day at St James' Park, I was up with the larks the following morning (assuming the larks also like a bit of a lie-in on Sundays) to watch the Sky TV's *Goals On Sunday*. Actually, a partiality for procrastinating in my pit might be prevalent on most other days of the week, but in fact I usually fall in early on Sunday morning (if only to fall down on the couch a few minutes later), for Jimmy Hill's *Sunday Supplement* – a particular favourite footie programme.

Lord knows why I enjoy the programme so much. I regularly get frustrated, to the point of throwing something at the screen, by the pompous piffle from the postulations of the four various gentlemen of the press rat-pack, seated around what is purported to be the rabbi's (as I believe was the bearded one's pet name on the pitch) parlour table. They certainly weren't short of subjects for discussion this week, as they prevaricated over the parlous state of the beautiful game in Britain. No one is more displeased by the deplorable scenes witnessed recently than myself. I stopped attending live matches completely in the late '70s and early '80s because being bashed up on a Saturday afternoon was not my idea of entertainment. Consequently I value as extremely precious the fact that, for the last few years, the missus and I have been able to follow the Arsenal around this country and Europe, more often than not wearing our colours with pride, without fear of putting ourselves in danger.

I recognise the authorities need to avoid complacency. The lunatics must not be let off the leashes, which have successfully limited their behaviour for so long. However, I rail against the media's abject failure to recognise its responsibility. It doesn't require any real perspicacity to appreciate that it is the profession of making mountains out of molehills which has a prime part to play in this problem's potential to be self-perpetuating. Apart from our players, few people batted an eyelid back in November, when the Spurs fans attacked our coach (ironically it was the Spurs' team bus on loan to us!) and threw anything to hand at anyone in red and white who had the misfortune to approach the touchline. Naturally, through my rose-tinted specs it seems reprehensible that there was no retribution for the sordid behaviour of our sworn rivals.

By contrast, such is the focus of the media's attention over the current furore that news of the unsavoury scenes at Stamford Bridge came to me via my sister, who is usually only vaguely aware of football gossip through her vicarious interest in my passion. Lamentably, the lower leagues have always been prone to the occasional crowd flashpoint, which in the past have merited a sentence or two lost somewhere in the match report, but now the slightest sign of hurly-burly is seen as headlines that might sell more papers. And as the brouhaha builds, the newsprint barristers bemuse us real football fans, with their cries for kangaroo-court sentences of matches behind closed doors and heaven forbid, perimeter fencing.

Most of us are constantly bemoaning the demise of the atmosphere at our grounds; the drama that takes place each week becomes more and more like theatre (but more expensive!), with audience participation limited to polite clapping in appropriate places (not to mention the obligatory panto villain, albeit no longer always in black). These days an electric atmosphere is a rare treat, but on such occasions there is a fine line between singing your heart out for the lads and wishing the opposition fans a journey home 'in a London ambulance'.

You couldn't wish to meet a more mild-mannered person than my partner, but I have even seen her in a paddy when we've been in close proximity to opposing fans and they've been needling us all game long. On Sunday I realised she's been coming to games with me for too long: I was dumbstruck to hear her threaten to throw a Liverpool fan's hat over the front of the upper tier should he jump up injudiciously if the Scousers scored. As far as I am concerned, the odd outbreak of malevolence is almost inevitable and the police get paid a fortune to contain it. So long as we don't return to the dark days when I was afraid to go to football, it is a small price to pay for a passionate sport. The alternative is the sterile surroundings in which American soccer takes place, which might just as well be watched on the box.

1 Three days after getting the key to the door, home-grown Stuart Taylor gets his Highbury debut against the Red Devils. Before being thrown into the Champions League cauldron and manfully filling the breech between the sticks in our crucial Xmas schedule, he's brought down to earth with a bump in the Worthless Cup (v. Grimsby, Highbury, 27 November 2001)

2 An auspicious day for the Arsenal and the NIMBY's nadir, as Islington council finally gives the gargantuan Ashburton Grove project the green light (10 December 2001)

3 Thierry throws his toys out of his pram after Poll's floodlit robbery; he's less apoplectic than any Arsenal fan, yet Titi ends up persecuted for his passionate outburst (v. Newcastle, Highbury, 18 December 2001)

1	2
3	

4 Dudek brings down Freddie for a penalty before the break, one of the ten-men turning points in our season, resulting in our first victory at Anfield in nine seasons (v. Liverpool, Anfield, 23 December 2001)

5 Robbie, Titi, Nwankwo and Paddy with their eyes on the ball and their gloves on their crown jewels! (v. Boro, Highbury, 29 December 2001)

6 A clue to the catalyst for the Arsenal's all-conquering confidence – the renaissance of the famous Arsenal spirit (v. Bayer Leverkusen, Highbury, 27 February 2002)

4	5
6	

7 Pure poetry in motion. Dennis scores the goal of the season
(v. Newcastle, St James' Park, 18 December 2001)

8 Most Gooners are caught off-guard, as the lionhearted Lauren proves he has the 'cahones' to cope with the pressure of the penalty-kick chopping block. It might have bobbled into the onion bag, but he and Sylvain celebrate the goal that gave us victory against the old enemy (v. Spurs, Highbury, 6 April 2002)

9 In case there are any doubters, Martin Keown proves yet again that his loyalty runs deeper than his dermis, as our 'red-and-white' blooded centre-back battles on regardless
(v. Boro, Old Trafford, FA Cup semi-final, 14 April 2002)

10 Tragically taken, but definitely not forgotten by the travelling Gooners, Rocky's name still rings around most grounds, wherever we go (en route to the Millennium Stadium, FA Cup final, Cardiff, 4 May 2002)

7	8
9	10

11 Joining thousands of other red-headed followers of the Freddie faith, young Ben looks more than a little beatific to be present in Cardiff for the culmination of the Arsenal's Cup campaign (the Millennium Stadium, FA Cup final, Cardiff, 4 May 2002)

12 The Romford Pelé pulls a rabbit out of the hat with a goal to grace the world's oldest knock-out tournament (the Millennium Stadium, FA Cup final, Cardiff 4 May 2002)

13 It couldn't have been scripted better, as we are favoured with a second to put a smile on the face of all 'Freddie's Dreamers', especially the mates of my neighbour from the West Upper – North London was drained of every last drop of red-hair dye (the Millennium Stadium, FA Cup final, Cardiff, 4 May 2002)

14 After suffering all those silverware-starved seasons at the wrong end of the Seven Sisters Road, having crossed the North London divide in the summer, Sol savours the moment, winning a Premiership title in his first season at the Arsenal. The stuff of nightmares for every Spurs supporter, Campbell kissing the cannon crest, as Old Trafford becomes the Theatre of Dreams for him, Ashley and Gooners everywhere (v. Man Utd, 8 May 2002)

15 Patrick's in safe hands as the players celebrate in front of the small group of Gooners in the 'Champions section' at Old Trafford, after Sylvain's goal secured the title and our unbeaten away record (v. Man Utd, 8 May 2002)

16 An example of the worldwide Gooner collective bellowing themselves hoarse in sports bars around the globe as the ball hits the back of the net in Manchester. Fifty-odd Finnish Gooners far outnumber the miserable Moaners in the Sports Academy Bar, Helsinki (8 May 2002)

17 The mere formality of a 4–3 victory at The Home of Football becomes an excuse for a Golden Boot Gooner party. Groundsman Paul Burgess was busy carting off the ticker tape even before it touched his pristine surface! (v. Everton, Highbury, 11 May)

18 Sol and Thierry remind Robbie how he helped the Arsenal to get one hand on the trophy before his unfortunate injury, just prior to the whole squad prostrating themselves to pay homage to Pires (v. Everton, Highbury, 11 May)

19 The following day's parade to the Town Hall sees a further proliferation of Gooners with red 'go-faster'
20 stripes and every possible permutation of this Freddie-fêting theme (Upper Street, 12 May 2002)

17	
	19
18	20

21 Never mind no room on top, it is down below where there is hardly space to draw breath, as the hundreds of thousands of Gooners lining the Islington streets proove the need for a new stadium (Upper Street, 12 May 2002)

22 'Mine's a Double' (Upper Street, 12 May 2002)

21

22

23 Mr Arsenal discovers a novel way to stay in shape, for another season . . . please?
(Islington Town Hall 12 May 2002)

24 Growing room for another three Doubles? (Upper Street, 12 May 2002)

25 Two front teeth and a Double, what more can a girl want! Gooner Sara's gratitude from across the big pond for a perfect finale to her pa's pilgrimage to The Home of Football after my help with a pitch at TA's testimonial (Boston, USA, May 2002)

26 The author and his missus, Róna, paint Islington red (12 May 2002)

There will be passion aplenty at Elland Road this weekend. I only hope it doesn't result in the nine yellows and a red witnessed at Newcastle, otherwise Leeds won't be the only side struggling to put a team together before the season's out.

22. On a Plane to Spain. Is His Mind on the Game?

Sunday, 20 January (Premiership): Leeds United (A) 1–1 Pires (45) 4th

Again the team that profited most from our table-topping clash with Leeds was Man United as they tightened their stranglehold at the top. The match at Elland Road certainly didn't live up to its billing. If this is the sort of uncommitted performance required for the refs to keep their cards in their pocket, then give me the dirty stuff any day. It would seem that the devil does indeed have all the best tunes and I would much rather we were singing with a little more heart and soul than was in evidence in this flaccid affair.

Stuart Taylor's staunch tour of duty between the sticks was over, as a broken finger gave Richard Wright an opportunity to reclaim his place for a few games; Seaman continued to linger on the injured list. Age and injuries were to condemn Lee Dixon to little more than the odd walk-on part when he eventually returned to fitness. In his stead, we were all becoming increasingly impressed with Lauren, who hadn't missed a match until an accumulation of six bookings saw him suspended (as far as my memory serves, not one of which resulted from malicious intent). Unfortunately, just as we were seeing signs of that vital intuitive understanding between this defensive unit, Ralphie disappeared with his Macaroon mates of the Indomitable Lions to the African Nations Cup. We would not see Lauren or Kanu again until the beginning of March.

I guess we really shouldn't complain in this instance, as otherwise Dennis Bergkamp might have been restricted to brief cameo appearances all season and not had a chance to blossom with this run in the side. I will gladly go down on my knees and sing 'hallelujah' in gratitude for the unbridled joy of witnessing Bergkamp recapture some of his brilliant form from a few years back.

Sadly, Robbie Fowler, our nemesis from a fair few nightmares at Anfield, continued where he left off at Liverpool. I hadn't even lit a second fag before Wilcox's cross found Fowler lurking in the box behind Ashley Cole and he met the ball with a powerful header past Wright's despairing dive. About the only memorable Arsenal moment was the mazy move for our equaliser, started and finished by Le Bob, via a delightful ball into the box from Dennis and a dummy from Thierry.

The only table we were top of was the disciplinary one, as our card count reached the half century. Yet the one clash of any consequence between Keown and Viduka was missed by ref Halsey. I imagine Keown to have one of those notebooks, in which, as an opposing striker, you really don't want him writing your name down. He was charged last season by the video panel for elbowing Viduka and having renewed roughhouse acquaintances, Martin came off the pitch to demand some justice from the same source, as Viduka had returned the compliment. He'd want to hope they didn't study the video too closely or they might have picked up his own petulant frenzy, when he threw a corner flag into the crowd. However, I wouldn't want to give the wrong impression of this game and my Man of the Match award would have to go to the travelling Gooners, whose efforts came over loud and clear on the gogglebox. Unless it was the Sky team turning up the crowd noise in an attempt to mask the paucity of entertainment in their production, there was patently a lot more passion coming from the terraces than the pitch.

Despite Wenger's constant assurances to the contrary, the rumours about Patrick Vieira's imminent departure continued to abound in the press. This week they were apparently sparked by the revelation that Paddy had popped over to Madrid but any sort of angle on this tired old story seemed to make it the much loved choice of lazy hacks on any quiet news day. In other transfer news the press still had Di Canio on and off the Man United menu on a daily basis, but in the meantime Fergie plumped for the not quite so hot-blooded Argie, Diego Forlan, pinching him from under the nose of his former pupil McClaren. For some reason Forlan favoured a move to United instead of Boro; go figure?

Monday, 21 January 2002

I am not sure whose appearance was least likely at Elland Road, mine or Tony Adams', as the club captain's niggling foot injury set his first-team return back another couple of weeks. If not quite dead, it feels like the big man is flogging a severely handicapped horse with his frustrating fight for match fitness. Still, along with every other Gooner, I live in hope of his comeback, to coincide with an all-conquering charge for the Championship. No doubt this too is the motivation of the man with the appropriate moniker of 'Mr Arsenal': to eke out those last few drops of the dwindling reserves of adrenaline required to lug himself, literally on his last legs, and a side which so obviously lacks his leadership qualities, in a triumphant, title-winning swansong. After having endured the treatment table for most of this season, I doubt Adams will have much enthusiasm for an arthritic encore and it would be a frightful shame for all concerned should the firework of his playing career fizzle out like a damp squib.

This show of sympathy is something of a struggle, since I am feeling so sorry for myself because my back is buggered again. I was devastated when it dawned on me last week that I had been struck down by a repeat performance of this debilitating problem, especially as I was looking forward to our encounter at Elland Road with such eager anticipation. Despite being unable to take a turn around the park with the dog, let alone a 400-mile round trip up north, I was extremely reluctant to let go of our Leeds tickets, living in hope of a miraculous recovery, right up until Saturday. Really I should have been grateful to find some suitable recipients at such a late stage, as I would have hated the thought of our tickets going begging for what promised to be a bloodcurdling contest (based on the heat of the Highbury hoe-down). As glad as I was of the 50-odd quid, which might keep me in fags for a week while I am back 'on the sick', it was with a heavy heart that I handed them over on Saturday night to a grateful Gooner, who couldn't grab them quick enough. It was the sort of game that I would normally get to, come hell or high water, yet there I was having to ask a stranger if he would be so good as to give the Gunners a shout on my behalf.

I am left with a similar dilemma about our tickets for the rearranged fixture with the Filbert Street relegation fodder on Wednesday. I would not want and can not afford to see the tickets go to waste, but with my desperate loyalty to the cause, I will doubtless end up leaving my decision to the last minute, under the illusion that the specialist might come up trumps on Tuesday. At least in my case, a cure is not out of the question (I hope!), which it appears is more than can be said for our crocked 'fox in the box'. After teasing us by bagging a brace in a reserve game, Francis Jeffers broke down yet again, suffering from the same chronic ankle injury which sidelined him for most of last season. In many respects it is an advantage that the Arsenal are not a PLC, but if they were, heads would be guaranteed to roll over what is undoubtedly an £8,000,000 ricket. Who knows, perhaps the medical man who passed Francis fit and the surgeon who removed 'all' of my disc, are one and the same. They certainly seem similarly shortsighted!

The only slight consolation in the Franny fiasco is that it is unlikely the club will have to cough up another £2,000,000 based on appearances.

Our chances were few and far between at Leeds and we certainly could have done with someone capable of capitalising on the two created in the first five minutes. With Bergkamp playing such a peripheral role for so long, in the absence of Kanu I was dying to see him make the most of a rare 90-minute run out. He is usually under unbearable pressure to perform when appearing with only 15 to go. It has been all too long since we've seen the best of Bergkamp, but as such a brilliant practitioner of the beautiful game, he is another player who deserves to go out with a bang, rather than a whimper. As far as I can recall, the only other incidents where I had reason to rave like a lunatic at an unresponsive telly, were Vieira's all too vague attempts on goal, with half-hearted headers (he should have heeded Fowler's lesson in the art of heading).

It is ironic that all week long the media had been building up Sunday's big match as the clash of the Premier League's 'undisciplined' bad boys and in every report I have read since, they've been bemoaning the absence of bookings as proof of a fairly boring game. They must have been grateful for Viduka's minor indiscretion with his elbow, as at least it gave them something to gloat about! Under normal circumstances coming away from Elland Road with a point would be perfectly acceptable. But in light of the fact that Leeds took all three points off us at Highbury and appeared to be there for the taking (in the second-half at least) on Sunday, I was extremely disappointed.

What has surprised me most in our matches against both Liverpool and Leeds is that neither of these teams, nor the Arsenal, have shown much evidence of the sort of fire in their bellies necessary for a sustained challenge against a United side which is only just beginning to show signs of a reluctance to relinquish their stranglehold on the title. On Sunday Martin Keown deserved the Man of the Match award. There was a moment in the game where he chased a ball in our penalty area, bowling over Sol Campbell in the process. It is this sort of hungry tunnel-vision that is required of a team with serious pretensions to the title. To date I haven't seen it present in sufficient numbers in the Arsenal side for me to believe we are capable of topping the table, unless gifted of the opportunity by the mistakes of others.

Myself, I spent most of Sunday's match praying someone would give Vieira the sort of dig that might anger him out of auto-pilot and into match-winning mode. I have no doubt that the attentions of the Leicester players on Wednesday will provide a little more motivation. I only hope his response doesn't result in me ruing these wishes come next week! Mind you, perhaps in his mind Vieira is already in Madrid. According to the gossip his mate Makalele took the keys to their training ground facility and gave Vieira the guided tour by night!

23. What a Difference a May Makes

Wednesday, 23 January (Premiership): Leicester City (A) 3–1
Van Bronckhorst (33), Henry (43), Wiltord (90) 2nd
Sunday, 27 January (FA Cup): Liverpool (H) 1–0 Bergkamp (28)

The last weekend of January promised an exciting fourth-round FA Cup tie at home to Liverpool but there was some Premiership business to be taken care of beforehand, which left us in a far more optimistic mood. On Tuesday night Steven Gerrard stamped his World Cup credentials on a gripping game at Old Trafford. There were plenty of *huzzas* from us in Highbury, when for a change it was United's opponents who pinched the points with a late strike, as Danny Murphy scored the Liverpool goal that kept the title race wide open. The Arsenal were breathing down United's neck by Wednesday night, with a victory at Filbert Street. We were now a point behind United with a game in hand.

With the Arsenal desperate to set the record straight after last season's FA Cup final robbery and the Scousers reluctant to relinquish their hold on the trophy things were set up nicely for a storming cup clash at Highbury. Sadly, a fantastic, passionate FA Cup encounter made the headlines for all the wrong reasons. The romance of the Cup had been revived the previous day, with the likes of Walsall winning at Charlton. Moreover Steve McClaren managed to put one over on his former boss by beating Man United. The horrible weather at Highbury was perfect for getting stuck in and the two teams duly obliged. With only ten top-flight teams left in the tournament there was plenty of incentive, with the likelihood that the victor might be close to a fairly trouble-free route to another Cardiff final.

It was just the sort of rumbustious affair that Ray Parlour revels in, so as sorry as I was to lose Pires' unlimited range of skills when he limped off injured early on, I felt we might benefit from Parlour's brawn. Hyypiä and Henchoz were rapidly developing into one of the best central-defensive partnerships in the country. So it is a shame to think that few will remember this match for the moment when Bergkamp bettered them both, with the extremely rare bird of a match-winning, glancing header.

Unfortunately, what brought this match reams of newsprint was the Carragher coin-throwing incident. This incident occurred in a frenzied six-minute period when ref Riley went red-card crazy. They'd been playing for little over an hour when Keown was first into the showers. As the last defender, he was left with little choice but to pull Owen down and most of us were grateful that he did because we didn't fancy Wright's chances in a one on one. Bergkamp followed Keown before the water had even warmed up, for a second bookable challenge which looked far nastier when portrayed in slow-motion.

The big screens at Highbury are reserved for 'non-contentious' highlights. Perhaps if the fans had seen the camera's view of what looked like Dennis's attempt to stamp on Carragher's ankle, the crowd might not have responded by throwing its toys out of the pram. Carragher became the third person to be sent off as a result of his impetuous reaction to being hit by a coin. The greatest pity was that we were deprived of Dennis for the last half hour as we had been royally entertained by his regal performance until then. Riley's rigid rule-book refereeing ensured an incredible atmosphere, but ruined a terrific game of football. Ultimately it was Carragher who cornered all the press interest, with talk of the police pressing charges against him and the offending Gooner (personally I like to think it was a disgruntled Scouser!). However, we were all concerned that the 41st and 42nd red cards of Wenger's reign could have a serious effect on our title challenge. Never mind about rotation, injuries and suspensions were leaving our squad so depleted that even Inamoto was in danger of getting a game.

Still, all that mattered on the day was that we were into the hat for the next round and when we came out of it again with a home tie against Gillingham, we couldn't have been happier.

Monday, 28 January 2002

Football is indeed a funny old game. Sam Hamman walks around the touchline at Cardiff and is castigated for causing a riot, while at Peterborough, barmy Barry Fry sprints down the side of the pitch to celebrate with the scorer and the Posh manager gets awarded a bottle of champers – as Sky's Man of the Match! The Barry Fry sideshow in Sky's live presentation was an amusing added ingredient. It was part and parcel of the high jinks and high drama of a weekend-long festival of FA Cup football. Having been stranded for days by my slipped disc, stretched out on my bed like a bellyaching beached whale, I was grateful for the distraction that left me glued to the gogglebox for most of the 48 hours. Some of the topsy-turvy turn ups which took place in atrocious conditions, as star players squelched their way through swamp-like surfaces, were a flashback to FA Cup football of yesteryear. Forget the economic vagaries, which resulted in only 17,000 watching Boro's last-minute knockout blow to United. Never mind the red-tops' sabre rattlers, who constantly rue the removal of the last remaining remnants of this tournament's romance. These days the atmosphere may take a little stoking and the overpaid participants a little prompting, but the oldest and greatest cup competition on the planet continues to retain magic aplenty.

Saturday's tasty Teesside upset was all the more palatable with the obvious chagrin evident in Alex Ferguson's post-match comments. It left me sorely tempted, come Sunday morning, to dose myself up on my elephant tranquillizers so that I could make it around to our seats at Highbury. In my head I had long since decided it would only aggravate my condition to spend 90 minutes fidgeting in my seat with the pain. It would be far easier to concentrate on the live coverage on the box. Nevertheless, the sound of the stadium announcer cut through the common sense, as it wafted through our windows 15 minutes before kick-off. It was an appeal to my heart that was hard to ignore. I was glad the choice had been taken out of my hands half an hour prior, when Róna had given my ticket to a gobsmacked Gooner kid who lives in our block.

Having experienced Highbury's lunar lack of atmosphere in recent weeks, I was gutted to miss this game. The increased allocation of away tickets in the Cup gave the Scousers the entire Clock End of the ground, which might be as good as the atmosphere gets this season. The only consolation watching on the box was the enthusiastic company of studio guest and confirmed Gooner, Ian Wright. Po-faced Alan Hansen stipulated at the start that Wrightie shouldn't attempt to kiss him if the Arsenal scored. I only wish they'd had a camera on the two of them when Dennis Bergkamp headed the only goal of the game, as I would have loved to see Hansen fending off Wrightie's affections!

However, if I had stopped at home for the sake of my health, it didn't serve much purpose. No matter how justified by the letter of the law, come the third of ref Riley's rash of red cards. I was in such an apoplectic rage that I wouldn't be surprised if I have slipped another disc after bouncing on my bed in frenzied frustration. I might have less cause to argue with Riley's decisions, compared with some of the ridiculous red cards we've seen this season, but I was absolutely mortified to see yet another great game ruined by the ref in the space of a manic six minutes of mayhem. Suddenly, from having six strikers out of the twenty-two on the pitch, with both teams starting with fairly adventurous formations, we were left with nineteen players tiring themselves out, for the most part timidly trying to avoid leaving themselves exposed. The supporters may have raised the roof as a result (indignation always gets us Gooners going), but for the millions watching live and on TV, we were cheated of 20 more minutes of marvellous football.

Thank heavens we have a satellite receiver, because for the vast number of viewers in the London area watching via an aerial, things got much worse. The FA Cup is the last bastion of domestic football's live broadcasts on the BBC. As such they made a major fuss over Arsenal–Liverpool, their flagship match that weekend. With 85 minutes on the clock, screens went blank across the whole of London. I assume a transmitter must have gone down, although Róna is convinced it was sabotaged by Sky. Fortunately I was able to turn over to their digital channel, because otherwise, with so much injury time to come, I might have been forced to make a mad disabled dash over to the stadium – unlike my poor mum, who was enjoying the extremely rare terrestrial broadcast of a live Arsenal game. The phone rang within minutes and I knew it would be her. After a few rings, she thought better of disturbing me in the dying throes of a match, perhaps thinking I might never forgive her if the distraction resulted in us conceding a goal. I imagine like many other livid Londoners, she ran upstairs to check the TV in the bedroom and then across the road to a neighbour, all to no avail.

She missed Michael Owen's last attempt on goal and it was only when Richard Wright tipped this ball around the post that I knew it was going to be our day. On the sunny Cardiff stage in May, Owen had two glimpses of our goal and scored on both occasions. Whereas he managed to fluff all four opportunities presented to him on this murky Highbury match day. Luckily nothing else of consequence transpired, or it would have been a nightmare when the picture was finally restored some minutes after the final whistle.

As calamities go, I guess this must come pretty high on the richter scale of rotten luck. Yet I can't really castigate my favourite commentator's TV station. His face looked extremely familiar (like an old family friend), but if it wasn't for Róna's cognitive capability, I would have walked right by John Motson last week as we exited the hospital. Stopping to chat with us as if he had all the time in the world, Mottie was a true gent. I only wish I'd broached him on some burning footie issue, instead of which we ended up comparing medical notes! With only Gillingham or Bristol Rovers between us and the last eight in the Cup and a point behind United, with a game in hand in the league, I wonder how Mottie would rate our chances?

24. *Victoria Concordia Crescit*

Wednesday, 30 January (Premiership): Blackburn Rovers (A)
3–2 Bergkamp (14, 75), Henry (21) 2nd
Saturday, 2 February (Premiership): Southampton (H) 1–1
Wiltord (40) 4th

Sadly the Arsenal were growing so accustomed to taking on the opposition with the aid of only ten men, that when Luzhny was the recipient of our eleventh red card of the season with about thirty minutes to play at Ewood Park, most of us believed it meant that the win was in the bag. Another breathtaking performance by Bergkamp and a sublime strike by Henry ensured we were two up after twenty minutes. It could have been three and game over if Wiltord hadn't been ruled offside, wrongly as it proved later, before burying the ball in the net. Yet in an all too familiar scenario, the Arsenal defence was guilty of switching off and Blackburn, specifically Matt Jansen, were the beneficiaries as they brought it level by the break, Jansen continuing where he left off with his hat-trick in the Worthington. Instead of cruising back into second place, just a point behind Man United, with a game in hand, we sweated it out until Bergkamp finally managed to bring home the bacon when he scored our third with fifteen to go.

Damien Duff ran Luzhny ragged all evening. Oleg 'the horse' must have lost a shoe at some point. At least I hope he had some excuse for the embarrassing slip which presented Duff with the ball for his assist in Rovers' second. Oleg's more of the cart variety compared to a thoroughbred like Duff and he must have mugged the poor man off once too often as Luz unceremoniously hacked down Duff for his first and then the tricky Tugay for his second yellow card. Once again Arsène's audacious tactics saw us start with three strikers, Henry, Bergkamp and Wiltord, with Sylvain playing wide on the right, but sadly all our sensational attacking play was stifled by the sending off, as Gio replaced Sylvain and we retreated back into our shell. I have Pires and Bergkamp to thank for poking their heads out sufficiently to seize the winner, as I was down to the quick with no nails left to chew!

After all the midweek excitement, a windy Saturday proved to be something of a damp squib. If the biggest difference between Wenger's team and the one managed by Graham was highlighted today by a record-breaking 26th consecutive game in the Premiership in which we've scored, it was also noticeable for our inability to keep a clean sheet. Moreover, we seem destined to ruin all our hard work undefeated on the road, with our lack of consistency at home. A draw at home to Southampton was definitely two points dropped and a gloomy afternoon only deteriorated when Vieira limped off early on with a hamstring strain. To add to the woes of our much depleted squad, Ashley Cole soon joined him with a long-term injury that was to rule Ashley out of the rest of our Champions League campaign, condemning him to the treatment room until the end of March.

The wind played havoc all afternoon with Richard Wright but he managed to clear the ball to a player in a red shirt as Wiltord started and finished the move for our goal. There was a certain inevitability to Southampton's equaliser, after Arsenal failed yet again to kill off a game at Highbury. Wenger brought on Edu for Bergkamp for the last 20 and it was the Brazilian who gave away the free-kick from which Tessem scored with a header, escaping the attentions of Upson and Campbell.

Elsewhere, the news from Old Trafford was that United had blown Sunderland away in the first-half, Newcastle had won 3-2 at home against Bolton, while any aspirations David O'Leary had for the Championship faded as Leeds lost 0–4 to Liverpool. It was now a four-horse race at the top.

Monday, 4 February 2002

After battling like lions to bring three points back from Blackburn, it was desperately disappointing to lie down like lambs and drop two points at home to Southampton on Saturday. Sadly I am beginning to appreciate fully the frustrations of supporting your team 'in absentia', as for the second time in a week, I was stuck at home, supine on my bed, still suffering from the reoccurrence of my slipped disc. At least I had the company of a live commentary on the radio, which meant I didn't end up having to hang my head out of the window, hoping for the crowd noise to come wafting the few hundred yards from Highbury and keep me abreast of events on the pitch. At least from the terraces, no matter how the match turns out, with my lung-busting efforts, I feel I've made my contribution to the proceedings. Somehow there is a complete lack of satisfaction to screaming my head off in our flat, empty save for our confounded cat and dog.

Mind you, if I had been at Highbury, no matter how bemusing the result, I certainly wouldn't have been involved in the booing at the final whistle. If only our fickle fans were as quick to encourage as they are to express their disapproval, it might have been a different story on Saturday. Unfortunately the majority of our modern all-seater stadia are populated by supporters who tend to be reactive, rather than proactive. The atmosphere created by an enthusiastic crowd might have been just the motivation needed to mask any sign of our squad's shortcomings, with a downright determination to dispose of the lesser footballing mortals before them. Besides, more than the odd goal up at half-time and they could have taken their foot off the pedal the second 45 and just played keep-ball – as appeared to be the case with United, after they'd secured a comfortable three-goal cushion against Sunderland.

Albeit that the 60,000 muppets (I was going to say Mancunian, but that's an oxymoron if ever I heard one!) at Old Trafford are not renowned these days for their motivational capabilities. However, aside from the 12th man potential of a vocal crowd (or in the Arsenal's case a replacement 11th man would be more appropriate), if I had to pinpoint one crucial difference between these two sides, the most obvious factor is that the Arsenal are currently lacking an inspirational captain in the Keane mould. Hopefully by now Tony Adams will have come through a reserve game without damaging those last legs on which he has been limping around so far this season. A comeback from Mr Arsenal couldn't be better timed, but even he has stated that he prefers to lead by example these days. I guess Wenger expected likewise from Vieira, when he rewarded his decision to stay by making him Adams' deputy.

Personally I feel such an honour should be earned on the pitch and with Patrick just about pulling his weight and little more, it sticks in my craw to see him wearing the armband. What we really require is someone who is prepared to ruffle a few famous feathers, by imparting the sort of blinkered focus on the ultimate prize that enables them to forget any feelings of fatigue. Moreover, I don't really buy tiredness as an excuse. We could have played Southampton next weekend, without a midweek game and still suffered the same consequences. They say the table doesn't lie and I was shocked to discover that on home form we are only 12th in the league, having dropped 17 points.

It seems Arsène has instilled such 'unbelievable belief' in his players, that at Highbury they simply expect success on a plate. All too often it is only when our opponents have the cheek to challenge our superiority with a goal, or our players become indignant over a perceived injustice, that they really pull their fingers out. As a result, on Saturday many felt we would have benefited from going a goal (or a man!) down. It certainly would have made for more exciting fare than this dowdy damp squib of a game.

Even with the sound on the TV and radio turned down, I could hear little noise coming from Highbury. It seemed the loudest cheer of the afternoon was the chant of 'What a Load of Rubbish!' that greeted the announcement about the Arsenal's new crest. This was one chorus of disapproval I certainly would have participated in. I never dreamt that the coin counters at our club could meddle with something quite so sacrosanct as the abiding image of the Arsenal which has lived with me all these years. For no matter what baloney we are told about copyright, you can guarantee that this is a financially fuelled fait accompli. The new design might look like the winning entry from a Junior Gunners competition, but it is not so much the look as what has been left out that I object to. After all, this is not a corporate logo which is due for a makeover, it is our coat of arms.

In an age when we find ourselves increasingly concerned by the mercenary motives of some of our players, it hardly seems appropriate to dispense with our 'Strength Through Harmony' Latin motto. To my mind this has always encapsulated the nebulous spirit of unity which first attracted me to the Arsenal and distinguished the club from the rest. Mercurial talents may come and go, but all our greatest triumphs have been grounded in these team-spirit qualities. Call me a sentimental old romantic, but I'd much prefer to see this constant reminder emblazoned on the chest of anyone privileged enough to don the red and white.

As suspensions and injuries begin to take their toll, we will discover whether the spirit in the current squad goes beyond skin deep. When I recall the bone-crunching bruisers of yesteryear, I find it laughable that we've been lumbered with this 'bad boys' tag. By comparison (with the odd exception) our current squad is comprised largely of a load of powder-puff pussies. I am hoping that as the media flack continues its relentless flight, it might foster the sort of bunker mentality which has in the past borne the most memorable fruit.

25. Pap Idols

Sunday, 10 February (Premiership): Everton (A) 1–0 Wiltord (62) 4th

There are any number of games in a season that we can look back on as the day we discovered our destiny. Considering the panoply of perfect football we were treated to during the course of ten months, some might think this single-goal victory at Goodison a strange choice. Elsewhere that weekend Man United won at Charlton, Newcastle picked up three points at home to Southampton and the Scousers put six goals past Ipswich at Portman Road. As a consequence a victory at Everton was essential.

In his 300th game as Arsenal manager, Arsène's ravaged squad left him making up a team from a motley assortment of players including the much maligned Igor Stepanovs. The weakest side Arsenal put out all season managed not only to maintain their 14-game unbeaten away record but took all three points back to London, with a smash and grab courtesy of Wiltord. When one adds the two blatant offences by Stepanovs in the area, both of which probably would have resulted in penalties if it wasn't for the visually challenged official, either the gods were smiling down upon us that day, or our fate was written. We received another five bookings, mostly unwarranted in such a timid affair, taking our toll for the season to a ridiculous 75. Yet what was most remarkable was that for the second time in successive games we ended up with 11 players on the pitch.

One of the products he advertises might revitalise Walter Smith's barnet but it was laughable that a sensible feller like the Everton manager expected the rapidly waning, 35-year-old Ginola to do likewise for his team's season. Amongst a Goodison crowd deprived of entertainment all season, he might have caused a few 'oohs' and 'aahs' early on with his flashy football, but an obvious lack of fitness soon saw the Frenchman fading fast. The other new addition to the Everton squad, a competitive Lee Carsley, might have been some consolation for the Toffee fans but seeing the lumbering double act in the last 20 minutes of Gazza and Ginola, both on their last legs, was quite pitiful. It is not surprising that Smith was out the door soon after.

Apparently much of the TV-viewing public was in the grip of the *Pop Idol* contest between Gareth and Will. My interest can be judged by the fact that I've just spent ages trying to suss out what Gareth Southgate must have been up to that week, to merit the reference in the last sentence below, but I am sure it must have been more interesting than the TV wannabee!

Monday, 11 February 2002

There was a time when Lee Dixon was often teased from the terraces by opposing fans. The cruel chant of 'If Dixon Plays For England So Can I' was probably testament to the fact that, as member of the most tenacious defence of the modern era, Lee was perhaps a little timid by comparison to the rest of his cohorts. That he received least recognition during a dumbfounding decade of doughty shut-outs, was evidenced by our dear dinosaur's surprising revelation that he had never received a Man of the Match award before Sunday.

Against Everton it was appropriate that a defensive performance should earn this accolade, particularly as he appeared 30 minutes into the match as a substitute. This was perhaps the most tedious first-half of football I've seen watching the Arsenal this season. There was only the odd post grazer from Ginola to set pulses racing, as the 'hair flair' Frenchman made his debut for the blues. After victories for the rest of the title-chasing pack, if Wenger was planking it, one would never have believed it from his team's frugal football.

By the break I was so frustrated by their failure to find the target against an uninspired Everton side (who should leave even bottom feeders like the Foxes feeling that they shouldn't give up the fight), that I felt I might have been better off watching Lauren in Cameroon's game against Senegal in the African Nations Cup final (Cameroon won after 120 goalless minutes).

With the protracted problem of my prolapsed disc, I was counting my chickens that I hadn't crammed myself into the back of a car for the four-hour journey north to Goodison. It might not have been the recommended road to my recovery, but after a slight improvement subsequent to a second epidural (and still no kids to show for it!), I was sorely tempted. I couldn't have coped with a third consecutive radio commentary after missing my beloved Arsenal's matches for a miserable month. Thank goodness live TV coverage put the mockers on such madness and common sense prevailed.

I am hoping to be fit for a gentle return against Gillingham on Saturday. During the week I received an e-mail from an old neighbour in the West Upper, who through marriage and a move away from London has been denied one of life's greatest pleasures far longer than my brief detention. He told me how much he misses the thrill of mounting the steps of Block X and the breathtaking view, as you catch the first glimpse of the expanse of snooker-baize-like green stretching before you. Well if I have been guilty of taking The Home of Football for granted in the past, his mail left me desperate to get back there. I only hope some of our walking wounded also make a timely reappearance.

Our squad may have been stretched to its limit on Sunday, but the unusual look to Wenger's chosen line-up left us all scratching our heads. The last time Arsène lumbered us with Igor Stepanovs in a league match was a romp against Joe Royle's relegation-bound Man City. After a promising start to the Latvian's career, it was the humiliation of his previous Premiership outing at Old Trafford almost exactly a year ago, which shattered his self-belief. Amidst a similarly unfamiliar defence, was it really necessary to remind him (and us!) of this anniversary with a recall? Ginola's all too sporadic strafing apart, having seen what little threat Everton pose, perhaps Wenger was proven right and this was the perfect fixture, as the first block in the rebuild of Stepanovs' belief.

It's been so long maybe Igor's forgotten that he's supposed to wait until after the final whistle to exchange shirts with his opponents. The sight of him recklessly risking a penalty in his eagerness to grab an Everton kit on two separate occasions (there's a joke in there somewhere about sticky toffees), left many Gooners desperate to see him disappear back to rejoin the deadwood, hopefully never to be needed again (or at least until next season)! Until Dixon appeared to put the poncey shampoo salesman in his pocket and bring an air of calm authority to our back line, I was convinced Ginola would spend the afternoon making 'the Horse' Luzhny, look like the donkey we all know him to be. Moreover, I kept expecting Gazza to take his bow and make such a monkey out of both East Europeans that Siberia might seem a safe option. However when the time finally came for swopping shirts, instead of a sexy six-pack, we caught sight of the party-pack which Paul is currently carrying around his waist. And that is not the only excess ballast which is in danger of weighing Walter Smith's side right down into the relegation dogfight.

If we survived two decent penalty shouts, we were due a spin on a lucky roundabout after suffering so many misfortunate swings. Nevertheless, aside from the lunacy of Henry's two-footed tantrum, another five pesky yellow cards weren't really warranted in a passionless contest, where hardly anyone else put a peevish foot in. It is hard to pick holes in some of our players' developing persecution complex after seeing the exact same tackles go unpunished in other fixtures last weekend. Why are we so rarely favoured by those refs who appear to appreciate that the football is far more important than a full-house hand of the petty punishments, which so often spoil our matches for all the paying punters? Could it be the number of televised fixtures which frequently finds us faced with officials whose egos force them to play to the audience?

There were times during Sunday's game when I was half hoping for a sending off, to inject some much needed heat into a far too frigid affair. But for a change, somehow we survived with 11 on the pitch. Although there was little to cause Dixon and Campbell any consternation, more miraculous, considering the concoction that included such vulnerable component parts, was the fact that we came away with a clean sheet. Not to mention the three crucial points achieved by the weakest Arsenal side likely to be seen all season. Hopefully that is, for with the likes of Lauren and Kanu finding their way back from Africa and with any number of vital players returning from suspension and injury, it will all be downhill from here. No doubt Gareth was similarly optimistic before Saturday!

26. Sadly Mr Arsenal's Number is Not Up but His Time Might be

Saturday, 16 February (FA Cup): Gillingham (H) 5–2 Wiltord (38, 81), Kanu (50) Adams (67), Parlour (88)

This FA Cup fifth round tie at home to the Gills proved a welcome relief from the tension of the relentless cut and thrust of the title chase. We were all delighted to see Tony Adams back on the pitch for the first time since September. Kanu had found his way back from the African Nations Cup in Mali, but Lauren was still on the missing list as the celebrations of his cup-winning Indomitable Lions involved a detour via Cameroon. Arsenal were desperate to get him back as the list of players injured and suspended was almost as long as the one of those available. As a result the diminutive Brazilian left back Juan got an FA Cup debut (not easily distinguishable from the mascot) and Edu a rare start alongside the forgotten Francis Jeffers. It was a really enjoyable match, as the Gills gave as good as they got, drawing level at 2–2 in the second-half. With the Champions League starting up again in three days with our match in Leverkusen, Wenger had rested Pires and Henry. Yet he is only too aware how much this competition means to us and to make certain there wasn't going to be any upsets, he brought both on with 25 minutes to play. There is also evidence of a resolve to right last year's wrong and with so many of the other big clubs already blown out of the water and a victory putting us only a couple of games away from a Cardiff final, there's a scent of silverware in the air.

After the fabulous ebb and flow of this old-fashioned cup clash, it was disappointing that, come Monday morning, the media were focused on another supposed elbow by Vieira. Wenger rightly called it a witch-hunt, with talk of barmy punishments being bandied about. It took the victim Iffy Onura to come out and exonerate Paddy before the press stopped building his pyre. Travelling Gooners might have groaned a little (I know I did) when the draw for the quarter-final involving three other London clubs threw up a second trip to Tyneside, so close to our league enounter in the North East. The vagaries of TV coverage resulted in this match being allocated a 5.35 kick-off and Arsène was really annoyed that no concessions were made to our Champions League match at home to Deportivo on the Tuesday. He even offered to waive the club's fee for an earlier kick-off.

Monday, 18 February 2002

Walking home from Highbury on Saturday, under bright blue skies and almost spring-like sunshine, I was positively beaming. What with easing our way into a quarter-final, my own interminably slow return from injury, alongside the comeback of our Captain Courageous for his first appearance since September and the prospect of Tuesday's resumption of European rivalries, all was right with the world.

The Gills fans who we commiserated with as they headed for their car didn't sound too downhearted. This match alone makes it a memorable season as far as they are concerned. Besides, they'd fared better than many a Premiership team, whose premature cup exit had seen their season scuppered even sooner, with little to play for but the prospect of a relegation dog fight. It might have been the final act of some fantastic FA Cup flight of fancy, but their team had done them and the 6,500 other Gills fans proud.

My neighbour in the West Upper wasn't quite so chipper for the majority of this contest, as he was dreading the prospect of a draw. He and his mates had paid to fly to our league game against Newcastle and he was horrified to discover that a replay at Priestfield would be played on the same date. While the match remained on a knife edge, I couldn't resist teasing him relentlessly that his trip to the Tyne was bound to be fogged up. It wasn't until Adams headed home our 3rd on 67 minutes that the frown finally faded from his forehead. He pocketed his pen, having previously sat with it in hand, as a symbol of his intent to write and demand that the club cough up for the cost of his flights. I suggested he'd have better prospects of getting blood from a stone!

The hero of the hour was Tony Adams. The rafters of the Highbury Library must have got a rare old fright, as they were raised by a resounding chorus of 'There's Only One Tony Adams', when our Captain Fantastic capped the celebration of his long-awaited reappearance by hitting the back of the net. To my mind, more satisfying than Adams' goal was his petulant response to conceding one. His surly two-footed stomp served to remind me quite how much I've missed our leader's 'they shall not pass' attitude. The Arsenal profited from an instant return on his inspirational capabilities and the much missed air of security he lends to our back line. Sadly his uniqueness has proved all too true, as his performance confirmed quite how much our side has been crying out for a competent captain. I can't help but speculate on the sort of summit we might have scaled aided by his presence these past five months.

With Robert Pires in such sensational form, the Arsenal might have many pundits' choice for player of the season, alongside a whole host of skilful stars who are coveted by other clubs. Nevertheless Tony Adams ranks alongside Roy Keane as the sort of catalyst which can combine a collection of individual elements into a close-knit compound, which is far stronger than the sum of its precocious parts. These continental cash cows might wait for Wenger's disciples to develop and purloin our best players one by one. Yet, no amount of pesetas (sorry euros!) can purchase the sort of leadership qualities of a player steeped in the principles of our sporting institutions.

With injuries, suspensions and players on international duty which would stretch the very strongest squads, most had arrived at Highbury in trepidation of a potential calamitous pratfall. After Adams had restored an air of calm assurance to the team, there was a complete turnaround. We left 90 minutes later daring to believe that there might be no limit to what this team can accomplish. Boy am I glad I savoured this moment, as it didn't last too long.

This mood of optimism began its downturn during *Match of the Day*, when Alan Hansen decided to rake over the coals of Sol Campbell's reputation. It was as though after Campbell's supposed culpability in conceding the goal in England's draw with Holland, Hansen had Sol in his sights. He then went on to point out the pettiest example in order to accuse him of poor positional sense. At least Sven was present in person (isn't he always?) on Saturday to judge for himself.

The draw didn't exactly see us jumping for joy over a second expensive trip to Tyneside only seven days after our league encounter was due to take place. Come Monday morning, I was then confounded by the news that Vieira could be up on another charge of elbowing an opponent. Have you seen the pictures? This incident was such small-potatoes that the next thing you know, the FA will have Monty Python up on video evidence for use of the elbow (nudge, nudge, know what I mean). If we are prone to paranoia, us Gooners might soon all be suffering from a persecution complex. It was the traumatic revelation that followed which proved to be the lowest blow of all, as I discovered the team travelled to Germany without Tony Adams. Not only must it have been devastating for him, after finally believing his injury had healed, but I dread to think of what defence Wenger will dig up to face Bayer Leverkusen.

27. Superstitious? Yes. But Stupid?

*Tuesday, 19 February (Champions League): Bayer Leverkusen (A)
1–1 Pires (55)*
*Saturday, 23 February (Premiership): Fulham (H) 4–1 Lauren (5),
Vieira (15), Henry (38, 59) 3rd*

Luckily Lauren made it back in time for our trip to Leverkusen. The story was that the Cameroon FA had withheld his passport for their visit with the President, but with defenders Adams, Keown, Dixon, Cole, Upson and Luzhny all unavailable, the boss was so relieved to have Ralphie back that they soon kissed and made up. With Igor making his second start since his Old Trafford torment and with Gio lined up at left-back against the most potent strike force in the Bundesliga, we were quaking in our boots. The vast majority of us would have bitten the hand off of anybody that offered us a draw beforehand, so we should really have been well satisfied. Yet it was impossible not to feel bitterly disappointed when our first European victory in over a year was snatched from our grasp with Kirsten's last-minute header. As angry as we were about the outcome, there were no complaints about what was a wonderfully resilient performance under the circumstances.

Another slick passing move resulted in Pires taking the lead, but the real plaudits were reserved for our defence. Arsène said that it was the hardest decision of the season so far to drop Richard Wright in favour of David Seaman's much awaited return to action after five months out injured. The bluff Yorkshireman's inimitable air of calm assurance seemed to spread amongst this unfamiliar back line and they were all absolute heroes on the night, especially after the ref had been bamboozled by Basturk's acrobatics into sending off Ray Parlour (13th and most ridiculous red card yet) with 30 minutes still to play. Sol had a header cleared off the line earlier on, but it was their 'backs to the wall' brilliance in the closing stages that really deserved our first clean sheet in eleven Champions League games and certainly did not merit the malicious timing of Bayer's equaliser.

Stepanovs' assured play dumbfounded his detractors and I blame

Trevor Brooking for Bayer's goal. Igor had their strikers under manners all night, until moments after Brooking tempted fate by naming him as Man of the Match on the radio and almost guaranteed that Kirsten would escape his attentions seconds later. Yet in a manner we would become used to over the next couple of months, Igor had stood in for Keown or Adams and had done better than we could have possibly expected. Since a medical analogy is quite appropriate, they say when you break a bone, it is unlikely to break again in the same spot because the marrow that leaks out to form bone as you heal ensures nature's repair is stronger than the original. By the same token, as our lot were dropping like flies, whoever came in to plug the gap in the team we just seemed to appear stronger each time as a unit.

At the end of the day, sadly, the last-minute goal in Germany would be the one many looked back on as being ultimately responsible for our exit from the Champions League (I felt it was the subsequent home defeat to Deportivo that we could have had some influence on). However, it was the incredible team sprit forged within our entire squad in these high-pressure circumstances which would stand us in such good stead for our domestic endeavours. Mind you, I can't imagine Dennis Bergkamp was a particularly happy bunny having undertaken a 700-odd-mile round trip by road, only to sit on the bench in Germany. At least for once it meant that nobody could claim his fear of flying was a factor in this European result away from home. As he would still be serving his suspension at the weekend there was some speculation that Dennis was merely using the trip to Germany as his excuse to spend a couple of days in Holland.

Good news for the club came the following day, when Transport Minister Stephen Byers hopefully put the final nail in the coffin of the protests over the new stadium project, when he gave Ashburton Grove the green light, refusing the public enquiry which might have delayed building plans for up to two years.

As Arsène tried to put his finger on the cause of our indifferent home form compared to our unbeaten away record, he decided to try and replicate the bonding between the squad on our travels. At huge expense, the club put the team up in a hotel the night before the Fulham game and subsequent home games. It certainly paid off, as we didn't drop another point the rest of the season!

There were 11 Frenchmen on the pitch in the Fulham game and plenty of flair football despite the snow flurries of the ferocious British weather. For three lads from Cork it was perhaps their one pilgrimage to The Home of Football all season. Having paid me a relative fortune for their tickets, I was more nervous than usual, hoping that they would not only see a victory, but an entertaining game. They were privileged to see both in a local derby which was taking place at Highbury for the first time since 1967. It was a match that continued to highlight the gulf in class between the top of the table and the chasing pack below.

Vieira slammed home his first goal of the season and Titi probably would have managed a hat-trick, which I guess was the reason he looked none too happy to see his number up on the board when Wenger gave Aliadiere, another Clairefontaine prodigy, his first-team debut. The contest for the Golden Boot was mirroring the Premiership, as the two from Henry took his total to 27, while Van Nistlrooy got his 28th in United's victory over Villa. In the two more contentious derby matches that weekend, Everton held Liverpool to a scoreless draw at Anfield and the Black Cats took a beating from the Toons at the Stadium of Light.

Come Monday, still with a game in hand, we remained three points behind United, with both Liverpool and Newcastle on our coat tails. Wenger had stirred things up at the weekend by suggesting the Worthless Cup has been so devalued that it would be much fairer to give European qualification to another runner-up in the league. I sometimes wonder if this is just Wenger's sense of mischief coming out, as he certainly got the goat of all my Spurs pals. They needn't have worried as it was Blackburn who won the Worthless final and took the first European place of the season.

Monday, 25 February 2002

The missus had the misfortune to be stretched out on a sun-bed in Tenerife on Saturday, instead of huddling up with me for some warmth in the hail storm which hit Highbury. Waking up that morning to weather which would have chilled a brass monkey to the bone, I was more than a little jealous. Still, no tan would have been worth the tease of text-message news that I'd forfeited the 4–1 fiesta against Fulham. Moreover, while it may not have been our most impressive home performance, I would have been gutted to have missed out on what were without doubt some of the most sumptuous, scintillating skills seen at Highbury so far this season.

In less satisfying early-season home games, I often found myself screaming at our mercurial footballing maestros to play the simple ball, frustrated by all the Fancy Dan flicks and bootless back heels, which so frequently failed to find a team-mate. Where far too few of these seemed to come off in previous contests, these same players couldn't put a foot wrong for much of Saturday's match. We were left marvelling at the magical entertainment of football of such an intuitive nature, one might have thought it a team that had been playing together since time immemorial.

The mazy patterns drawn by our slick passing and prescient movement were all the more surprising considering the makeshift make-up of the side. Even the Arsenal's sizable squad has been stretched to the very brink by the boundless blight of injuries and the scourge of scandalous suspensions. So when stand-in left-back Van Bronckhorst limped off at the weekend, we were all left wondering what possible permutations are left to Wenger for Wednesday in the way of a defensive hand to deal the Deutschlanders.

We've spent the vast majority of matches at Highbury sitting on the edge of our seats, either regretting or awaiting the relief of the final whistle. Not since August have the Arsenal availed themselves of their home-team advantage and afforded us the therapy of being able to relax in the comfort of a two-goal cushion. This rare treat meant that we left Highbury in fairly optimistic mood. Despite the crucial absences which leave us with such a dodgy defensive line-up, in all other areas of the pitch we appear to be hitting the sort of form which inspires confidence in our side's cavalier capability to outscore any opponent.

With the Arsenal going strong in all three competitions, it seems I got caught up in all the tabloid talk about it being our most successful season since '98. However, it has taken donkey's years of disappointments to grow my customary skin of pessimism – a necessary protection – and if I shed it on Saturday afternoon it was rapidly replaced come Sunday evening. While I revelled in the way our North London rivals rolled over in the Worthington Cup, it came as a timely reminder that reputations count for nothing.

A little bomb from the Bundesliga came later that evening which reinforced my pessimism. Bayer Leverkusen had beaten Borussia Dortmund 4–0, leapfrogging them into top spot in the German League. If you were to believe the papers (hardly the most perspicacious source!), qualification for the Champions League quarter-finals is a mere formality for the Arsenal. Recent experience has shown that at the highest level European games are rarely the sort of goal fests which flatter our strengths going forward. Invariably such contests can turn on a single lapse in concentration and with our ever-changing back line, it is just such balls-ups which might prove to be our Achilles heel.

At present, when we get the breaks and games go for us, we look like the world-beaters that I know we have the capacity to be. It is when our backs are up against the wall that the cracks begin to appear and the absence of a natural leader leaves an air of insecurity to our play. Perhaps Tony Adams will prove a temporary solution and they can wrap his crippled limbs in cotton wool so we could count on the air of authority our old warhorse lends to the team for our most crucial encounters. But if we are to offer a serious challenge on all fronts, the result of every match between now and the end of the season will be significant. It is evident Adams' battered old body will not be able to cope with the twice-weekly torture of a frenzied fixture list.

I sold Róna's ticket to a young South African Gooner on Saturday. I have calculated that our season tickets work out at over £48 a match. Yet despite this knowledge, when one of us has been unable to attend in the past I have tended to subsidise the recipient of our spare ticket because I've been downright embarrassed to ask for such an extortionate amount. It is crazy when I think of how I slogged my guts out and left myself partially crippled in the process of stumping up a King's ransom to renew our season tickets last summer. The undoubted entertainment this entitles me to might be something which is impossible to value in mere monetary terms, but on Saturday I could only bring myself to take £40 from this feller. And even then I had to ask if this price was acceptable, after pointing out that the box office would have charged a flagrant £50 for the same seat.

Such are my superstitions that after winning at the weekend in the company of my new pal, I am reluctant to change this routine on Wednesday. I am convinced that it is in the Arsenal's nature to end up having to go to Turin needing some kind of result in the last group game. Yet I would forever blame myself if we were to lose on Wednesday night. With Róna not returning until Friday, it would have been my fault for forsaking my South African pal in favour of the person who had previously been promised her ticket. To solve this dilemma, I have just been over to the box office, to beg an additional ticket from an extremely accommodating Arsenal employee. So surprised was the South African to secure a seat at this late stage that he didn't flinch at the £50. As for the three compadres from Cork, whose tickets I sorted for Saturday's game, I'm afraid my dire financial straits ensure that my superstition doesn't quite stretch so far as 150 smackers!

28. The Return of the JEDI (Just Exquisite Delightful and Inspired!)

Wednesday, 27 February (Champions League): Bayer Leverkusen (H) 4–1 Pires (5), Henry (7) Vieira (48), Bergkamp (83)
Saturday, 2 March (Premiership): Newcastle United (A) 2–0 Bergkamp (11), Campbell (41) 2nd

Who knows whether it was United's 5–1 victory over Nantes which renewed Alex's appetite, or part of some Machiavellian boardroom master-plan with his horse-racing cronies that went wrong. However, I am sure we weren't the only ones to be bitterly disappointed that Fergie changed his mind about his retirement and signed up for another three years.

There was a sense of the well-oiled Gooner machine beginning to grind into top gear when we had all but disposed of the best the Bundesliga had to offer, within ten minutes of kick-off at Highbury that night, in what was our most impressive European result of the season. It was all the more remarkable considering that Gio was out of football for up to nine months after tragically tearing a ligament and Parlour had picked up a suspension after last week's red card. Two additions to the litany of players already lost to Wenger for this fixture. Gio was the fourth player to go lame playing at left-back in the last few weeks and if it wasn't for the return of the versatile Lauren, we would have been running out of options (especially as an oversight meant young Juan wasn't registered for the competition).

One might have thought the position was cursed but then things weren't much better anywhere else in the pitch. I never imagined the day would come when the Arsenal would be running low on centre-backs. Yet Campbell and Stepanovs not only coped admirably but Igor also almost got on the scoresheet. There could be no complaints about their inability to keep a clean sheet, since the blasted volley for Bayer's consolation goal was arguably the best goal of the night. High praise indeed, on a night when all four Arsenal goals were collector's items.

I found myself sitting in front of Sol's best pal and Spurs player Steffan Freund. I therefore couldn't resist giving it some serious welly, when joining in with the chant of 'Are you watching Tottenham?' No true fan of the game should miss out on this footballing nirvana. I was fast running out of superlatives to adequately convey the calibre of football we were watching . . . and it only got better!

Arsenal travelled to St James' Park without Thierry Henry who had a stomach strain. It was over two months since Titi tore into Graham Poll after the reciprocal match at Highbury and he still hadn't been called up in front of the FA. Yet we knew he faced an eventual suspension, so this was an opportunity to see how we coped without the man responsible for half of our 57 goals. I could say that with Wiltord and Bergkamp up front the join was seamless, but in fact Dennis took centre-stage and grabbed all the limelight for his unique goal. It was amazing as I was only talking earlier in the week to a French footie journalist who described one of Bergkamp's tricks from the Leverkusen match as an '*aile de pigeon*'. It's typical – as the inventors of the beautiful game, we have dour descriptive terms, like 'nutmeg' and 'step-over', yet we haven't got a term for this tasty tidbit they call a pigeon's wing. I wasn't certain I understood exactly what he meant, so having seen Dennis perform this tantalising trick to open our account at Newcastle, leaving Dabizas for dead and the watching millions dumbfounded, when I caught up with my pal a couple of days later I asked him if the move had been an '*aile de pigeon*'. His emphatic response was: 'No, THAT was a Dennis Bergkamp!'

I should tell you that the Toons took us all the way and that the score-line didn't really reflect the balance of play but Dennis's goal was a thing of such rare beauty, it is all anyone needs to know about this game. With the match being a pay-per-view offering, Dennis's goal alone should have guaranteed that Murdoch garners a few more million from subscribers.

After smashing up his motor en route, I am glad my mate Nell made it and in hindsight, I wish I'd been with them, as the trip home was a helluva lot jollier than our journey back from the North East the following week. We were top of the league and would have remained there if referee Dunn hadn't ruled out the goal United conceded at Pride Park. Nevertheless the momentum was building, as May drew nigh. Only a point behind our old foe, the pressure at the top of the Premiership increased.

Monday, 4 March 2002

Despite the distasteful last-minute drama, as ref Dunn disallowed Derby's winner on Sunday afternoon, it was a delightful departure from the norm to see United suffer at the mercy of fate's fickle favour. We breathed a huge sigh of relief on seeing their luck finally begin to level out at long last.

By contrast, the positively exquisite performances this past week would suggest we cannot put a foot wrong at the moment. On Friday we were horrified to hear that Thierry Henry, currently in the form of his life as this season's most prolific scorer, had also succumbed to the injury epidemic which has stretched our squad to its extremes. At this point in the season, many clubs are plagued by the same curse. Yet there are few who could have said on Saturday they had easily an equal, or even better team on the treatment bench, as the one that turned out on Tyneside.

There is a growing feeling around Highbury that the force is finally with us and it doesn't seem to matter who the Arsenal's very own Obi-Wenger Kenobi selects to fill the breach – everyone seems to slip seamlessly into the boots of all our sidelined superstars. It is being whispered quietly for fear of tempting fate by appearing too full of ourselves, but the thought I've heard reiterated most often in recent days is that this could be '98 revisited, with the added ingredient of Champions League spice.

Shmeising Bayer Leverkusen last week and sticking it to the sneakier members of their squad was supremely satisfying. Beating the Bundesliga leaders 4–1 is about as good as it gets and it was our Highbury high of the season so far. However it was far from being the breeze the score-line might suggest. It is just that at the minute, with the ball at our feet, we are breaking from defence with such incision, intuition and precision, that every attack appears to have an inevitable momentum, whereby the ball is bound for the eventual inertia of the net.

I hadn't given the Glasgow final a thought before now, but suddenly it is not the unrealistic fantasy it was for the sorry bunch of losers who slumped to successive away defeats to lowly Mallorca, Panathinaikos, Schalke and Deportivo. What an incredible transformation of the team which only just scraped into the second stage. It is a privilege to be present to witness football of such a mesmerising calibre that we were all left with our jaws on the floor in dumbfounded delirium.

Aside from the sensational skills, if there is one image which left its imprint after Wednesday night, it was the sight of the team hug to celebrate Bergkamp's beautiful strike; therein lies the clue to the catalyst for the Arsenal's all-conquering confidence. There is little tangible evidence that you can put your finger on, but avid Arsenal watchers can attest to the burgeoning bond between this group of players. Perhaps Wenger pulled a masterstroke in his attempt to curb our Highbury inconsistencies by putting the team up in a hotel prior to recent home games. There are signs of a developing selfless team ethic which is so rare in the modern game, whereby it doesn't matter who plays, who scores, or who assists, so long as it is all for the greater Gooner good. For someone bred on Bertie Mee's 'Boring, boring Arsenal', where team spirit was our greatest solace, I truly rejoice in its return, especially since I was so scared we might have seen the last of this sentiment.

Such fabulous football and the narcotic effect of the Arsenal spirit aroused the notion of cramming my crocked back into a car for the five-hour journey to Newcastle. Eventually I resigned myself to saving my sore body for next Saturday's quarter-final, when a specially arranged train to Tyneside means that at least I will be able to stretch my aching limbs en route. I was celebrating my sagacity on Saturday when I had the fabulous pleasure of frame-by-frame coverage of the further incredible feats of Dennis Bergkamp. I might have missed out on the wonderful atmosphere, but those who saw the goal from up in the gods at the opposite end of St James' Park had to wait until they arrived home to fully appreciate what had taken place before their eyes. Moreover, my good mate Nell didn't even make it home. I considered myself fortunate not to have finished up in his backseat, as he ploughed into the car in front, the fifth victim of a five-car pile-up which closed the motorway earlier that day. Having been stranded on the hard shoulder, it was only due to the good grace of a passing Gooner that they even made it to the match. As Nell advised me by text message: 'Just like the team that's gonna win the Premier League. We shall be moved!'

29. Delicious Dinner Date or The Last Supper?

Tuesday, 5 March (Premiership): Derby County (H) 1–0 Pires (69) 1st
Saturday, 9 March (FA Cup quarter-final): Newcastle United (A) 1–1 Edu (14)

Arsenal were doing something right because Fergie was feeling the pressure. It produced the sort of verbal salvo which is becoming an annual tradition. Despite the fact that Dunn had rescued a point for them at Derby, he laid into the ref for making decisions which could have cost Utd the title. It was a blatant attempt to intimidate any subsequent official who had the misfortune to be allocated a Utd match. Fergie followed this with an attempt to fire up Derby by suggesting they weren't likely to be quite so motivated when they came to Highbury.

ARSENAL ON THE DOUBLE

After blanking the media for much of the season, suddenly there was no stopping a fulsome Fergie. He got in a timely broadside just a couple of days before Henry was finally due to come up in front of the FA. The following day's tabloids were full of his allegations concerning a conspiracy in the association's delay in dealing with both Henry and Vieira. I kind of preferred the peace and quiet of Fergie's self-imposed ban but then we wouldn't have the pleasure of Wenger's witty self-effacing responses.

Obviously the intention was to distract us from the task at hand, defeating Derby and overtaking Utd. The feelgood factor from his recent appointment may have been wearing a bit thin, but John Gregory should have been proud of Derby's admirable display. Compared to what had gone before it was a below-par performance from the Arsenal and they successfully stifled us for much of the game. Bergkamp and Pires eventually rose above this mire of mediocrity with 20 minutes remaining. Combined with the pleasure of our first clean sheet since August, it was enough for a good old-fashioned '1–0 to the Arsenal'. We went two points clear at the top, at least until Spurs' complete collapse at Old Trafford the following night (like they were going to do us any favours!). It would remain nip and tuck all the way, from here on in.

The following day Thierry Henry received a three-match ban for the incident with Graham Poll. It was longer than any of us hoped but far shorter than we feared. Still Wenger was raging. His argument was that Henry was the victim of the amount of live TV games played by Arsenal and the amount of media hype around the incident. Conflicting reports ensured many heated arguments about which matches Henry would miss. In the end, the club decided not to appeal, so his ban began immediately with Saturday's cup game, but he would be available for either our clash with Utd, or the semi-final. Henry's long-awaited ban had been hanging over the club like the Sword of Damocles for so long, resulting in so much speculation that it was almost good to get it resolved. It seemed to have a calming effect as at last we knew what had to be done and who would be available to do it. Additionally, whether manufactured, or genuine, Wenger's righteous indignation would be used as additional fuel to fan the flames of his team's passion.

Arsène rang the changes for our trip to St James' Park, with Richard Wright returning, as he would in every round, Freddie Ljungberg back fit for the first time since January and with an eye to Tuesday's clash with Deportivo, Dennis and Le Bob were left on the bench. Also on the bench amongst the various young prospects who were benefiting from experience in the first-team squad as a result of all our injury and suspension woes, was Kolo Toure, a new arrival from the Ivory Coast who was setting the reserves on fire, according to terrace gossip. It must have been a nerve-jangling experience just warming up on the touchline in front of 50,000 raucous Geordies, in this fervent FA Cup tie.

The look of unbridled joy on Edu's face as he celebrated a rare goal was a pleasure to behold. Sadly, as so often happens with an early lead, it ensured we sat back and began to soak up the pressure from which, eventually, Robert belted home their equaliser. With Man United having the weekend off, the last thing we needed was a replay to be squeezed into a congested fixture list. The only consolation on the interminably long train journey home was the realisation that at least the replay would count in Henry's suspension, so after all the fuss he would only miss one league match against Aston Villa.

It would have been a treat to trounce Tottenham ourselves in the semi, or the final, but Chelsea ended Tottenham's season for us. With a linesman hit in another coin-throwing incident, few were sad to see the back of Spurs and their hooligan element. On this evidence, it will be another 12 years before they manage to beat the Blues again. The draw guaranteed capital interest in the Cup final, as Fulham were to play Chelsea and Boro drew the victor in our replay with the Toons.

Monday, 11 March 2002

By the time you read this, the Arsenal might have pulled off a highly prized place in the Champions League quarter-final, in their penultimate match. Obviously I am praying that Tuesday night's results will render guaranteed qualification and a relaxing jaunt to Italy, but from the very day of the draw, I have fancied that the Arsenal were fated to a final, full-blown, ding-dong of a duel with the mighty Juve. For the boys to have earned themselves a breather with a meaningless last match would be too much to ask for and decidedly un-Arsenal-like. Whatever the outcome, our midweek dinner date with such a delightful footballing side as Deportivo is a delicacy that will undoubtedly set all genuine football aficionados drooling.

Nevertheless if you had inquired of the 5,000 Gooners who travelled to Tyneside on Saturday, many making the tortuous trip for the second time in seven days, there would have been few who would have been happy to forsake the FA Cup in favour of three points on Tuesday. Sure, there will be thousands of Gooners who didn't go, who might tell you that this domestic trophy is a mere trifle compared to the kudos of the Champions League. Some are suggesting that only parity at the European top table, by securing this ultimate prize, will be sufficient to prise Patrick Vieira away from the clutches of his shameless Spanish suitors. Personally I have a feeling that this particular writing has long been on the wall (or more's the point, on some pre-contractual arrangement) and Paddy's move to Madrid is already a done deal. Perhaps he's become less reckless with age, or it is a result of the close attentions of officials and the opposition. Yet while Vieira's performances continue to attract the plaudits, many who study his input every week cannot ignore their inkling of a commitment which is more Marcel Desailly than Tony Adams.

I idolise Vieira and am positive he will continue to play a major part (FA suspensions permitting!), as long as perhaps the best midfield player on the planet privileges us with his presence at Highbury. In this day and age, it's hard to begrudge him his opportunity to milk Madrid's monetary madness for all it's worth. Yet money does not maketh the man and one might have thought the poignant experiences of his mates Anelka and Petit might have put him off. Moreover, if it wasn't for Wenger's tutelage they might not be talking telephone numbers. I am not alone in despising the thought that the days of his Highbury domicile could depend on a demonstration that the Arsenal are no longer Champions League chumps.

Call me a sentimental old fool, but whether I'm paying five bob (I wish!) or £50 and whether they're earning fifty grand or sweet FA, my sole stipulation is that the bearer of the Captain's armband and his team-mates sweat blood for the cause. I certainly couldn't support the inconsistent likes of Chelsea, with their characteristic ability to hammer Spurs a couple of weeks after being humiliated by them. No matter which dance the Arsenal ends up doing with destiny, I am happy to schlep from Land's End to John O'Groats (who knows, perhaps even with a reel round Glasgow en route?), so long as it is to see a side which can express the same commitment to the club in combat with the crème de la crème as they would in a relegation dogfight (heaven forbid!).

There was plenty of desire on display at St James' Park on Saturday, both on the pitch and from the 50,000 voices reverberating around what has become one of the most impressive stadiums in the country. Not having brought any oxygen for our Nou Camp-like ascent, we looked for a lift to save us from the stairway to the gods. Surrounded by stripey-shirted Toons in the elevator, I found myself staring at the sea-horses that made up the crest of a middle-aged lady's United earrings. With Wenger having confined two of our most crucial gods to the substitutes bench, I attempted to alleviate the heavy air of apprehension in this confined space by suggesting that they were likely to fare better than the previous week's beating. They parted with a pessimistic quip which could only have come from a supporter sentenced to lifelong seasons of disappointment. I wish it had not been us cast as the bad guys in this particular drama.

It was strange travelling up on a Saturday for a tea-time kick-off on Tyneside, with only one other match involving Premiership sides taking place that afternoon and the three remaining cup games the following day. On TV they are constantly trying to talk up this famous competition, denying that the romance has been ruined. They certainly don't help themselves with such an insane schedule. As usual we whiled away the train ride reading the sports sections of the papers and the oft-repeated details about Shearer's distaste for touring Tyneside on an open-topped busload of FA Cup losers. They also romanticized about Bobby Robson and how righteous it would be for the honest endeavours of a true Geordie to be rewarded with a trophy. I knew which side the neutrals would be favouring, when even my ma passed comment on this pensioner and his silverware-starved side. I was grateful to be on a train full of 500 Gooners, or I myself might have arrived on Tyneside singing 'Ha'way the lads!'

Considering Wenger's disrespectful starting eleven, we definitely got away with it at St James' Park. We had plenty of time to reflect on this fact during an eternal train ride home. After an hour delay at Darlington we ran into nighttime repairs on the track. Despite being a dry train (or perhaps because), some gormless Gooners' frustrations fuelled a nasty fracas which necessitated another wait, whilst the police were called at Peterborough. When we finally crawled into Kings Cross at 2 a.m., I had to marvel at the Travel Club's ability to conjure up 50 taxis on a Saturday night in Central London to ferry Gooners as far a field as Portsmouth, Reading, Brighton and all points in between. Although it would be pointless applauding their charity, as doubtless the cost will be included in next season's ticket-price increases!

A replay and any subsequent Cup matches at Highbury would be over and above the seven games included in our season tickets. This meant an additional 50-odd quid per match which would be passed on to us along with any increase in next term's astronomically priced season tickets. There is also the congestion to be considered, which could see grief or glory come in a frantic flood of fixtures. Yet neither potential drawback would cast any doubt on the Gooner desire for progress. Not in a cup that owed us a large slice of fortune after we were floored in last year's final by the iniquitous icing on our cake.

30. May The Force Remain With Us

Tuesday, 12 March (Champions League): Deportivo La Coruna (H) 0–2
Sunday, 17 March (Premiership): Aston Villa (A) 2–1 Edu (15), Pires (60) 2nd

Our Champions League clash with Deportivo was the biggest anticlimax of the season. Our defeat in Spain way back in November was in another age, long before the Arsenal's season had begun to simmer, let alone bubble along on the boil as it was now. Since we'd already had a taste of the seductive football the Spaniards were capable of, on paper this game had all the hallmarks of a classic contest. Sadly, it is on the pitch where the match is played, not on paper. Only Dixon was missing from the side that battered Bayer Leverkusen so emphatically. He was replaced by Luzhny but it would be wrong to single out Oleg for the blame. Although the rest of the names of the players that beat the Germans were listed on the team sheet, too few of those capable of influencing a game actually showed on the pitch, as the majority hid for most of the evening.

If Vieira has pretensions of winning European trophies with the likes of Madrid, then this was the sort of game he needed to stand up and be counted, dominating the midfield as we know he can, instead of playing one-touch football, passing the ball and the buck at the earliest opportunity. Paddy sometimes has the air of someone who is no longer prepared to do the donkey work, hunting the ball and preventing the opposition from playing. With a team like Depor it was fairly obvious they would punish us if we gave the time to do their skilful stuff.

I am also not certain that resting players from the starting line-up at Newcastle was the best move. At this time of the season players develop a match–rest–train rhythm and it is often best not to disturb this groove. In my opinion the only Arsenal player to come away with any credit was Freddie Ljungberg. It was probably too late at 0–2 down already, but he was the only player to show the necessary intensity if we were going to get anything out of that match.

We didn't and had qualification taken out of our hands, which meant that our match in Turin could well be meaningless. I was so looking forward to battling it out with Juve for a place in the quarter-final, I am not sure whether this, or the fact that the Scousers took a giant step towards going through and Man United qualified both with scoreless draws, was the biggest wind-up. It was also frustrating knowing that in the pressure-cooker situation of the knockout stages the Arsenal were capable of playing better than both these teams.

Newcastle might have dropped two home points to Ipswich, but with Liverpool taking all three at Boro and Utd winning at Upton Park (despite the best efforts of Nigel Winterburn and his team mates), it was vital that we bounced back immediately. This time it was Pires who stepped up to the plate in the absence of Henry, with a goal that some suggested was the same quality as the Bergkamp stunner at Newcastle. Myself, I think that Dennis' was absolutely inimitable, whereas the one scored by Pires was merely exquisite; he ghosted past Boateng and coolly chipped the ball over a stranded Schmeichel's head. The timing of it was probably more crucial then Bergkamp's goal, as Seaman had just pulled off a superb penalty save, only for Le Bob to go down the other end and make it 0–2. On such instances do games turn, or even seasons for that matter. It was a safe bet that these Arsenal goals were guaranteed to monopolise the Goal of the Month competition. This was Edu's first start in the league, having played a largely peripheral role up to now on the bench. It had taken him some time to adjust to the pace of the Premiership but having scored that crucial goal at St James' Park in the Cup and then chipping in with another at Villa Park, he was at last looking more at home in Arsenal's midfield.

Monday, 18 March 2002

It was a fair kop, guv, last week. We were undone by a better side on the night. Sounder minds than mine can evaluate the implications in our *'jeux sans frontières'*, but the one statistic shouting at me was that these craftsmen from La Coruna included eight Spanish nationals, while Seaman and Sol Campbell were the only contributors from these shores to Wenger's multinational force. The most devastating consequence from this defeat to Deportivo was the potential destruction of that 'winning feeling', which had been steadily accruing in the Arsenal camp, until last Tuesday night.

Before Christmas the loss of extremely influential players like Henry, Adams, Keown and Cole would have left us dreading the team news prior to each game, bemoaning the weaknesses of Wenger's increasingly limited choice of replacements. In recent weeks, though, our run of victories had begun to instil in Gooners everywhere an air of invincibility. Our sublime skill going forward meant that it did not matter who Obi-Wenger Kenobi picked to plug the growing number of gaps, the air of confidence about the camp was such that each and every member of the squad was capable of cutting the mustard. Until a club of La Coruna's calibre tore our defence asunder and exposed the fact that while still waters run deep, squad strength can only be stretched so far. At the highest level in European competition there is no substitute for experience in defence. Alex Ferguson might have been ridiculed at the time for risking United's season on a replacement for Stam whose pensionable age entitles him to a free pass for public transport, but how our back line might have benefited last week from the calming influence of a cool, collected Laurent Blanc.

Frustrated by their failings a few months back, I would often holler at Henry and his pals to play the simple ball. However I have been happy to eat humble pie, as the practice of Pires, Henry and Bergkamp has made for the ultimate in footballing perfection of late. Yet where against Leverkusen they managed to bang in our first two attempts on goal, against Depor, not only did they fail to capitalise on a couple of early opportunities, poor old Thierry couldn't put a foot right all night. Considering his sensational form, it is hard to begrudge him the odd stinker. I only wish he had accepted the fact that it wasn't his night and let someone else take that penalty. As he stood facing the North Bank with the ball on the penalty spot, you could sense his apprehension. Just that week I had read a quote from Gazza about the penalty process, in which he described the goal posts shrinking and the keeper growing before his eyes. Seeing Henry in a similar predicament, I imagine I was amongst a majority present who wouldn't have fancied putting our money on him converting this one. Sadly Molina's save signalled the death knell against Depor. It was a great pity, since Ljungberg's arrival on the pitch had brought about an injection of enthusiasm. Having secured the penalty, who knows where the momentum might have taken us if we had managed to get on the scoreboard.

In the past, anything but a victory at the Highbury Library has seen the fickle faithful heading for the exits long before the final whistle. I've been disgusted by expressions of disapprobation from the disgruntled few. It was a rare sight to see the vanquishers applauded off, rather than our vanquished heroes being booed. Either this was a magnanimous gesture to a marvellous display from the Spaniards, or merely our only means of ingratiating ourselves with the Galicians, in the hope that having qualified for the quarter-final, they won't give up the ghost against the Gerries this week.

In the space of 90 minutes, all our old inferiority resurfaced. Just as the beautiful dream had begun to boil, the gas had gone out and no one had a coin for the meter. A draw would have been sufficient for our fantasies to continue simmering sweetly, instead of which I suddenly feared our season could fall flat in the space of three successive failures, leaving us destined for our perennial place as also rans. Consequently Sunday's match at Villa Park wasn't just crucial in terms of a continued assault on the Championship, it was vital for the feelgood factor. With the frantic schedule of fixtures facing us in the next few weeks, winning is imperative for the momentum that masks fatigue.

The tragic tale in the Sunday papers of the plight of poor Paul Vaessen, who passed away last year aged 39, saw memories of 1979 come flooding back. This was the man who literally had the world at his feet, with his goal in the semi-final of the Cup Winners' Cup securing the Arsenal's victory in Turin, against a Juve side whose home record in European competition had been unblemished for a decade. A subsequent four-match semi-final saga against Liverpool in the FA Cup saw our weary legs undone in the final, on Wembley's wide expanses, by Trevor Brooking's talented West Ham. Apparently Brian Talbot collapsed on the coach with exhaustion, but still managed to turn out four days later for one of the biggest nights in the Arsenal's history: a European final at Heysel. Despite 15 games in 45 days David O'Leary managed perhaps his most memorable performance in red and white, to mark the mighty Mario Kempes out of the game for 120 minutes, only for Valencia to win on penalties. The perfect example of a season which promised so much, but ended so painfully empty handed.

Let's hope that moment on Sunday when 'Safe Hands' gambled on the right direction to produce a stunning save, will galvanise the Arsenal, in order that we might run the gauntlet of the ghosts of the more recent past. Even without their top scorer, I can't help but feel that United wouldn't have made such heavy weather of a decidedly workmanlike Aston Villa. The core of Ferguson's side might be favoured by the fact that they are habitually accustomed to the pressure and have positively thrived on it in the past. Yet it's been a while since they've been bothered by anyone breathing down their necks, let alone the binary breath of both the current challengers for their crown. As far as I am concerned, our titanic encounter at Old Trafford can't come soon enough and I am saddened at the thought that an FA Cup semi-final place will cause a postponement of this peach in the Premiership run-in. We might see a repeat of '98, when Overmars exorcised any inferiority complex, or heaven forbid, a tonking like last term to put us southern upstarts firmly in our place. Or a stalemate could see the Scousers steam past us both. It will certainly prove more conclusive than the vacillating views of the string of morose managers who in defeat each week are expected to opine on the outcome.

Another silverware-starved season might be insufferable for us Gooners, but when I ponder on a weekend including an imperious lob from Pires, the boy

Beckham's virtuoso volley and the fact that the Arsenal have not failed to score in 31 league games, without doubt we've not wanted for some of the most wonderful football it has ever been my privilege to witness.

Despite endless explanations, I still remain completely confused about the convoluted qualification permutations this week. If, after an amazing 0–3 Arsenal triumph, the cameras should focus on a bemused Gooner 'boat-race' in the stands of the Stadio Delle Alpi, it'll probably be me, not knowing whether to jump for joy because we've qualified, or to cry for having fallen at the final hurdle before a knockout stage which could favour any team with a bit of luck on their side.

A Triumphant Reprise or a Requiem for Rodders?
Reprinted from *The Gooner*, *121*, 25 March 2002

I wrote this piece in the immediate aftermath of the Gillingham match, inspired by our captain's return after a lengthy five-month absence. However, another niggling injury set him back a further month. It might have been too late for TA to play a part in our erratic Champions League campaign, but since his eventual league comeback coincided with the following six 'clean sheet' steps on the road to Premiership paradise, it somehow seemed an appropriate point to honour his awe-inspiring contribution to the Gooner cause over so many marvellous years.

Like most gullible Gooners, I tend to stick with the same Arsenal T-shirt during a winning run. If results are less consistent, when getting dressed for a game, I will go through my massive collection in the hope of finding the one which the force might be with for that particular match. When my choice of T-shirts hasn't been helping our fortunes and I need to pull out all the superstitious stops for a match that really matters, invariably I will don the old faithful, the cock of the walk in my cupboard: my 'Donkey Won the Derby' souvenir from '93. I have to refrain from reaching for this magic bullet too often, for fear that frequent spin cycles might wash away the wonder, along with the picture of that memorable moment.

This T-shirt made it to such an exalted position, atop a huge pile, not only because it represents such a special occasion, but also because this particular goal (rather like the one he scored against Everton in '98) epitomises everything that is great about our club. Hopefully I might get a chance to flaunt my favourite T-shirt at another FA Cup semi, or even a final. Between times it has been my front-line offensive weapon for festering the wounds of many friends of the forces of darkness.

Mr Arsenal soaring to slam-dunk our way into another Wembley final with his head, wreaking revenge for Gooners everywhere, after a tormented two-year wait and our leader striding forward to leather it home against Everton, to put a perfect lid on our league title – these are two of my most vivid memories from a momentous decade. With the blow-by-blow denouement of our domestic conquest, I am still hoping that our captain might cap his career with another sensational moment of synchronicity. I would guess that TA still salivates at the thought of signing off with just such a swansong. What else would motivate the man to put himself through the punishing schedule required of him to regain fitness and instil in him the patience of Job, which has seen him through so many infuriating setbacks.

Mercurial footballing maestros may come and go but Adams has been part of the Arsenal fabric for so very long that few of us can imagine a squad that doesn't include TA's name at number six. For us Gooners, we know the end must be very nearly nigh, when we are left with the likelihood of losing our omnipresent leader, The Home of Football and the club crest, all in one cruel connivance of fate. It has been obvious all season that much of our inconsistency has been due to the apparent insecurity which pervades our half of the pitch, when our opponents are in possession. We can be world beaters with the ball at our feet, but at other times the team has lacked an authoritarian focal point. Nevertheless it was only when the great man finally got a game against Gillingham that I fully appreciated quite how hamstrung we've been in the absence of Tony's titanic presence. With both Adams and Dixon on the pitch there was almost a nostalgic air of invincibility about us. Yet it was the papers that portrayed the moment at the start of the second-half, when Adams stood towering over our schnip of a Brazilian debutant, lending him the benefit of all the donkey's defensive years. Few stars remain in this egocentric era of the game who relish their responsibility to retain the vital elements of the team ethic.

It's not that it hasn't been an entertaining season without Adams so far, as we've been privileged to witness some of the most amazing artistry ever seen at the Arsenal. But imagine how much better we might have fared with a few more clean sheets. For a moment there I thought TA's triumphant comeback might kick off an all-conquering run-in, taking us all the way along the high road to a May Day in Glasgow. This delicious dream was devastated with details of Rodders suffering another dodgy reaction. Could this be confirmation that our captain is truly limping around on his last legs?

Disregarding Vieira, as I cannot condone a captaincy waved as a carrot to keep someone at the club, Sol, or anyone else for that matter, will struggle to stand in Adams' sizable shoes. Yet I was hoping we might get an entire last season from our leader, so that the likes of Campbell might learn the ropes from Captain Fantastic. The misadventures of our injury-ravaged antiques have meant I couldn't have been further off the mark. In his modern incarnation, TA doesn't appear to be the sort of person to continue playing until Father Time finally jabs his arthritic joints with the scythe. Unless he surprises us all with a worthwhile contribution for another season, it looks as though our expectations should be limited to the odd crucial contribution to the conclusion of the current contest.

Adams' presence in the dressing room alone would undoubtedly prove a major advantage, but playing the unsung hero would hardly be a fitting scenario for the curtain call of such a colossal playing career. It would be far more appropriate for the fates to favour our one club captain with a few more chances to unwrap the cotton wool from his crippled limbs and let the good times roll for one last big exit.

In this cash-crazy sport of ours, where a contract for a couple of seasons is now considered sufficient for a loyalty bonus, we might never see the likes of Adams again. When working your way up through the ranks is perceived as a minor miracle, what price his wholehearted, career-long commitment to the cause? 'No one player is bigger than the club' is an oft-repeated cliché. Yet Tony Adams and the Arsenal are synonymous and no matter how inevitable his eventual retirement, it is painful to think of the place without him.

31. Give Me Domestic Drudgery Any Day

Wednesday, 20 March (Champions League): Juventus (A) 0–1
Saturday, 23 March (FA Cup quarter-final replay): Newcastle
United (H) 3–0 Pires (2), Bergkamp (9), Campbell (50)

Standing on the terrace of the Stadio Della Alpi with the Gooners that made up a large proportion of the extremely limited numbers in the vast void of this cavernous stadium, I was amazed to pick up the rather ropy transmission of Radio 5. It didn't prove to be such a blessing when the first news I heard about the match in Spain was that Depor had rested all their star players. I was clinging in vain to the thought that the Spaniards relative second-eleven would all be fighting to avoid Real Madrid in the quarter-final, when the really sickening revelation came from someone in Spain, who was watching live on TV, to say that the Germans were all over them and at 0–2 up we might as well go home!

There was a glimmer of hope when we heard that they had sent their big guns Tristan and Valeron on in the second-half. There was a brief buzz of excitement with the news of a Depor goal, but by that time it was already 1–3 and it was too little, too late. It was adding insult to injury when the Italians scored and although there was plenty of industry from Arsenal in response, there was no end product. I reckon even the ref must have felt some sympathy for us when he awarded Henry a decidedly dodgy penalty. It summed up the night when their keeper made a brilliant save from the spot and so we went home without even the consolation of being able to celebrate a goal. Róna and I had a great trip to Turin, spoiled only by our reason for being there!

It was likely that this demoralising end to another European campaign would have an affect on Saturday's cup quarter-final replay. The fact that this was positive was doubtless related to the positive return to full fitness of Tony Adams. The timing of his and Ashley Cole's comeback from injury, both keen as mustard, was just the boost we needed. Better still Champions League football was the furthest thing from our mind when Pires scored with our first attack of the game. Arsenal were purring from the off and had hit the bar before we scythed through the Toons defence for Bergkamp to score a second. I felt sorry for some of the Geordies, as they must have left at the crack of dawn to make this ridiculously timed noon kick-off on a Saturday.

If this triumph wasn't enough for us to turf out the nightmare of Turin, I came home to watch the score updates on the box from the civilized afternoon games, waiting for news of the inevitable last-minute goal at Old Trafford. It never came, as Steve McClaren's Boro side made our day and our smiles even broader by beating United for the second time this season. We'd become so accustomed to our players dropping in and out of the team, with the plethora of injuries they've managed to pick up, that no one batted an eyelid when Robbie Pires limped off after 30 minutes, having already played his crucial part in putting us through to the semis, scoring the first and making the second. It was therefore distressing news on such an upbeat day, to discover later on that Le Bob might be seriously crocked.

Like the return of Caesar, the Scousers had hung out the flags for Houllier's triumphant midweek return to Liverpool as his side ground out a victory over Chelsea which took them one point clear of United at the top of the table. We were two points behind in third but now with a potential six points in hand having played two games less. In a sad coincidence, just as Liverpool's French hero returned, we lost ours for the remainder of the season. We discovered quite how fond we had become of Pires when it was revealed that he faced the prospect of surgery on his ruptured knee ligament and his World Cup dreams were dashed.

It was a real tragedy because Robbie was playing the best football of his career and having developed into our most influential player since his timid start last season, many thought he would be a shoo-in as many of his fellow professionals' favourite for Footballer of the Year. We saw his confidence blossom in the early part of the season to the point where he was attempting all sorts of audacious tricks that I doubt he would have dreamt he was capable of pulling off prior. More's the point, this was the player who came to us from Marseilles, where apparently the fans would moan at him for failing to *muscler ton jeu* (get stuck in). He sat on the bench for his first game at Sunderland wondering what he was doing here, not fancying English football after seeing the 'crazy tackles' flying in. Though he might have started a little timidly as a result, his game has developed at Arsenal to the point where we can have little complaint about his all-round contribution.

In fact, though his attacking instincts might occasionally leave Ashley Cole exposed when our opponents are in possession, we have all become so enamoured with his ability to tear the opposition apart in attack, that there are plenty at Highbury who would prefer he went and had a cup of tea and a quiet fag should Arsenal lose the ball, instead of endangering himself with any petty donkey work. Myself, I am harder to please, as I expect even the most gifted to play their part in defensive duties. In the past I might have been guilty of criticising Pires for being a bit of a pussy, but even I was warming to his tenacious attempts to fulfil his responsibility to the team. It was therefore not just a tragedy but a sad irony as far as I was concerned, that Robbie's season and his World Cup summer was ruined, as a result of the ligament-wrenching, awkward landing he made when attempting to ride the clattering challenge from Dabizas. The tournament in Japan and Korea should have been the perfect stage for Pires, in the prime of his career, and I only hope Germany 2006 doesn't come too late for him.

Monday, 25 March 2002

I was lying on the bed, staring up at the fresco on the ceiling of our palatial hotel room in Turin, some hours before our humiliation at the hands of a phalanx of Fiat-owning, bench-warming *bianconeri*, playing devil's advocate over what domestic trophies I might be prepared to dispense with in order to dine with the elite at European football's top table. Like any other right-minded Gooner, I can't wait to see the Arsenal conquer the crème de la crème, en route to their eventual coronation as crowned heads of Europe. Taking our rightful place as European rulers by establishing a Real Madrid-type dynasty would be wonderful, but personally I would settle for taking club football's top prize just the once (to start with!). Not only so that I might sing 'by far the greatest team' with absolute conviction, but because it would be beautiful to obliterate at long last any inkling of an inferiority complex compared to some of our more corpulent European cousins. Many of us live for the moment that will finally enable us to open our programmes at the start of the season, to see the one trophy which has to date eluded us, listed there amongst our role of honours, for all eternity.

Unlike some slightly more presumptuous Gooners, the three-trophy 'T' word had not passed my lips, for fear of tempting fate. Yet as I debated this matter prior to the Juve debacle, I decided I definitely wasn't prepared to concede either the FA Cup or the Premiership, in favour of progress in Europe. Not to mention paying such a hefty price only to see us embarrassingly nailed in the knockout stages. With the possible return to fitness of those two stalwart rocks of Keown and Adams at the heart of our defence, if Deportivo hadn't done the dirty on us (it galls me to think of the gracious round of applause we gave them at Highbury) and we had made it through to the quarters, a Glaswegian finale to this fabulous season might not have been such a fanciful fantasy.

Albeit if there is one lesson to be learned from the way Liverpool levered themselves into the later stages, it is the patent fact that at the highest level it is not scoring goals that counts, but a defence which is capable of keeping them out. And if we are honest with ourselves, all thoughts of being kings of the continent should remain in cloud-cuckoo land until our current squad can conceive of keeping a clean sheet against the very best. Cryonics would have been the perfect solution. If only we could have frozen our fab five dinosaurs a few years back, defrosting them just for special occasions! I feel for poor Captain Fantastic, Pugwash, Able Seaman and dear Dicko, since fate might well have dealt most of them such a lousy last European hand.

Although the defeat was mighty disappointing, it was more the manner of our undignified European exit which I found so depressing. With my extremely limited knowledge of Italian, I usually find a few words of the lingo are met with an incomprehensible, rapid-fire response. So my attempts to communicate with the taxi driver who collected us from the Stadio Delle Alpi degenerated into fairly universal hand signals. Assuming that he wasn't referring to a recent shag, or making a pass at me, I construed his vulgar gesture to suggest an appreciation of the commitment and spirit of sides from these shores (obviously he hadn't seen the match!). Qualities which are traditionally associated with our football, but are so often found wanting from players abroad who change team shirts as often as their pants! This taxi driver obviously didn't see our last match either when the eight Spanish nationals in the Depor side danced past an Arsenal team with only two Brits. Could it be a mere coincidence that the two teams who qualified for the quarters from this country both contain a sizable core of countrymen, be they English, Irish or Scottish?

ARSENAL ON THE DOUBLE

I was scared I'd been barking up completely the wrong tree, when this Sicilian came to a screeching halt en route to our hotel. However, he was merely responding to the sirens from the police escort for the bus loads of Gooner daytrippers, heading straight to the airport. I was disconsolate despite the consolation of a third delightful day in 80-degree sunshine, so Heaven only knows how miserable they must have been, without even the pleasure of feeling the sun on their backs. I fancy it was a somewhat funereal flight home. I can remember when an appetising duel like Arsenal v. Juve was a once-in-a-decade delight, which would guarantee lifelong memories of a full-house and a fantastic atmosphere. Whereas the weekly encounters in the Champions League have ensured we've all become far too blasé about such common occurrences. For evidence of football's bursting bubble, you need look no further than the blight of the *bianconeri*'s bare terraces. As far as the football match itself was concerned, I have to say our trip to Toon town will leave a far more lasting impression than our lame struggle to get our leg over with 'The Old Lady of Turin'!

My loyalty to the Gooner cause is such that I love away matches far more than our home games, on account of the fervent atmosphere one finds amongst the travelling faithful. Constant Champions League qualification will eventually present a scenario in which I am likely to be far from alone in no longer being able to afford to follow my team to every match. I adore the fact that our European adventures have taken us to so many far-flung corners of the continent that I would have never dreamt of visiting if it weren't for football. Yet I absolutely abhor the fact that there might soon come a time when I am forced into another damn digital subscription in order to watch the Arsenal play via sterile television coverage. It certainly doesn't bode well for the inevitable advent of a Euro League which might well replicate the non-partisan, vacuum-packed product of the philistine sport played on the other side of the Atlantic.

I returned from Italy plagued by pessimistic thoughts that our 'big-stage' stars wouldn't be able to raise their game for the remainder of our season, after our ignominious European exit. Although with season-ticket renewals just around the corner (including the cost of extra cup games on top of any increase!) I have to admit to feeling somewhat relieved at not having to tax the plastic with two further foreign trips, after it took a pasting on all those irresistible treats to comfort us in Turin. Thankfully my pessimism was totally misplaced, as our imperious cup performance proved that defeat has only hardened their desire not to end another season empty-handed. It was a heartwarming experience that suggests the Arsenal spirit is alive and well and coursing through this squad!

32. A Whirlwind Against the Wilting Wearsiders. Whither Next on this Long and Winding Road?

Saturday, 30 March (Premiership): Sunderland (H) 3–0 Vieira (2), Bergkamp (4), Wiltord (30) 1st
Monday, 1 April (Premiership): Charlton (A) 3–0 Henry (16, 25), Ljungberg (21) 1st

With bothersome international friendlies behind us, we could focus on the fixtures of an all important Easter weekend. A dazzling performance by Dyer, in front of the omnipresent Ericsson, helped Newcastle to hammer Everton 6–2 in the live TV match on Good Friday. Of the top four, we were the only other side playing twice over the long weekend, because United and Liverpool both had the distraction of Champions League quarter-finals the following week. It was imperative that we made the most of both matches.

I had been looking forward to seeing relegation-threatened Sunderland play and to see if their loan-signing, Patrick Mboma could breathe some life back into the Black Cats. We strolled around to Highbury in good time for once, intent on not missing any more opening-minute goals, having just watched the Leeds late show at Elland Road as they tried in vain to rescue something from their 3–4 defeat to Man United.

You could almost touch the mood of anticipation in the spring sunshine, with all the Gooners gathered in and outside the pubs around the ground. Many had arrived early to watch the midday broadcast of United's match and had drunk themselves into a state of eager exuberance. I wondered if United had gained an unfair advantage, with our lot under the pressure of knowing their rivals were already back in the dressing room with all three points in the bag. I needn't have worried, for if we were toiling under the tension of it all, the rampant response of our team suggested they couldn't be more relaxed.

Our rivals all hoped that the injury to Pires might put paid to our Premiership challenge. Though it was saddening to see Le Bob appear on the pitch in civvies before the game, to pick up another Player of the

Month award, it seemed as though his personal disaster and that of Van Bronckhorst had only hardened the resolve of the team. Our concern may have been more for the consequences than for the actual record itself, but it was an incredible fact that we had now scored in 32 consecutive games. What's more, Titi's prolific performances would sustain his challenge for the Golden Boot. But it was great that so many others were making a contribution to our tally, in a manner not seen since our last successful campaign. He might have had to wait until Monday to increase his total, but this didn't stop Henry from revealing the almost obligatory message underneath his Arsenal shirt, which on this occasion read: 'Gio, Robert. Thinking of you'. On another record-breaking day, the Arsenal managed an entire 90 minutes, their tenth match in a row without a red card!

It was a surprise when Harry Bassett accepted the Foxes hot-seat, when their fate already appeared to have been decided. Although their fans kept faith to the very last, as Bassett new boy and ex-Gunner Dickov banged in a couple against Blackburn. Leicester's first win in 17 saw Souness' Worthless Cup winners faced with the unlikely prospect of relegation and European qualification in the same season.

With the Queen Mum rumoured to have an affinity for the Arsenal, I guess I could have shown a little more consideration for the event that was consuming the nation. Despite the blanket media coverage, her passing only really impinged on my consciousness on account of my fears that the fixture list might fall victim to the FA's mark of respect. I know she 'toughed it out' with the cockneys during the blitz (according to the endless reminders), but death hardly came as a shock at her age and there are far more unfortunate souls deserving of our sympathies.

3–0 up after 30 minutes might have enabled us to take our foot off the pedal and play the remainder of Saturday's game with an economy of effort but it was Tony Adams' first two successive games since September. So not wanting to risk the rigours of two games in three days, he was rested for our visit to the Valley. Charlton put up far more of a fight in front of their fans than Sunderland's sorry performance, but once again the Arsenal flew at them with such pace in our attack that it was all over in the first-half – bar the shouting, as our end of the stadium shuddered to the sound of 'We Are Top of The League'. I joined in with more enthusiasm than ever, knowing that we weren't just keeping the seat warm, waiting to be leapfrogged by our rivals once again. No matter how superstitious I am about not tempting fate, intent on remaining pessimistic to the last, for the first time I found myself moved to the point where I couldn't prevent myself from daring to dream the not so impossible dream.

Thierry had failed to find the target in the last four games, but he was on song here, back to his irrepressible best, with two goals giving him two opportunities to flash his tribute to Gio and Robbie to the thousands of Gooners behind the goal and the millions watching on TV. It also meant he was the first Arsenal player to score 30 goals in a season since Ian Wright in 1997. Freddie Ljungberg also seemed to have taken it upon himself to put the misery over Pires out of our minds and to put all our rivals in no doubt about the direction in which the Championship was heading. His terrific late runs into the box were to become a trademark of this title run-in.

Whether it was the 'go-faster' red stripe in his hair, or the fact that like others in the squad, his enforced absence for a large chunk of the season had left him with fresher legs than some of our opponents. Perhaps it is Wenger's wise husbandry of his resources that deserves our respect, because up to this point we were familiar with the sight of Freddie being pulled off with 15 or 20 left on the clock. Whereas from here on in we would get used to seeing sluggish opposing defenders made to look like they were standing still, while Freddie charges around, his enthusiasm up to 90, for the entire 90.

We've seen plenty of individual evidence of what Paul Merson termed 'unbelievable belief', but it was at the Valley that I first recognized its potency, when applied to each and every single squad member. It was the few moments of mutual admiration after the final whistle, as the team came to our end of the ground to express their appreciation and we lauded them with the heartiest rendition of 'We Shall Not Be Moved' ad infinitum. I saw Martin Keown saluting us, shaking both fists, his expression bristling with pleasure while his eyes burned with steely determination. With our twelfth unbeaten game on the road and the six goals in two games (with two clean sheets to boot), we'd gone from top gear into overdrive. If we weren't certain, the Gunners' body language screamed the all important answer. Nothing was going to stop them now.

The only blot on such a stirring Easter weekend landscape was Graham Stuart's shuddering retributive tackle on Ashley Cole. We felt it from behind the goal, so heaven knows what it was like to be the recipient. For a while there we were terrified the dreaded left-side curse had struck again and Ashley would be another to fall by the World Cup wayside.

Monday, 1 April 2002

For a moment, I almost felt sorry for the couple of thousand amongst the Black Cat collective, as they ran out of their nine lives in less than five minutes. I have a soft spot for Sunderland. Apart from the usual suspects, where my disfavour is too deep rooted (eg. Spurs, Chelsea, United), I have some sympathies for the long-suffering supporters of most sides that aren't quite so privileged as us Gooners. Occasionally our advantage seems so unfair, that if we were playing in the school playground, to ensure a more even contest, I might offer them the likes of Wiltord or Luzhny (depending how desperate they were!). Still, there's little room for sentiment in this barmy business.

Expectations under Wenger have become so inflated, that after a few silverware-starved seasons, many Gooners are far too blasé about our uncompromising consistency. It confirms how brilliantly our club goes about its business. Besides, it is a minor economic miracle given the gate receipts of competing continental and domestic clubs, who can squeeze 20,000 or 30,000 more fans through their turnstiles every week. It is no wonder the club are so keen to move to a bigger stadium, so long as Highbury's limited capacity continues to cost us a fortune.

I am long enough in the tooth to recall the last time the Arsenal approached Easter attempting to rally against a serious risk of relegation, way back in '76. Yet during Arsène's era, we've grown so accustomed to challenging for the Championship that I couldn't possibly imagine the fears of those fans facing the nemesis of Nationwide anonymity.

There is no shortage of admirers for what is arguably the Arsenal's most entertaining side ever. In a discussion with a Spurs-supporting pal, I surprised him by revealing that we continued to gain admittance to the ground for our ninth cup game (excluding the Worthless Cup), even though the cost of only seven is included in our annual subscription. He left himself wide open when he questioned how the club would go about claiming payment in arrears, if someone gave up their season ticket. With relish I responded that while it may be a regular occurrence at his club, a three-year waiting list ensures it is extremely rare at ours. Mind you, I wonder if we'd be as whimsical as those at White Hart Lane, if like Tottenham's turncoats, our tickets didn't come with a warranty of such wonderful football.

It is another month before May and the end of a sizzling season. Already I am sweating over our season-ticket renewals. It will be a substantial financial sacrifice, but when you consider how the current squad are breaking all records, with an unbroken run of a goal in every game, going to Highbury is far from a grind. By contrast, my utmost respect is reserved for the trusty Trojans of the relegation candidates, those who stump up their hard-earned spondulicks every season, buoyed by the sophistry of silly-season speculation, optimistically believing they are about to storm the Bastille of what is now an annual bi- (or at most tri-) partite carve up.

They might happily hold this hallucination close to their hearts, but in their heads, the height of their humble expectations is limited to the distraction of a decent cup run, during their habitual endeavours to hang on to their Premiership status. Don't get me wrong, I'd be a wobbling, whining blancmange if the boot was on the other foot and I was currently pondering the ignominious prospect of playing the likes of Preston and Portsmouth. I'd much rather contemplate our chances of the Championship and cups and whether we'll cope with the absence of poor Robbie Pires, whose presence might have proved crucial on the wide expanses of Old Trafford. At least season-ticket holders at every Premiership club should get good value for their money this term. The top six are chasing European qualification and every club from seventh down is only a couple of calamitous results away from being dragged into the trapdoor dogfight.

It is too little, too late for Leicester, but their surprising success on Saturday shows that they have yet to give up the ghost. It suggests that no team intends to see their season out with a whimper, following the sort of glut of dreary, meaningless matches of yesteryear. Mind you, it is not something I should be crowing about, when it leaves mid-table Charlton chomping at the bit against the Arsenal. Previously we might have mown down such a side, because their players were preoccupied, already daydreaming about basking on a Florida beach.

I feel so much for the fans of the relegation rearguard, that I have no desire to see any of them doomed. With an arbitrary yen for the axing of our most arduous away trips, one might have thought I'd be thankful to kick one of three trips to the northeast into touch. It is not just my admiration for Peter Reid's achievements. A whole host of managers regularly attempt heroic Houdini acts at the bottom of the pile. They usually have budgetary restraints that would bamboozle the prodigal bunglers who appear hell-bent on blowing their benefactors' last million beans. Sunderland are one of the most accessible and family oriented clubs in the league. With a sensible pricing structure, local kids can obtain a season ticket without having to strip the lead from the roof of the nearest church. Moreover, the Stadium of Light has perhaps the best atmosphere of all the new stadia and is one of my favourite outings. Not forgetting my affection for the Arsenal old boys, Stefan Schwarz and Niall Quinn. Quinny remains the consummate professional on the pitch, not to mention a far better player than many give him credit for. The wily ways which enable him to continue performing at the highest level never fail to impress.

Having served together for so long early in their careers, it was a fitting coincidence for Niall Quinn to be involved in what turned into a celebration of Tony Adams' 500th game in red and white. They are the last of a dying breed, of loyal 'do or die' dinosaurs. As a selfish striker, Jeffers was hardly likely to pass up an opportunity in front of goal. Sadly the scally sub couldn't have read the script, as Adams lumbered forward on his arthritic limbs at the death, in the hope of crowning the occasion with his 50th goal for the club. It may have been a black day for the Wearside Cats, but confirmation of a cakewalk for the Arsenal came, as our opponents mounted two attacks before Captain Fantastic ambled back from nosebleed territory.

The Arsenal are making a habit of kicking off at a cracking pace. It's been my misfortune to miss a handful of goals which have hit the net as I've hurried around Highbury. Consequently I made certain I was sitting comfortably before kick-off on Saturday, but I am beginning to believe it is a conspiracy to cure my tardy tendencies!

33. A Five-minute Life Lesson in Not Larging It Too Lasciviously

Saturday, 6 April (Premiership): Tottenham Hotspur (H) 2–1
Ljungberg (24), Lauren (86 pen) 1st

Having gone clear at the top, a point in front of the Scousers and two above United, with a game still in hand, our forthcoming fixture at Old Trafford was looking increasingly like the title decider. Although with this game scheduled for the weekend of our FA Cup semi-final against Boro, the two clubs still had to agree on a rearranged date for this titanic clash. It had crossed the minds of each and every one of us that if we won the other five remaining league fixtures, we could lose to United and still win the Championship. Yet it wasn't just winning the title that was important. It felt as though our 'friends' in the north had been preparing themselves in case events shouldn't go their way, with suggestions in the media that if they didn't win the title, it would be United that had thrown it away, as opposed to the Arsenal winning it. Consequently I don't know about anyone else, but as far as I was concerned it was imperative that we beat United to prove that the title hadn't been won by default.

As far as the pundits on the box and in the press were concerned with Spurs, Ipswich, West Ham, Bolton and Everton being the five of our six remaining victories required to bring the title to Highbury no matter what happened at Old Trafford, the derby match was the only one Arsenal were in danger of losing. We've had our fair share of semi-final encounters with the old enemy in recent times but I can't remember such a significant league clash since that momentous night in 1971. With them slumming it for so many years, our results are often more important to Spurs fans than their own matches. As far as they were concerned this was a chance to derail our Championship charge. While a draw or (heaven forbid!) a defeat wouldn't be fatal for us, the fact it was so important to them made the outcome equally mammoth for us (the summer would be no picnic if we were condemned to months of their merciless teasing!).

Again United's 0–1 victory in their noon kick-off at Filbert Street meant we would be playing catch-up. However it might be their last taste of the heady heights for the remainder of the season. Up to now I had felt quite happy chasing the Championship, but after the victory at the Valley, the tension really began to mount. Overnight we had become the outright favourites and after spending four seasons relentlessly trying to recapture the ultimate domestic prize, suddenly it was all there for us to lose. To be honest I am always a lot more comfortable when Arsenal are the underdogs and I was nervous that this shift in perceptions and the resulting intense pressure was bound to have a negative effect on the pitch.

Kick-off signalled the start of a month-long nerve-wracking roller-coaster ride. The tension on the terraces was mirrored on the pitch with the football fluctuating from the sublime to the ridiculous. We dominated possession and made Spurs look ponderous at the back with our pacey passing and slick movement. Tottenham had turned up with the sole intention of denying us the victory. I am not sure whether George Orwell sat on either side of the North London divide, but if he'd turned up during this game in his time machine, he would have sworn the participants had already swapped shirts. Spurs may have won their first silverware in eight years with George Graham's guidance, but he would, always be considered an Arsenal man. There were hallelujahs all round, with the return of the messiah, when Hoddle replaced Graham at the helm. We couldn't resist the irony of Hoddle's entertainers coming to Highbury, with the negative intention of preventing the Arsenal scoring, and so the Spurs fans were serenaded all afternoon with the song 'You've Got Your Tottenham back.'

Vieira was one booking away from a suspension which might have meant him missing the Cup final if we made it, or even the cosmic clash at Old Trafford. I spent much of the match praying Paddy wouldn't be provoked into losing his head. If Spurs couldn't beat us on the day, it appeared as though they were intent on making sure the repercussions were as damaging as possible. They had three bookings in the first-half, all for fouls on our French midfielder. This was the elegant Edu's most impressive match for Arsenal yet; he began pulling the strings in our midfield, managing to play his cool, calm passing game amidst that cauldron. Mercifully, midway through the first 45 Dennis finally found his range as he tore Spurs asunder with a defence-splitting peach of a pass that was perfectly aligned with Freddie's red stripe (with a built-in adjustment for the wonky bit at the back!). I could have sworn the numbers on the digital clock on the front of the East Upper had changed from the time Freddie clipped the ball, to when it finally groaned its way inside the goalpost. I reckon the resulting noise must have been the loudest eruption at Highbury so far this season and if we'd have come home to find the pup had messed the carpet I would have quite understood (besides I would be struggling for control of my own bowel before this game was over!). It was such a massive release of all the tension which had been building up that even the librarians in the West Upper tried to muddle through the words of Freddie's new theme tune.

Hearty renditions of two new terrace tunes had first been heard at the Valley a few days earlier. I should have known there and then that we were onto something special, as the last time a decent, tuneful ditty was introduced into the somewhat limited Gooner repertoire was Vieira's song in '97. For the benefit of the unenlightened, Freddie's song is a reworking of the Andy Williams classic 'Can't Take My Eyes Off Of You' with the lyrics: 'We love you Freddie 'cos you've got red hair. We love you Freddie 'cos you're everywhere. We love you Freddie 'cos you're Arsenal through and through'.

There is something about Ljungberg, the irreverent, DIY red stripe, the all-action enthusiasm that makes him, amongst many others in this squad, one of us and so, just like the Vieira song four seasons back, the Freddie song became the theme tune of our assault on the title. Whether it was inspired by Ljungberg's goals, or inspired him to score the goals, we'll never know, but it certainly can't do a feller's enthusiasm any harm to have 30,000 proclaiming their love!

It is one of the reasons I always find myself singing the praises of our unsung heroes. When Lauren stepped up to the plate to pull all three points out of the bag, I wanted a means to express my adoration of him and all our heroes that afternoon. Five minutes earlier, the whole season flashed before my eyes when Poyet went down in our penalty area. I told my Spurs pal back in August that I thought the Uruguayan was the bargain buy of last summer, because I always felt most threatened by the Blues when Poyet was making his runs from midfield. Little did I know then that these words would come back to haunt me at such a harrowing moment.

I probably wouldn't be writing this book if ref Halsey (again!) wasn't from the 'two wrongs' school of thought and Richards hadn't presented him with an opportunity to award us a penalty in return five minutes later. Most clubs celebrate the award of a penalty with wild abandon, but at Arsenal we've become so accustomed to looking this gift horse in the mouth (actually looking at it over the bar, round the post, in the goalie's hands, anywhere but the bleedin' goal!) that the immediate ballyhoo becomes a stifled buzz of speculation, as we bet amongst ourselves whose chance it is to put their head on the penalty chopping block. This turns into an uneasy hush while we search for some confirmation of the condemned and the butterflies in 30,000 bellies begin to flap with absolute abandon because they know even if we don't, that the spot-kick won't hit the net!

Often with hindsight one can spot some slight telltale trait when a player would rather the goal open up and swallow him instead of the pressure of the penalty. There was nothing on Lauren's face to suggest he was fazed by the thought that a whole 38-game season might stand or fall on his tap of the ball. Some were more confident than others, having seen him score from the spot for Cameroon. Yet when it came to it Lauren probably hadn't scuffed a ball as badly all season. It might have bobbled towards the goal but it ended up in the old onion bag and that is all that mattered. The previous five fearful minutes with our hearts in our mouths and our indignation at its most intense, ensured an even rowdier explosion of emotion every bit as deafening as the first.

Delirium truly reigned, with the demolition of all decency as such a civilised crowd lost itself in the lyric of the other new, candid incantation. To my mind, getting carried away is what going to football is all about. Hard as I try to avoid it, I often find myself conscious of the sensibilities of the genteel Gooners in the West Upper and perhaps constrained by my middle-class conditioning, am even a little embarrassed when I suddenly realise I'm all alone in joining in with the ribald roasting of a referee. It was therefore beautiful to hear thousands in the West Upper bellowing 'F***k all, f***k all, f**k all and the Cockney Reds are going outta their heads, 'cos United will win f***k all!' High old times indeed at The Home of Football.

Monday, 8 April 2002

Despite suffering the 90-minute climax to their relegation catastrophe, I had to admire the unwavering fealty of the Foxes fans on Saturday. Leicester let me down with their limitless inability to take advantage of a lacklustre United. While I agonised over the TV coverage, our pets were left positively petrified because I was constantly springing out of bed, screaming like a banshee at the box. Yet all due 'respek' to their fans, who rose to their feet for the last few minutes, for a rendition of a rousing chorus to confirm their unfaltering feelings for this football club. Perhaps it's the huge gulf between the height of expectations, but I found myself contemplating the likely contrast in the reaction of the Highbury faithful if our season was drawing to a close in such calamitous circumstances.

Thankfully the opposite is true and us Gooners are gobsmacked with gratitude, struggling for superlatives to do sufficient justice to such a fabulous and fortuitous finale to the domestic football calendar. It might have helped our cause, by taking some pressure off, if United had dropped a couple of unexpected points in their midday match. In truth, they probably did us a favour, as the last thing we needed going into that afternoon's derby duel, was the knowledge that we could afford to take our foot off the pedal. The facts were as clear as the crisp blue sky that greeted me, as I nipped out to give the gold dust of two tickets to a Green Gooner pal and his missus, over from Cork for the match. Against the forces of darkness we had to win or wave goodbye to the points advantage and the momentum that has everyone (apart from the most persistent of us pessimists!) believing the title is in the bag.

It was the sort of bracing, bright Saturday afternoon which is just perfect for playing football. I wandered on to Blackstock Road, where crowds outside the Gunners and the other boozers were spilling off the pavement into the road, as the boys and gals supped their bevvies in the spring sunshine. There was a blatant big-match buzz in the air. Leaving White Hart Lane in November after Spurs' gut-wrenching, last-gasp equalizer had felt like a defeat for us and a definite victory for the enemy. This was undoubtedly a more decisive derby date. It was Spurs' last opportunity to give their season some raison d'être by putting the mockers on our championship merriment, in what might well prove to be a title-clinching encounter.

The Corkonian couple profited from the nonappearance of my two closest Spurs pals. I've been fortunate to find them tickets to this fixture for the past few years. However they'd wasted a fortune on a limo, in a vain attempt to make the most of their Worthless Cup experience. And after the Cardiff fiasco, I guess they couldn't face further humiliation and the thought of fronting up £50, in all likelihood of another affront to their club's credibility. Ridiculously generous odds of 7 to 1, in a two-horse race, made Spurs a far more propitious punt than any runners at Aintree. Although, as far as my mates were concerned, they might as well have the same odds as any of the 'hope-in-hell's' chance' National horses.

And so it proved. The Arsenal may not have blown them away in the manner of the first-ten-minute massacres meted out at Highbury recently but, in the first-half at least, our football was of such a superior calibre that I was pleased my pals couldn't make it. I would have probably felt obliged to spend half-time stewing over some slight saving grace, that I might offer as consolation. Doubtless this would have been the fact that at only 1–0, nothing was decided. For all our dominance, I felt we should have saved some of the fancy football, keeping it simple until we'd established a comfort zone.

My neighbour in the West Upper sat down for the start of the second-half, unable to hide his delight. He discovered he was £200 wealthier, having picked the winner of the National. We may have been shivering in our seats, with the biting arctic breeze, but he was radiating a warm glow. The Arsenal were taking the Totts to the cleaners, where he'd taken his bookie. Yet from the moment the words 'it's a wonderful day' left his lips, I feared fate would have its ears on. When Poyet went down in the penalty area, there was an extremely pregnant pause pending clarification from the ref. This was just the sort of decision that would never go against a home side with more fervent, 'in yer face' fans. I don't think any of us could grasp the fact that the ref had the gall to give Spurs, of all sides, such a controversial penalty and Teddy Sheringham, of all players, a humdinger of an opportunity to have the last laugh.

Mercifully it was just the gods having a little giggle at our expense, before ref Halsey evened matters out with an equally debatable decision in the dying seconds. Thierry Henry didn't take to the turf in pain, it was the weight of the responsibility as the appointed penalty taker that had him rolling around. Having missed two recently, his reluctance was perfectly acceptable. It is not a task that anyone should undertake unless totally confident. After a moment of euphoria, a huggermugger hush fell upon Highbury as the deliberations of 35,000 Gooners drowned out the hullabaloo. Bergkamp's blunder at Villa Park, which bequeathed United the treble and several other similar 'so near, yet so far' moments flashed across the mind.

Though I would have much preferred to have avoided all that unnecessary anxiety, there was a silver lining to this five-minute storm cloud. Our victory was so much sweeter for having snatched it from the jaws of a draw, which would have seen the hated enemy full of hubris, having handed our rivals back their title chance. And until his eventual cock-up comes around, at last it looks like we have someone, in the lion-hearted Lauren, with the 'cahones' to take a spot-kick. It was such a momentous, frazzled five minutes in a Machiavellian season, that even I was moved to forsake sobriety for a medicinal snort. My Corkonian guests accompanied me to an Irish-owned hostelry where the craic was ninety, as we celebrated 'D-Day'.

It is the partisan passions which make this derby such an occasion. Unfortunately the fatal mixture of too much alcohol and melancholia often results in an already intimidating atmosphere being inflamed past the point of all propriety. In my experience, White Hart Lane is the usual scene of such sorry events. After Saturday's match it was obvious something was afoot in Highbury, when the revellers in the boozer found recreation in the riot police's floorshow outside. With horses, shields and batons, they justified their overtime by doing a can-can across the street. I guess for fear of losing his windows, the landlord lowered his blinds and locked the doors. Now if only I could have earwigged the resultant phone calls and explanations of those trying to excuse their unavoidable absence from home, because they were locked in the pub!

34. About a Bore

Sunday, 14 April (FA Cup semi-final): Middlesbrough 1–0 Festa (39 og)

This was the week the whole nation went metatarsal mad after Deportivo's Argentinean assassin assaulted the country's most highly prized asset. You couldn't open a paper, or turn on the TV without a minute-by-minute account from the flunkey who files Beck's toenails. Duscher may have done for David, but Depor couldn't stop Utd cruising into a semi against Leverkusen, to the sound of Gooners groaning 'if only'.

Sunday's semi-final at Old Trafford felt like a dry run for our league encounter with United. The two clubs were still wrangling about the date of this duel. United were proposing Tuesday 6th May, in the somewhat presumptuous belief it might give them an extra day to prepare for the Champions League final if they should beat Bayer in the semi. However, Arsène wasn't happy, since this would mean only two days' rest if we made it to the FA Cup final on the Saturday prior. He wanted a further 24 hours in case we needed to recuperate from running around the wide expanses of the Millennium Stadium.

Indeed we were destined to be running around Cardiff come 4th May but not before Bob Wilson's grandson had led the team out in the semi at Old Trafford, looking the part with the replica red stripe in his hair that was fast becoming endemic amongst us Gooners and not before 90 minutes of some of the most dire football Arsenal fans had seen since we lost to Charlton in November. We were like the Ferrari Formula 1 team forced to take a driving test with a strict examiner and 60,000 backseat drivers. All the tension of recent weeks seemed to suddenly take its toll, as even the simplest of passes went astray in the opening period. All the pace with which we could tear any opponent apart was strangely lacking, as if they expected a fuming Fergie to pop out any minute to flag them down with a flashing red nose and threaten them with a speeding ticket if they dared to try and win a match on his pitch.

McClaren had turned Boro's season around since the New Year and despite the enforced absence of the influential likes of Ince and Whelan, his game plan worked a treat. His team worked their socks off, putting us under constant pressure and panicking us into plenty of mistakes. With Vieira still walking the suspension tightrope, we were pooping ourselves on the terraces throughout this physical encounter. Festa can't have many friends left on Teesside. I almost felt sorry for him when he replaced the injured Ehiogu and scored a cracker from a corner just before the break, as he put the ball in his own net.

It is a mystery how Ericsson managed any of the hanky-panky alleged by the media when he seemed to spend all his time on the terraces. He witnessed the decimation of his latest squad as Campbell became the second hamstrung stopper (poor Ehiogu would miss out on his sole chance to stake his claim in the squad). At least Keown's return to fitness from a hairline fracture of his leg meant that the Arsenal would narrowly avoid another centre-back crisis. Nevertheless, Adams was out on the day and so Vieira was forced to drop back and bolster our defence.

In fact it was all hands to the pumps as Boro blitzed us towards the end when Kanu was sent on to try and relieve the pressure and waste as much time as possible with his corner flag jiggery-pokery. This contest turned out to be a real test of the Arsenal's character. A sentimental throwback to an old-fashioned '1–0 to the Arsenal'. The nervous exhaustion took its toll on the terraces, but was without doubt worth whatever it took out of the team because it would be strength of character which would see us through the following few weeks.

After the semi, we struggled back to our hotel room, where we were both so 'cream crackered' that it was a real effort to stay awake long enough to discover who our opponents in the final would be. Walking through the crowds streaming away from Old Trafford on our way back, I couldn't help but notice the relatively blank, blasé expression on the faces of the fairly silent Gooners. It is similar to the sang-froid I see so regularly from the Arsenal fans on their way home from Highbury. I often marvel at the fact that an onlooker wouldn't have a clue whether we'd just won, lost or drawn due to the general lack of exuberance amongst us. I couldn't help but wonder how much more boisterous the Boro fans might be, if they'd been departing The Theatre of Dreams with their reveries remaining intact, brimming with jubilation at the thought of only their second FA Cup final ever.

Monday, 15 April 2002

It was over an hour later than planned, when we hurried out of the house on Sunday morning (so what else is new!). The area had already begun to adopt its *Fever Pitch* persona, with hordes hanging about outside Highbury, waiting to board the convoy of coaches assembled along Avenell Road. A little further, by Finsbury Park station, we passed a gaggle of Gooners, gaily adorned in an assortment of Arsenal apparel, gorging on a liquid *petit déjeuner* a couple of hours before their dry train departed. By the time we turned off Stroud Green Road, I had already tired of triumphantly tooting the horn, on passing each and every partisan in their red and white regalia (the Gooner gold is far too recent for this reflex act of recognition).

As we joined the motorway north, accompanied apparently by the majority of north Londoners, the sun was splitting the trees, creeping up into a clear blue sky. I felt a bit of a party pooper, with virtually every other passing vehicle part of the marauding Arsenal army, proudly flying scarves, flags and banners in and out of windows. I soon stripped off my sweater so that my (hopefully lucky) T-shirt, chosen carefully from my massive Arsenal collection, might at least be visible. Merging with the masses was the odd Boro *charabanc*, bedecked in identical colours. It was as though we were all part of one continuous, brightly coloured cavalcade, where one might find Wenger and the lads at its vanguard. His head would be poking out the top of a half-track with an arm outstretched, screaming: 'Forward to Old Trafford, to the Final and onwards to the title!'

Grateful for a gorgeous day and a fairly clear road, I waited until we'd passed Birmingham and the scene of the second semi, before making a pit-stop. We headed straight for the petrol pumps, passing by the service station swarming with all those who had set out at a similarly early hour in the hope of avoiding the tortuous traffic tailbacks suffered on previous semi-final sorties. I felt for the poor unfortunate female at the cash till as we paused briefly for a caffeine pick-me-up. It was criminal that no one had bothered to convey a warning about the invasion of hordes of football fans, with the inevitable hooligan element. She was distracted from her duties by the task of writing down the registration of every single vehicle at the pumps. In response to my query, she revealed that she had found out the hard way, having already been ripped off by several rogues doing a runner!

No need for signs up north – it was the first few splatters of rain on the windscreen that signalled we were approaching Manchester. In a little more time than it took Haile Gebrselassie to lose the London Marathon, we had our feet up in a hotel room overlooking Old Trafford. As we settled down to some pre-match entertainment on Sky Sports, I was afraid that so far it had all gone far too swimmingly for my liking. I first felt some feelings of foreboding a few days prior. It was the presumptuous attitude of many Arsenal fans which preyed on my mind. On the Internet, some seemed to believe that beating Boro was such a foregone conclusion that they were already counting their Cardiff chickens, with their concerns that Arsenal should not be allocated the unlucky end in the Final. I continued to fret more fervently with the television pundits who gave Boro the hope of the 'Bob' and 'No' variety.

Old Trafford is a stadium on such a scale that you could easily spend 15 minutes sprinting around the perimeter in search of the turnstile shown on your ticket. So when we eventually exited the hotel, only a few minutes before kick-off, to find ourselves directly facing the correct entrance, I wasn't sure whether to be grateful, or gutted. I was terrified that this might be the sort of trip where absolutely everything might be marvellously tickety-boo, apart from the main event. According to my mad logic, I was almost ecstatic about the Everest-like assault necessary to attain our exorbitantly priced seats, somewhere in the gods. The cover on the stand prevented us seeing any higher, as we were wondering whereabouts on the roof were those poor Gooners who had paid 15 and 20 quid less for their tickets! Perhaps they'd been seated strategically, to secure a roof that hasn't been raised by such a wonderful atmosphere for many a Mancunian moon?

Give me a grotty seat any day if it will guarantee us a good old-fashioned '1–0 to the Arsenal'. Of late we've become so accustomed to scintillating football that watching the Arsenal grind out a gritty result was almost a rare treat. It shows how far we've come, when not so long ago we would have been begging our players to hang onto possession in the 89th minute, no matter how slim our lead. Whereas on Sunday you might have heard the moans when Kanu was sent on at the death to take the ball to the corner flag from a free-kick on the edge of the area.

These days, against a side like Boro, there's a sense that we are better than that and I was certain that our failure to attempt to kill the game off would be punished by an equalizer, extra-time and capitulation to penalties. But then I've always been a 'nothing's over, until it's over' type of pessimist. An all too brief interlude of heavenly euphoria at the point of victory was soon impinged upon by the purgatory of apprehension and all those worst-case end-of-season scenarios. Albeit should the silverware end up on the Arsenal sideboard, you can be sure you'll hear about it ad nauseam, for the next decade or so.

35. Slowly, Slowly Catchy Monkey. But can Our Tickers Take it?

Sunday, 21 April (Premiership): Ipswich Town (H) 2–0 Ljungberg (68, 78) 1st

Sol Campbell's hamstring strain misery proved to be to Martin Keown's advantage when he replaced his team-mate in the England squad (having been particularly miffed to have been left out in the first place). Despite Wright's run in the Cup, the fact that Seaman has kept him out of the first team suggested he might miss out on the World Cup as a result of his move to Arsenal.

Off the pitch, the Arsenal signed a £10 million shirt sponsorship deal with MM02. The rebranded phone company (Cellnet) will replace Sega on the Arsenal shirts with their 02 logo, which David Dein assures reporters is lucky (referring to the score-line at Anfield '89). The deal allays all-round fears of a downturn in sponsorship revenue as a result of the ITV Digital collapse. Robbie Pires resigned himself to surgery on his knee but some consolation came by way of pipping Van Nistelrooy and Beckham to the Football Writers Association Player of the Year award – which Bergkamp won in the '98 Double season.

Once again a live Sunday game on Sky meant we were playing catch up with Liverpool and United. Chelsea put in a horrendous home performance, crashing 0–4 to Man United, while Liverpool's 2–0 defeat of Derby left John Gregory's side seven points from safety. With Adams, Parlour and Cole all returning to fitness, confidence was high at Highbury, but nothing less than a win would do against Ipswich, even though we still had that vital game in hand.

The picture on the front of the match-day programme spoke volumes about the efforts of the Arsenal squad of late. It portrayed Martin Keown in a Terry Butcher-type pose, oblivious to the blood pouring down the side of his face as he applauded the travelling Gooners after the semi at Old Trafford. We started brightly enough, laying siege to the Ipswich goal in the first-half. Although we peppered the woodwork we couldn't get that all-important goal. Then five minutes before the break Ipswich came millimetres away from taking an onerous lead. There were two schools of thought at half-time. Some were hoping that the wake-up call which had left our defence needing a change of shorts at the break, might ensure the focus that would prevent any further lapses in concentration. Or there were others who believed that our goal was leading such a charmed life in those last few weeks that Ipswich weren't going to score even if Seaman was only permitted to make saves using his pony-tail.

You might think that the Arsenal finally took the lead by means of the fantastic way Freddie swivelled and shot in one explosive instant but those seated in our immediate vicinity know this was just the outcome of sending someone out to buy the lucky Smarties! I think it must have been a very rare moment this, as it was the first time I've seen Arsène express his genuine emotions publicly: he sank to his knees with a clenched fist pointing towards the heavens. He made a joke later about falling over, but it occurs to me that he might think that such public expression of emotion would make him appear more vulnerable, or more susceptible to the sort of verbal assaults Ferguson would resort to in the next few weeks. We all know Arsène is as sincere as they come but I have to admit that it was brilliant to see his veneer of calm slip for one second, to reveal himself as one of us. There was more relief for us all when Ljungberg poached a second, as we had been on the edge of our seats suffering the most terrifying, tension-ridden football and at last we could relax for the last ten minutes, in the relative comfort of this two-goal cushion. Departing Highbury into the sunshine of a balmy April afternoon, after four long seasons, it felt like we were at long last in touching distance of the Premiership prize.

Monday, 22 April 2002

We might be cresting a heavenly horizon, in our quest for a similar haul of silverware, but that is where the comparisons with the class of '98 end. In Wenger's first full season, his transitional team weren't quite so burdened by the weight of expectation. He was more than a little fortunate to find the perfect chemistry, which was the catalyst in creating a pack of hungry hounds. The Arsenal were the underdogs with little to lose, as they stalked a quarry whose name was already supposedly on the title. We played with the belief that gave all a licence to express themselves and virtually everyone took their turn at banging in beautiful goals.

Sadly we slipped up the following year. The Mancunian prey escaped our clutches, as the hunt was eventually held up at an Elland Road hedgerow. In the two successive terms, our dogs hardly saw the Red Devil rabbit, before it disappeared in the distance, leaving us sniffing fresh air with something of an inferiority complex. This season we've had the scent of victory, ever since the indignity of our pre-Christmas slip up against the Toons. We've played some of the most entertaining football it has ever been my pleasure to witness. Nevertheless, having finally battled our way into sight of the booty, the scintillating football seems to have stuttered in the face of a fear of failure. In the space of the last two matches the thought of having everything to lose seems to have dawned on the lads and a tension has developed, which just doesn't allow for our delicate skills.

Naturally the loss of the inspirational wing play of Robert Pires and a permanently rammed treatment room hasn't helped. Albeit that we are far from alone in having to cope with the curse of a calamitous casualty list. From a core of 24 central combatants (excluding the peripheral players), who have combined in various configurations to make up the vast majority of the Arsenal line-ups, 19 have sat out parts of this season, suffering from serious injury setbacks. The cause of an apparent increase in injuries is obvious to me. Squad rotation and the demise of replays means that modern players might not play as many matches as their counterparts of yesteryear, but they are trained to a peak of fitness which would have frightened the life out of their flabby forebears. Yet there is a fine line between ultimate fitness and physical failure. The game is now played at such an incredible pace that many are often playing on the point of exhaustion, just one tired tackle away from harming a hamstring, or a lacerated ligament.

One of the most gratifying sides to such a great season so far has been the evidence of Gooner grit. No matter which member of Wenger's multinational multitude has bricked up the Arsenal wall, each time it has been about to buckle under another broken bone, or every subsequent strained sinew, they have all performed admirably, with no adverse effect on our famous Arsenal spirit. In fact it seems to have only encouraged us to endure, no matter what fickle misfortunes fate throws at us.

Ipswich proved to be such obdurate opponents on Sunday that it is a wonder their Jekyll and Hyde extremes haven't driven George Burley to distraction. Without the pressure applied by Liverpool and United playing leapfrog, a win wouldn't have been nearly so vital. We might have relaxed and not been able to muster the enduring intensity required to eventually triumph over the Tractor Boys. It might have been our Achilles Heel in the past, but that is successive games where we've ground out a result. Even more significant perhaps is fortune's favours. I might be such a pessimist that I won't put it in writing until the battle is beyond all doubt, but if there is one thing that gives me an inkling of the outcome, it is the fact that we can count on the force of fate in our corner this season. Success via a last-minute penalty against Spurs, an own goal in the semi, such are the fickle fine details which haven't been our destiny in the recent past.

When Reuser hung in the air, for an eternity, hoping to head home a sitter from about Ipswich's only threatening first-half attack, 30,000 sat there aghast. It felt like a pivotal moment, as we all fatalistically feared he was about to bury our Premiership trophy with the ball. Bouncing propitiously off the goalpost, it was as though we had the protection of a goal-proof forcefield. Mind, it wasn't as if Ipswich weren't on the receiving end of the rub of the green (or the goal!). In the past as our opponent's crossbar rocked from our fourth flirtation with the woodwork, you could have guaranteed a huge groan of resignation in recognition that it just wasn't going to be our day. Whereas on Sunday, suddenly the Highbury Library found its voice, urging the Arsenal on at a volume not heard all season (they were even warbling again in the West Upper!).

The epitome of this 'we ain't gonna take it no more as also-rans' attitude was Tony Adams. Leading by his inspirational example, he took it upon himself to lumber forward with the undiminished desire of a captain who was going to demonstrate how to conquer. We last had the reassuring presence of both Adams and Keown in the same side at the start of the season. With the soon-to-return Campbell, the third of this staunch triumvirate, our prospects of success seem a whole lot safer, at the feet of such 'never say die' stalwarts. I wouldn't be aggrieved if the likes of Keown and Cole had a break this summer, instead of busting their balls for the Bulldog cause. While the ever-present Eriksson considered their progress, come the final whistle it was his compatriot with the go faster stripe who deservedly received all the plaudits. But by then Sven had shown his own turn of pace, managing to tiptoe out of the stadium to avoid the media mêlée!

36. Mine's a Double!

Wednesday, 24 April (Premiership): West Ham United (H) 2–0
Ljungberg (77), Kanu (80) 1st
Monday, 29 April (Premiership): Bolton (A) 2–0 Ljungberg (36),
Wiltord (44) 1st

Three nights later we were back at Highbury for a repeat performance. This was our game in hand, which meant that if we could continue a nine-game winning streak against West Ham, we could go four points clear of Liverpool and five ahead of United. Basically, beating the Hammers would mean that we could have what is rightfully ours, i.e. the

Championship trophy, out of Utd's cabinet and halfway back to London, if not quite locked away safely with the rest of the silverware, while United were busy being knocked out of the Champions League by Bayer Leverkusen.

In what was almost an exact repeat of Sunday's game, nearly to the minute, we had another nerve-jangling 90 minutes. This time, however, come half-time, few could ignore the significance of the fact that the vast majority in the stadium had seen the ball go over the line for a West Ham goal, except for the all-important match officials. If our luck was indeed evening itself out for the season, then we'd not only been repaid in spades for the Poll fiasco against Newcastle but must be so far over our credit limit by now that I seriously hope the balance doesn't get carried over! When Kanouté was one-on-one with our defence, I breathed a sigh of relief to see he was faced by our captain, but for the second time this season my relief turned to panic as the pacey striker went past Tony Adams like he was one of those training-ground dummies. Sliding the ball by David Seaman, Kanouté would have only had to apply a soupçon of speed and Ashley Cole wouldn't have reached it in time.

This game didn't bear comparison with some of the wonderful football we'd seen played at Highbury, the pressure and tension put the kibosh on that, but I imagine it was nonetheless an engrossing spectacle for the neutral. For us it was like 70 minutes in a dentist's chair having your wisdom teeth pulled with no anaesthetic! Like Sunday's match it felt like a goal might never come, until Bergkamp again finally found Freddie in the box with another slide-rule pass. With a toe-poke that was his fifth pivotal punt in the last four games, Ljungberg almost single-handedly wrapped up the title race and ensured the stuffed shirts in the West Upper were partying on down with wild abandon once more – as if we'd all found the gas after having our teeth pulled. It was Freddie's 15th goal of the season in all competitions.

Thierry Henry was still lagging behind Van Nistelrooy and Hasselbaink as the Premiership's top goal-scorer. Yet, similar to '98, what was crucial to our success was the fact that Pires, Wiltord, Bergkamp and Freddie had all weighed in with contributions of more than ten goals. Tonight it was Kanu's turn to conjure up a second goal with Ljungberg's assistance, which enabled us all to sit back and relax in our seats and enjoy the last ten minutes of this match, savouring our exalted position, with a beautiful bit of breathing room between us and the competition.

After sweating it out for Vieira's almost inevitable tenth booking during the previous three matches, ref Steve Dunn put me on a right downer when he took Paddy's name at the death. Confusion reigned for a few minutes. Calendars were studied and phone calls made as many panicked at the prospect of Patrick's suspension for the Cup final, or the crunch game at Old Trafford. When the definitive confirmation filtered down from a few rows behind, I greeted the news almost as gratefully as I had Kanu's goal, as we discovered that Vieira's creditable self-control had seen him past the watershed date. Our midfield maestro would be available for both matches.

The brilliant thing about the weekend was that no matter what transpired we would still be heading to the Reebok on top of the league. On top of the world more like. It meant we could relax for perhaps the first time this season. For a while I was bothered by the thought that with the footballing world focused on the forthcoming battle between us and United, there was the possibility that a draw between the two could leave Liverpool to sneak past us both. Their defeat at White Hart Lane blew this improbable theory out of the water. However, if I gained some pleasure from seeing the spontaneous combustion of Liverpool's challenge at White Hart Lane, it was nothing compared to the thrill of knowing the agonising dichotomy for Spurs fans who were horrified that their own team's triumph had given the Gooners another leg up to the title.

On the drive up to the Reebok on Monday, we were shocked to hear that Henry had joined the list of players with niggling strains (too many games played at such great pace), but we had grown so used to players dropping like flies that it wasn't cause to panic, even when it was our top goal-scorer who would be rested that night (he ended up on the bench). It was Wiltord's turn to step into the breach, only just back to fitness himself from the injury picked up while 'training' with the French squad. Like all those before him, he adapted to what was required of him, playing as an out-and-out striker when he'd spent most of the last few months playing out wide.

The atmosphere amongst the 3,000-odd Arsenal fans that night was without doubt the best all season. Over the years I can recall odd occasions when I've been in grounds around the country and I've been green with envy about the uninhibited expression of their passionate fans who have got behind their team from start to finish, coming into their own when they turn the volume up to try and raise their side's game. Whereas the reserved Londoners by comparison are so much more fickle, quick to boo and often only prepared to 'sing when they're winning'. However as the effect the title run-in had been having on the Arsenal's form peaked at the Reebok, it was brilliant to be surrounded by all those who had turned up with their metaphoric boots, prepared to do whatever we could for the cause. In those first ten minutes it appeared as though the lads were going to lose their nerve at the last hurdle and after standing there anxiously watching each of them fail to find a player in the same colour shirt with the ball, it was as though we collectively decided that we were not going to let this happen.

It had already occurred a few times on away trips in recent times, where the crowd starts singing 'Arsène Wenger's Red and White Army' at a speed and for a duration where it feels like a Buddhist chant (or how I imagine Buddhist chanting to be). I know it sounds as ridiculous as believing I can affect a result on the day by a change of underpants, or know how I feel a score-line is going to turn out by my bowel movements (actually that's currently my most reliable method of forecasting!), but this is something more than that. The voices of 3,000 singing together for 20-odd minutes, rising to a crescendo and falling a few times along the way, but still non-stop, creates an energy that feels truly powerful. There have been times away from home when I have been convinced we've somehow sucked the ball into the net. Well in Bolton that night it was as loud and as long as ever before. We chanted consistently during that 20-minute spell of decidedly dodgy football until eventually it felt like we had a calming effect on the lads' nerves, to the point where they started passing the ball around and we eventually stopped singing. Two minutes later the ball was in the back of the net. Yet again it was another sublime Bergkamp and Ljungberg combination that made and scored the goal. Far be it from me to take absolutely anything away from our Dutch master, as some of his moments of breathtaking skill these past months were just sensory overload for any football lover. Yet I am convinced we deserved some credit for playing our part in this particular goal.

We had travelled to Bolton expecting it to be one of the least rigorous games in the run-in. I didn't expect Bolton to be so focused that they managed to give as good as they got, for a time. When Freddie finally made the breakthrough it was the cue for absolute delirium and more non-stop celebrations but of the more random sort, as we serenaded the lads with the entire repertoire. We'd done our bit with the conscientious effort that went into our 20-minute mantra and despite singing ourselves hoarse and being all hand-clapped-out, we now knew that we had one hand on the trophy and we were going to have a ball. The two climactic games in Cardiff and Manchester would both be memorable, extra-special occasions, but for me personally, somehow neither would quite match the transcendent quality to the atmosphere at Bolton that night.

Superstition is a cross borne by most football fans all season long, but at extremely tense times like these one can be driven to distraction. Most are fully aware that it is a load of mumbo-jumbo, but it doesn't stop us from being terrified of the disastrous consequences which might result from the slightest change in our routine. Ray, my neighbour in the West Upper, neglected to shave on the day the current winning run began against Everton. Despite the protestations of his wife, he had a healthy beard by now which he didn't dare shave off. Myself, I hadn't made it to the Jewish Passover celebrations at the home of my uncle who sits opposite in the East Upper. So I ended up collecting from my mum the present he had for me of an Arsenal-embroidered *kapul* (Jewish skullcap). By pure coincidence it had remained in my pocket when I wore the same trousers to the match the following day and since we'd won, that was it, it became a permanent fixture in my overcrowded pockets from then on.

Our puppy, Treacle, was nearly a year old, but we still hadn't managed to cross that bridge of leaving her alone in the flat for fear of her chewing the place to pieces. So far this season Róna's son, Reuben, had managed to look after Treacle on match days, but the West Ham game was the first time we were without a dog-sitter. It actually turned out to be fortuitous that Róna decided to start watching the game live on the box, unable to leave Treacle on her own for the whole game. No sooner had I arrived at Highbury alone when it dawned on me that I had left the lucky *kapul* on the bedside table. Having failed to find the target in the first 45 and after the tension had been turned up a notch by the goal-line incident before half-time, Ró dashed around to the ground at the break not so much to watch the second-half live, but to bring me the *kapul* as I just couldn't bear the thought of the responsibility if we failed to win.

I was relating this long-winded tale to Nell in the car on our way to Bolton, as if to suggest that he had me, Ró and the *kapul* to thank for the three points against West Ham. It was only when I finished and he turned to me for confirmation that I had brought the precious object with us to Bolton, that it dawned on me to my horror: I had again left it at home! Strangely enough I had been loading a bag with everything I usually take to try and cover every eventuality on an away trip (gloves, scarves, binoculars, batteries for the radio etc.) when I came across an Arsenal hat that I don't think I had worn since our last successful season four years back. Pinned to the hat was a badge Ró had bought me when we had gone with her dad to see an Ireland game at Lansdowne Road a few years back, in order that I would at least be wearing something green. The badge had a shamrock on it and as a result of our fabulous season that year, it soon became a lucky omen. So if you are looking for anyone to blame for

Arsenal's lack of success during the following three seasons, look no further, as the hat with the badge still pinned to it had gone into a draw that summer, not to surface again until the day of our trip to Bolton.

Consequently there I was trying to convince Nell (and myself) as we headed north to the Reebok that everything would be alright, for if we should be forsaken by the God of the Jews that night, we would be guaranteed the luck of the Irish!

Monday, 29 April 2002

If I was a betting man, I would have been inclined to put a few quid on Ipswich pinching a couple of points off United at Portman Road on Saturday, but I certainly didn't expect the turn-up at Tottenham earlier in the day. Speaking to my Spurs pals, apparently they instinctively partied when Poyet put the ball in the net just prior to the break. It was only when they sat back down that the consequences dawned on them and they began to baulk at the unbearable thought of playing such a prominent part in putting the title on a plate for the arch enemy.

I guess they must have been more than a little relieved when Van Nistelrooy's penalty-winning performance that evening earned United all three points and at least saved them (for the moment!) from suffering a long summer of galling Gooner gratitude. Their relief was shared by many, including my missus. Róna has been trying to visit the folks in Dublin for the last couple of months, but the crowded football calendar has made it almost impossible, without passing on a couple of important matches. After missing the celebrations for her mum earlier in the month, she finally settled on spending her own birthday with the family, as it meant forsaking only the one fixture. When I phoned her on Saturday after Spurs had won, she was horrified to hear that an Ipswich victory could result in us rejoicing our title triumph at the Reebok on Monday. Having travelled the length and breadth of the country in my company, sharing all the peaks and troughs in our pursuit of the ultimate domestic prize for so many seasons, it just wouldn't have felt right not to have her by my side for the big one. Besides, she wasn't the only Gooner to have some misgivings about such an impromptu end to this marathon championship saga.

The tremendous tension of these past two games has taken its toll on all our tickers. Ashley Cole sliding into the goal-mouth, to hook the ball back over the line against West Ham, must have shortened my life span by another couple of years. Highbury was one of the first grounds to have the Jumbotron screens, but the club have always strictly adhered to their agreement only to show non-contentious replays. Consequently everyone in the ground understood the implications when this incident wasn't included in the half-time highlights, as the indignant Irons' fans hollered 'show us the goal!'. It was the sort of timely twist of fate which left even this eternal pessimist mulling over the possibility that perhaps (just perhaps mind!) our name is on the trophy.

The thought of all our hopes disappearing in a disastrous draw against West Ham was sufficiently traumatic to leave us all thankful to take a title triumph any way it comes. And if that man Van hadn't managed to take the ref for a ride with his penalty ruse, we wouldn't have exactly refused an opportunity to settle matters at the Reebok. It would have been truly wonderful to go to Old Trafford with the trophy in our hands, sufficiently relaxed to taunt our rivals for the entire 90 minutes. Nevertheless, it would seem suitably poetic, the possibility of actually taking United's title on their own turf. So although I felt the Tractor Boys deserved more from their doughty performance, I wasn't too downhearted about this result.

To win the league but lose at Old Trafford would lend credence to the contentions of the anti-Arsenal contingent in the media, that ours was a championship conceded by United, as opposed to a triumph of our own making. Whereas taking the title in a winner takes all, clash of the titans, in The Theatre of Dreams, would without doubt seal our incontrovertible credentials as the country's current top club and might at long last lay to rest the last remnants of any inferiority complex.

In the meantime all thoughts of the possibility of such a tantalising prospect must be postponed. As I write, we have the small matter of Monday's match against Bolton and Saturday's second string to our Double bow to deal with. It might prove providential that at least one of our competitors maintained the pressure and like last weekend, we go into our game at Bolton knowing we cannot afford to relax. The Arsenal's sparkling football might have suffered from the strain of the constant nip and tuck at the top in recent weeks. Yet so far the unrelenting tension has had a tremendous effect on our team spirit, resulting in totally committed performances, without a single stain on Spunky's clean sheets.

At this stage the winning momentum is paramount and if we could have afforded it, any relaxation at the Reebok might have proved costly, with calamitous feelings of fatigue causing the cracks to show at Cardiff. Besides, it would be marvellous if we could manage an entire season without losing a game away from home, not to mention extending our unbeaten record. If the momentum is masking any signs of tiredness in the team, I certainly can't say the same. Over the next two weeks, I will either be leaping like a lamb with all the joys of spring, or end up becoming the bald old wrinklie that I currently feel. Knowing the Arsenal's notion for never doing things the easy way, it is likely to be the latter. At Highbury last week there were small huddles at halftime, as everyone tried to concoct a cunning plan in an attempt to avoid the congestion of 70,000 travelling from London to Cardiff along with all the Bank Holiday traffic. Mind, much of the cynicism in the media about a London Derby Cup final being played in another country relates to the fact that much of the capital's media rat pack can't abide the idea that they themselves are forced to travel so far from London like the rest of us plebs.

It is a peculiar phenomenon that the Arsenal were everybody in the media's darlings when they were the underdogs. As always, the moment we became the favourites they all began gunning for the Gunners, with the sort of fervour they favour, for felling anyone who has the temerity to triumph. I only hope that with the sweet, sweet scent of victory in our nostrils, we'll keep our eyes on the ball, instead of their bogus claptrap. Our rapture rises to a crescendo as we creep along the final furlong, but with the winning post in sight, hidden behind my bellowing bravado, I'm petrified – in a palpitating funk with the fear of failure!

37. Porthcawl Portents

Saturday, 4 May (FA Cup final): Chelsea 2–0 Parlour (70), Ljungberg (80)

We'd beaten Bolton on the Monday night, despite Alex Ferguson's best attempts to motivate our opponents with his usual caustic verbal intervention. He should have known better by now that he was likely to come off second best in a bout of mental sparring with our manager. Instead of dignifying his remarks with the overwhelming statistics Arsène could have used to prove otherwise, he came up with probably his best one-line put-down to date with his comment that everyone thinks they have the prettiest wife at home. According to reports I read, Ferguson had to be assured that this wasn't actually a reference to her indoors.

I spoke to my pal Nell on Friday afternoon to find out where in the Millennium Stadium he would be sitting, as he'd wangled himself a helicopter ride into Cardiff. I assume HM Inspector of Taxes would be expected to foot the bill, as one of his mates tried to write off this jolly as a legitimate business expense. Nell told me he was out and about, scouring London for red hair dye in order to do a Freddie streak on his own barnet. Apparently it was impossible to find, since every single shop and hair salon he tried had sold out of the colour red. We only fully appreciated the scale of the run on red hair dye when we arrived in Cardiff to discover about half the 30,000 Arsenal fans present had attempted their own tribute to our Swedish hero, with red streaks almost de rigueur amongst the Gooners.

Getting to Cardiff for the final was a different prospect altogether from the easy journey that used to take me to Wembley. We ended up in the queues of vehicles full of football fans that combined with the rush-hour traffic to create the mayhem on the M4 around Bristol on Friday evening. It seems the idea of getting to Wales early was hardly original. After an exhausting drive of almost six hours I was almost disappointed to wake up the following morning to hear from mates on the phone as they covered the journey in a couple of hours, wondering what all the fuss had been about.

It was the second successive season that my Welsh Gooner pal Chris had the rare treat of the mountain coming to Mohammed, after he'd spent so many seasons schlepping the other way down the M4 to Highbury. Although I was tempted to avail ourselves of his local knowledge after I had searched in vain for some accommodation, I didn't dare risk it. Like everyone else, superstition decreed that it was imperative to alter every external factor which could have been responsible for last year's misfortune. So we drove past Cardiff to spend the night in a guest house, 20 minutes further down the motorway, a five-minute walk from the seafront in Porthcawl. It was a little surreal the next day to be basking in the glorious sunshine on the golden sands of a relatively deserted beach only a couple of hours before kick-off.

We spent an idyllic half an hour soaking up some rays before it was time to put on our football hats. Amongst the myriad of T-shirts in my Arsenal collection I have a couple of the horrible synthetic tops which I've received as presents over the years, but the only replica kit I will wear is the '71 shirt because it is cotton (not to mention the fact that my fondest football memories are from this period). With the weather turning out so fine, it proved to be an unfortunately warm selection, but as my weapon of choice for that particular afternoon it had to be worn. Like many others, I have a mental check-list of must haves for every football match, not just because they are useful, but because I cannot bear the prospect of seeing an Arsenal side sweat blood for the cause only to end up defeated due to the fact that I had forgotten to bring the fruit Polos. So having stopped at a newsagent to stock up on the obligatory sweets for a dry throat, tissues for a runny nose and batteries for a dead radio and having made sure I had the binoculars (an ever-present, the further us fans seem to end up from the action and the worse my eyesight gets over the years), scarf, lucky hat complete with attached shamrock badge and the *kapul* (the gods had been good to us so far, but there was no harm in making sure we were covered!), we made the short journey back to Cardiff.

Half an hour later we had left behind the best nature has to offer, the wide open expanses of an enchanting beach, for the very worst of rampant commercialism, as we queued amongst a brightly coloured crowd in various dulled states of inebriation, waiting to hand over an exorbitant seven quid for a programme. It seemed far too much to pay for something that will lie around the house, unread, collecting dust for the next ten years, until the day I can find nothing else to read in the karsey, but like any other game, I would have kittens if I ended up going through the turnstiles without the security of a programme in my hand. I think the Chelsea fans in the queue believed I was trying to wind them up when I gleefully revealed that it was good news for us Gooners that John Terry had surprisingly not made Ranieri's starting line-up.

As far as most Arsenal fans are concerned, Chelsea have replaced Spurs as the target for our enmity. Yet we remain the Spurs fans' most hated rivals and as a result the atmosphere at our encounters with Chelsea might not have anywhere near the distressingly bad vibes of the North London Derby, but there is often a noticeable amount of ill will in the air. Whether it is the congenial welcome from our hospitable Welsh hosts, or the fact that most have set out so early that they are too tired or too blathered for any bother, but on both our trips to the Millennium Stadium, the atmosphere in the city and around the ground has felt pleasantly mellow. Last year it was such a hot day that I can recall walking to the ground and seeing a few poor sods, abandoned by their pals, propped up against the castle wall in such a stupor that they were bound to end up having missed the match, with little to show for their day out but a hangover and a bad case of sunburn.

As a modern arena, the sightlines at the Millennium Stadium are marvellous. No matter where you sit you are guaranteed a decent view of the action on the pitch. To be perfectly honest, I couldn't care where we were sitting, I was just happy to be there on the day. However, I am tall enough for it not to matter but from Ró's perspective, some inches below me, there have been times when she would have seen far more if she had stopped at home and watched on the box because she has been stuck behind tall folks who insist on spending much of the game standing up. I couldn't prevent myself from getting wound up the previous year, when we had followed Arsenal all over the country (and the continent) and had ended up with seats behind the goal and all the pals I know who rarely stray from Highbury were sat along the sides. I am always presented with the same dilemma when applying for tickets because past experience has proved that a higher price often does not guarantee a better view. So I thought I would be extremely clever this time around. I went to all the trouble of finding a seating plan of the stadium on the Internet, printed it out and handed it in with our application for tickets. You can imagine that I was more than a little disappointed to find we were not only sat behind the goal, but as far away from the pitch as possible, in the very last row.

Our vantage point may have given us a great view of the tactical deployment of both teams, but I was glad of my binoculars and radio, which showed me which of the ants in the distance was doing what, to whom. The only consolation of the back row was the corrugated metal behind us, which I ended up banging until my hands were raw, in an attempt to drum up some life in the strangely subdued atmosphere around us. Maybe we sounded louder on TV, or they were making more noise at the Blue end of the ground, but from where we were sitting the crowd weren't making much of an effort.

Ranieri's invitation to Di Matteo was truly a selfless gesture. Let's face it, the Italian manager is not going to have too many opportunities to lead his team on to the pitch for an FA Cup final and passing this honour to a player whose career was cruelly cut short by injury ensured my esteem for the man went up considerably. Needless to say, the smartly turned out Wenger walked out holding the hands of another of Freddie's admirers, our mascot with the ubiquitous red streak. Stuart Taylor might have been between the sticks at Watford, but it was Richard Wright's goal minding that had carried us through the remaining five matches en route to the final. With his move to Arsenal also probably responsible for Wright's World Cup plans falling by the wayside, I am glad it was Arsène and not me who was left with the decision of who to leave out. In the end, though we all agreed Wright had got a bit of a raw deal, few could argue with Wenger's reasoning behind playing Seaman. After all he was the keeper in form. As a partnership, Hasselbaink and Gudjohnsen were proving to be the most deadly pairing in the Premiership on their day. I guess Wenger believed Parlour would be more helpful in snuffling out this threat than Edu. It turned out that Wenger needn't have worried too much, as this wasn't going to be their day.

I might be a sentimental old romantic to believe that this squad of players has changed since last year to the extent that their supporters' feelings matter to them more than an hour or so after they've left the pitch, when they are back in the dressing room dreaming of the new Porsche that they're going to treat themselves to with their bonus. However, what is obvious now that wasn't evident before is the fraternal feeling of camaraderie that has seen this collection of individuals meld together into a squad with a shock-proof spirit. From the not so cryptic messages worn by Henry under his shirt, to the comradeship seen in every goal celebration, this squad is the embodiment of *'Victoria Concordia Crescit'*. What a sad irony this sentiment returns to our squad at long last, in the season that it is lost on our new simplistic crest.

Cup finals rarely produce fabulous football because it seems like the players feel there is too much at stake to be able to relax and let their fine art flow. Meanwhile in the first-half, any flowing football from our end was almost immediately snuffed out by an imperious Marcel Desailly, stepping out each time as if taking candy from a baby. Perhaps it all looked so easy for him because the likes of Henry and Vieira had too much respect for this elder statesman of French football. Yet when Desailly decides to put on a rare peerless performance, I have to wonder what satisfaction he gets from treading water the rest of his time at Stamford Bridge.

Spunky was certainly the busier keeper, diving full stretch to palm away a couple of stinging efforts from Lampard. It was 20 minutes before Arsenal fans had anything to get excited about, when Ashley Cole's pin-point cross resulted in almost the first goalmouth action at the other end. We have all heard how much the FA Cup means to Dennis Bergkamp and the stories about him watching it on the box as a child in Holland. Having made such an incredible contribution in '98, an injury ensured he missed out on the entire climax to the season. Then he had that nightmare penalty miss at Villa Park in the semi against Utd, sealing our fate and sending Utd on their way to the treble, only to finally get on the pitch last season with such awful consequences. So desperate was I for him to finally get there this time around that I was convinced he was going to get injured or suspended in the lead up to the final.

Then as Dennis met Cole's cross and he sent a looping header towards Cudicini's goal, for a second there I thought it had all come good at last. Unfortunately, the ball fell the wrong side of the post and although it turned into a wonderful day, there was a sad irony that after all these years, on a stage that was made for Bergkamp, in a team which complemented his amazing talent, Dennis ended up having a fairly ineffectual role on the match as a whole. I couldn't see the expression on his face when he was subbed with 20 minutes to go, as Wenger sent on Kanu to titillate us with his time-wasting ball skills, but in the celebrations that followed the final whistle I detected an air of regret about Dennis. All anyone else cared about was the trophy, but I had the distinct feeling that Dennis was dissatisfied because he hadn't been able to stamp his distinctive mark on this match.

I can't imagine the match made for good entertainment for all the millions watching on the box, but none of the Gooners gave a hoot so long as we ended up with our hands on the all-important trophy. Ray Parlour had only scored one other goal all season and that was against Gillingham, so I bet the bookies didn't end up paying much out on him being first scorer. Perhaps Chelsea didn't fancy him to score either, as no one went to close him down as he ran towards the Chelsea penalty area, minutes after Jimmy-Floyd had departed the scene. With such a world-class squad at Highbury these days, the whingers who sit around us in the West Upper are left struggling for a scapegoat. Poor Ray might not be as naturally gifted as some, but he usually makes up for anything he might lack in the silky skills department by putting all his heart and soul into most every game.

My dear old dad has been gone for a few years, but my mum still does an impersonation of him cursing Parlour. She has become much more of an armchair Gooner since and as a result I am permanently trying to persuade her that it would be worth having the carbuncle of a small satellite dish on the exterior of her new house, because Sky's live coverage of our games has to be a little bit more enthralling than sitting in front of a Teletext screen on a Sunday afternoon (especially when the Arsenal games of late involve waiting for around 70 minutes before a digit will change on the screen!). However in those days Parlour was without doubt the name most familiar to her because she'd be standing upstairs, ironing, and all she would hear was the sound of my old man venting his anger at Ray Parlour. When I eventually brought Mum to a game, I guess it was instinctive to join in with all the others, coating off our blonde bombshell. I was quite surprised she was so vocal (at least I know where I get it from) but similarly I imagine she was a little bemused when our Shirley turned out to be not quite such a schmock as my old man had said.

The arrival of Wenger resulted in recognisable change in Parlour, as his football began to benefit from the influence Arsène had on all the players' lifestyles. It wasn't quite the epiphany of his Essex pal Tony Adams, who seemed to be reincarnated overnight into a totally different being. I am sure our Captain wasn't able to turn his life around at such lightning-fast speed but considering the huge debt of gratitude we Gooners owe him, I couldn't be more pleased to see how much more content he seems these days. Nevertheless, no matter how much more important it may be in human terms, strictly speaking as a selfish Arsenal supporter there was some sadness in gaining the sensible captain who led by example because it meant sacrificing our more vocal, lunatic leader. There has been many an occasion when we weren't playing so well in the past couple of years that I would have given anything to have the old Adams back on the pitch, intimidating opponents, castigating officials and chastising his team-mates with a necessary boot up the backside. Yet despite sacrificing some of his attributes on the pitch for such worthwhile and doubtless imperative personal reasons, no matter how tranquil our Tony has become, he retains such an imposing presence that he will always remain an irreplaceable, inspirational captain.

Parlour meanwhile has become so supremely fit that whilst he is running his socks off, week in, week out, he just doesn't deserve to be the fall guy for our fickle fans. I have to bite my tongue these days when I hear them laying in to him for the odd misplaced pass that any other player could get away with without comment. My missus is not nearly so content to keep her own counsel and will often come to his defence with a sarcastic comment of the sort she mutters as if under her breath, but just loud enough for the intended individual to hear.

I have no doubt all these hypocrites were celebrating as loud as everyone else, lauding the Romford Pelé after he leathered the ball from 30 yards out (similar to any good fishing tale, the distance gets longer with every telling!) at Cardiff that afternoon. Nine times out of ten one of Parlour's such speculative punts would head for Row Z, to hoots of derision from his own fans and I am certain that no one was more surprised than him to see it nestle in the top corner of the net. It was a stunning strike worthy of winning an FA Cup alone. They were up on their feet at the other end of the ground a few minutes later but we ended up with the last laugh, teasing their presumptuousness having long since seen the offside flag.

In a spectacle that was somewhat short on the skilful football expected of two sides loaded with international heavyweights, if Ray Parlour's potshot was worth the entrance fee alone, then I guess we all got great value when Freddie came up with an equally exquisite second. Where Parlour's was all power, Freddie's seventh goal in seven games was fabulous finesse, as he put another cherry on top of our cup cake by curling the ball around Cudicini with the perfect precision of a player who is so on top of his game that he was wheeling around in celebration before it hit the back of the net. Freddie might have been the obvious choice for Man of the Match, but for my money the Romford Pelé at the very least deserved a share of it. It was the cue for the Blues fans to begin streaming out the stadium. No matter how quick they were to beat the rush, you can be certain theirs was a much longer journey home.

Naturally we would have preferred to have avoided last season's Millennium Stadium mugging. We had been by far the best team on the day but when we began dreaming about the trophy just a few minutes too early, it was stolen out of our grasp by a team that didn't know when they were beat. All our miserable memories might have evaporated the moment ref Riley blew the final whistle this time around, but the feeling of euphoria was so much sweeter for all our suffering. At least it meant our lads were guaranteed to take nothing for granted, as they celebrated long and hard, savouring every last moment on that pitch. Because they knew that no sooner would they be showered, dressed and heading back for London before Arsène would be demanding that they focus fully on the match only four days away at Old Trafford. As the first trophy in our assault on a momentous Double, there was some sense that we were just changing ends at half-time.

However, it didn't stop everyone having a tremendous time while they could and I can picture now the sight of Sylvain Wiltord going crazy on the Cardiff pitch, with such exuberance that he reminded many of Ian Wright. As Arsenal fans we are extremely privileged to have participated in our fair share of such special occasions. I very much doubt we could ever fully appreciate how it feels to spend a lifetime supporting a team that struggles every year with little realistic chance of ever making it. Nevertheless, although we've reached three FA Cup finals in the last five years, I have grown accustomed to making the most of every one. Like all other fans, I am filled with expectation when we start anew every season and while Arsenal might have better prospects than many, you never really know if or when you might next get a chance to drink in such success.

With the constant threat of injury and the onset of age curtailing any player's career, football is a far more fickle sport for its participants. We'd already heard too much distressing talk about Tony Adams' imminent retirement, but even if he can be persuaded to stay on another season, we know he can't continue indefinitely. Hopefully David Seaman and Martin Keown will continue contributing to the Arsenal cause for some time to come but they are nearer to the end of their careers than the beginning. We watched them all as they paraded the Cup and as the youngsters larked around enjoying their moment in the spotlight, our OAPs took their time drinking every last drop from their triumphant moment in this, the oldest knockout competition in the world. Looking back it was obvious that Lee Dixon was about to announce that he was calling time on his distinguished career. In the games he played in recent months he was always last off the pitch, having acknowledged the fans away from home and doing likewise with each stand at Highbury. It was a shame he didn't get on during the game at Cardiff, but you would have never known from the way he participated in the resulting revelry. My abiding last image of Cardiff that day was Dixon enjoying the pictures being shown on the big screen, standing all alone in the centre circle, bottle of champers in hand, slaking his thirst on both the booze and the last few drops he could squeeze from such a delicious day.

Monday, 6 May 2002

I have been walking around with our tickets to Old Trafford on my person for the last couple of weeks, not prepared to leave them at home where they might fall prey to the outside chance of fire, theft, or act of God! I had a call last week from someone whose mate was willing to pay £300 for a seat amongst the limited number of Arsenal fans making the trip to Manchester, in the hope of seeing our side secure the title in The Theatre of Dreams (hopefully our dream, United's nightmare!). Personally I see this occasion as our reward, after a long, arduous season spent schlepping all over the country in support of my team and I can't bear the idea that such a precious prize can now be snapped up by the highest bidder amongst the Gooner glory boys!

Not having the foggiest where we're going to find around three grand to renew our two season tickets, I would be a liar if I said the thought didn't cross my mind. Yet in truth, if some calamity should prevent us going, I would prefer to give our tickets away to a deserving cause, rather than go against my strict principles of never selling a ticket for over the odds. Assuming a draw or better, I imagine that like Anfield '89, it'll be the sort of historic occasion that will go down in Highbury folklore. No doubt in years to come, one could fill Old Trafford four times over with the number of Gooners who will lay claim to having been there on the night. Only an earthquake or a flood will force me to include myself among such fibbers.

Obviously I will expect United to do their utmost to poop our party. I am counting on the prospect that they might find it hard to lift themselves to provide the kind of potent force that ran riot against us last year, without the proposition of playing for their places in an upcoming European Cup final (I don't mean to rub it in, honestly!). Some might suggest the Arsenal's strength will be sapped after Saturday's Cardiff carnival. I am convinced that to the contrary, our FA Cup victory will ensure that we won't be troubled by tiredness. They will trot out at Old Trafford charged on pure adrenaline.

And should the fates decide not to favour us with an unforgettable evening, it won't exactly be a disaster to have to delay further celebrations for four days. As desperate as I am to complete the Double on United's doorstep, we have a delightful double-edged sword, with 30,000 Gooners waiting to savour sure-fire success at Highbury on Saturday.

I was standing in those hallowed marble halls last week, collecting our cup final tickets, when it dawned on me that I was dreaming of doing the Double for the third time since my indoctrination as a child. It feels almost greedy being a Gooner, when there are some supporters who suffer a whole lifetime, longing for the sight of a single piece of silverware. Believe me, success loses none of its shine, since I feel the same hair-raising tingle of excitement now as I did as a ten year old. I joined a queue of people waiting to see my pal in the box office and marvelled at his patience as he listened sympathetically to all the highly plausible pleas for the gold-dust of tickets to the remaining momentous matches. He must have no shortage of best mates at the moment and he certainly proved to be mine, when he not only produced our tickets, but the splendiferous surprise of a cheque for £279!

I bounded out of there with a smile broader than Broadway, with our weekend in Cardiff paid for courtesy of a refund from the club. Apparently this was because we'd been forced to vacate our usual seats for the last three matches in the Champions League. I only hope the club doesn't cotton on to the fact that they could save a fortune in future by sitting their corporate guests a few seats further away, instead of us! Despite feeling so unexpectedly flush, we weren't tempted to join all the Gucci Gooners in their various lavish attempts to leave the Bank Holiday motorway madness behind (which included more affluent mates who made their way to the Millennium Stadium by the Orient Express, helicopter and chauffeur-driven stretch limos). We tried to avoid the traffic jams by staying the night before and after the match in a humble B&B, on the beach in Porthcawl, 20-odd miles past Cardiff. We were fortunate to have found any accommodation, since on Saturday morning I overheard a local proclaim that there had been fans prepared to pay £400 for somewhere to lay their head the previous night. Heaven only knows what price they were offering for tickets.

Amongst all the cars we'd passed on our way down, gaily adorned in their club colours, were the occasional unfortunate travellers with 'ticket wanted' signs sprayed across their windows. Wembley has a unique aura and is a helluva lot more convenient, but Cardiff and the marvellous Millennium Stadium is a wonderful day out for any footie fan. There is a lesson or two to be taken from the Welsh in staging such a sporting occasion. Nevertheless I cannot condone the corporate takeover of our fans' day out. Ian Wright and Mark Bright were both bemoaning this fact on their radio roadshow that morning. After a steady stream of people came up to the mic and told how they were the invited guests of one company or another, with little or no knowledge about the club they claimed allegiance to, Wrightie bawled out: 'Are there no real fans out there?' Like myself, he felt for the frustrations of the genuine fan, sitting at home without a ticket, being forced to suffer the asinine remarks of those whose loyalty was limited to the lunch and free booze on offer on their corporate jolly.

Perhaps my slight disappointment with the singing from our end of the ground was in some part due to the presence of so many fair-weather fans. More likely everyone's early arrival and a warm afternoon caused the quaffing of such copious amounts of alcohol by kick-off time, that just getting to their seats was as much as many could manage! Mind you, after the cacophonous choir of only a couple of thousand at Bolton a few days prior, this was bound to be a bit of an anticlimax. Nerves might have meant that the football was a bit frantic, but for atmosphere this was the best game of this and many a season. It was evident to us all during the opening minutes that a bout of the heebie-jeebies was preventing our lot from passing the ball to one another. It resulted in a 20-minute spell of singing which sounded like a Buddhist mantra. I haven't heard the like from the Arsenal fans for many a moon. If we were left speaking in tongues on the terraces, it certainly seemed to temper the tension on the pitch and I swear we can take some of the credit for the first goal!

Don't get me wrong, Saturday was indeed a magical Arsenal moment, making up for last year's mammoth disappointment, when we sat for an hour outside the Millennium Stadium waiting for our minibus, suffering the friendly 'You Woz Robbed' jibes of the celebrating Scousers. Yet as such favourites this time around, knowing how unlikely it was that the team would let us and themselves down two years on the trot and what with winning the toss for the lucky North Side and all, there seemed to be a certain inevitability to the whole occasion. Even when Chelsea appeared to have the upper hand, with Desailly dominating supreme, it occurred to me that since we had entertained, but eventually lost, last season, the reverse would be true this time around. And so having removed the element of risk, in my mind at least, it wasn't quite such a religious experience.

However we are guaranteed all the nerve-jangling excitement anyone could need at Old Trafford tonight. Before Saturday's game we had a gorgeous stroll in the sunshine on a beautiful sandy beach. Where someone had scrawled with a stick in the virgin sand 'Chelsea', I inscribed underneath '0 Arsenal 2'. Perhaps we'll have to leave extra early today, to pass through Porthcawl for another portentous prediction?

38. Final Throes. Glows and Woes

Wednesday, 8 May (Premiership): Manchester Utd (A) 1–0 Wiltord (57) 1st
Saturday, 11 May (Premiership): Everton (H) 4–3 Bergkamp (4), Henry (33, 72), Jeffers (83) 1st

There were quite a few Gooners who had their own lucrative double on Saturday by backing Arsenal to win the Cup and Ferguson's horse, Rock of Gibraltar, which came home a 9/1 winner. One might have thought this cash-rich consolation would have cheered up the horse's owner but according to the media Ferguson finally cracked at the press conference held by United the day before the big game.

Well, apparently Fergie begrudgingly deigned to give the Arsenal some credit with a comment about Arsenal's form of late being worthy of Champions, but not without adding the rider that United had scored the most goals and played the most attractive football. It might not have been much of a compliment but it seems it was enough to cause Fergie to choke on his words because it was at this point that he began effing and blinding like nobody's business at the invited media. If Fergie doesn't like the heat, I don't know why he didn't stick by his decision to get out of the kitchen. When Wenger was broached by the media on the matter, our mischievous manager wanted to know what all the asterisks were about.

It was worrying news to discover that Henry was out and Bergkamp on the bench. Whereas once upon a time I might have been left feeling like the game was up, it was no longer the end of the world, merely another problem for the Gunners to negotiate. Besides, apart from Wiltord's crucial contributions, all the other goals had been coming from midfield and neither of these two had scored a goal since Easter. I was also surprised by Tony Adams' absence, as I would have thought this would be one game he would have been desperate to play in, despite the fact that he had played for 90 minutes in the Cup final four days prior.

Ferguson's diatribe had reminded me of our cat and the display she puts on, hissing and spitting, when cornered by a dog with her back to the wall. I expected his mood to be reflected in the way his side would come out fighting when the bell rang on Wednesday night and they didn't disappoint. However, there was no sign of our lot taking their foot off the pedal, having secured their first piece of silverware. They all left the FA Cup final banquet (and I assume headed for bed!) an hour before the midnight curfew. Like us, I imagine they were desperately keen to set the record straight after last season's 1–6 humiliation.

The match against Boro seemed to have served little benefit for the team, as they were falling all over the place in the early stages and Vieira even sent someone off for a change of boots. The rest of the first-half they continued their intimate acquaintance with the turf, with the aid of United's tactics. There were three atrocious challenges, each of which might have been deserving of a red card, instead of the yellows that were shown. Ironically, these were issued by Durkin, the referee who had sent Gio Van Bronckhorst off at Anfield for diving, when Gio had gone over without even making an appeal.

Scholes went right through the back of Edu for his booking and we couldn't help but laugh when this dangerous assault resulted in Ferguson springing to the touchline. I don't for one minute believe he was sportingly jumping from his seat to protest about his own player's challenge. Even Rivaldo would have struggled to make the GBH on Edu look any worse than it actually was, so perhaps Fergie was just reminding the officials in his customary intimidating fashion that a red card was likely to result in them being removed from his Christmas list. Whatever the case, it occurs to me that this would have made a perfect picture for a caption competition in *The Gooner* fanzine. No sooner had Edu stepped gingerly to his feet, when moments later we had a repeat performance by Phil Neville on Wiltord. It seemed as though Sylvain had released the ball minutes earlier and Neville was so late that he'll end up with a tardier reputation than myself.

At least Roy Keane had an excuse for his violent kung-fu-style, studs-in-the-chest assault on Patrick Vieira. Keane was obviously not prepared to accept Paddy taking the mick out of his team-mates, as moments earlier Vieira had arrogantly bypassed Scholes in midfield merely by flicking the ball over his head (which didn't exactly require a sand wedge with a *schnip* like Scholes). Who am I to argue with Fergie, but personally I think he got his tactics a little wrong in this first-half. He seemed to have got his players so fired up with his fighting talk, which would have been fine if this was a boxing match. They appeared to forget they were supposed to be playing football. In the past this has always been United's route to success over Arsenal and with our weakened team (up front at least), it would have been their best bet. I must be a masochist to even bring it up, as it is bound to cause nightmares, but when Giggs ran through the Arsenal defence like a dose of salts at Villa Park a couple of years back, nobody was left admiring the winger's physical strength!

At least the intensity of the action on the pitch ensured the atmosphere was well stoked on the terraces. There was no need for any such inspiration in our corner of the ground but it guaranteed that the remaining 60,000 didn't spend the entire half in muppet mode. It was different at Bolton because the Reebok holds less than half the capacity of Old Trafford. So the Gooners gathered in one stand behind the goal knew that we could be heard loud and clear, in order to try and influence proceedings. Whereas at Old Trafford we are always allocated such a small percentage of the capacity and stuck high up in one corner of the ground, that you feel the need to holler twice as loud as usual. And holler we did, as heartily as possible for much of the entire 90 minutes, because we were determined to do our little bit, no matter how insignificant a part, for a team that had come to Old Trafford so focused on their task that they were getting along just fine with 11 men. Don't get me wrong, it wasn't as if this was a chore, as we were positively revelling in such a rare opportunity to delight all night long in songs about United's dreadful season and our sensational one.

In the usual half-time search for old friends, in order to share a minute of this special moment with them, I managed to track down Ray. He wasn't so easy to recognise by now as the beard he'd been cultivating since the start of our current run made him look more like my grandfather, the rabbi, than the Ray I knew from the West Upper. We couldn't resist sharing our recollections of the corresponding point in the corresponding fixture last season.

My mate Nell turned out to be sitting, in fact standing as I don't think we took our seats for the entire game, only a couple of rows behind. This was great when the moment we'd all been waiting for finally came 12 minutes after the break. When Barthez only managed to palm away Freddie's shot and Sylvain Wiltord was first on the scene to stick the ball in the net, Ró and I went absolutely mental with the entire Arsenal section. It is usually myself who has to try and afford Ró some protection from all the flying arms and legs in such exuberant circumstances, but for once it was everyone else trying to get out of our way, as we were able to dive over and share the most poignant high-five of the season with Nell. Euphoric football moments don't come much better than this. The entire match is a bit of a blur but after the goal I can't recall a single incident on the pitch. We were far too busy with all the ecstatic celebrations, endless teasing of our rivals and counting down what must have been one of Fergie's painfully slow clocks until the moment when the Championship was finally ours.

Happily, for all those who would be at Highbury three days later, the Championship presentation was arranged for after our final game of the season. However it would have added to United's embarrassment if it could have taken place after the final whistle that night. Nevertheless, it didn't stop us from making the very most of this momentous occasion. All the nerves and pent-up emotions of the past few weeks evaporated in the rapturous rejoicing that followed in our corner of Old Trafford, with the lads going doolally down on the pitch, as we sang their praises and informed the stewards that 'We're not going home'. As the team let their hair down (although I can't recall seeing Spunky untying his ponytail!), some cheeky fans had come prepared to rename our corner of the Stadium: they unrolled a big white flag which stated loud and proud 'Champions Section'.

According to the papers, Ferguson was man enough to appear in the

ARSENAL ON THE DOUBLE

Arsenal dressing room to offer his congratulations and Wenger made an effort to appease the surly Scot by finally accepting his offer of a post-match glass of wine (oh to have been a fly on the wall for that one!). I can't escape the analogy with the sport of boxing in this gesture. After all the pre-fight hype where the fighters exaggerate and talk up their hatred of one another to sell tickets to the bout, they occasionally appear to get so caught up in the whole circus. By the time they step into the ring the animosity between the two often seems almost genuine. However after a hard-fought 12-round bout, no matter what bad feelings there were before, you usually witness the two boxers giving each other a mutual hug, since now they both share a great respect for one another because they are the only two people who can truly appreciate how deep they had to dig both physically and mentally to last the distance in such a gruelling bout.

The party began again three days later, as our final game of the season signalled the start of an exhausting three-day celebration, which finally climaxed as far as I was concerned with Tony Adams' testimonial match against Celtic on Monday night. Our game against Everton turned into little more than a sideshow in the celebratory carnival that day. The streets around Highbury were awash with colour long before kick-off, as everyone seemed to arrive early to toast the Gunners' third Double with their pals, or to buy the obligatory flags and Double T-shirts from the stalls around the ground for the parade to the Town Hall the following day. Taking our seats in the ground, we all found little red and white plastic flags on every seat along with balloons liberally sprinkled around for people to blow up at the appropriate moment.

Before kick-off at Highbury there was an assortment of presentations to be made on the pitch, including Dennis Bergkamp's Goal of the Season award from ITV, Freddie Ljungberg's Player of the Month award, Arsène Wenger's Manager of the Month award and three awards for Robbie Pires, including the Football Writers' Player of the Year award. Amongst all the joy of this fabulous occasion, there was a hint of sadness, as we were saying a fond farewell to Lee Dixon after 14 years' service to the cause, and goodbye also to Gilles Grimandi. Moreover, after 39 years at the club as player and goalkeeping coach, the Arsenal were saying goodbye to one of its favourite sons, Bob Wilson, who'd finally decided to retire. With all the padded tops and gloves worn by modern-day keepers, I retain an enduring image of Wilson fearlessly diving in where it hurts, wearing nothing but a skimpy green top and white shorts.

As far as the match was concerned, we were most interested in whether Thierry Henry could add the Golden Boot to an ever-increasing lengthy list of achievements at the club this season. Studying the details in the programme before kick-off Van Nistelrooy, Hasselbaink and Shearer were all shown as having 23 Premiership goals, with Titi lagging one goal behind all three. Jimmy-Floyd was still out injured, so Chelsea's match was one game we didn't have to worry about, while the other two were involved as United played Charlton and Newcastle were down at Southampton. There was also the matter of continuing our goal-scoring record to 39 consecutive matches and increasing our run of league victories to 13. Naturally it would have suited better if it had been Henry who scored, but everything was hunky-dory when Bergkamp put us a goal up after only four minutes, making Arsenal the first team to score in every Premiership game in a season.

It felt like Everton had neglected to read the script when there was a threat of them pooping our party as they went 1–2 up with Radzinski's goal after half an hour. As an Everton supporter at the match wrote: 'It was like being uninvited guests at the birthday party who, having spilled red wine on the beige carpet, then leave with the two best-looking women.' At least Everton's lead only lasted three minutes after Henry weighed in with his first goal since Charlton on April Fools' Day. As far as I was concerned – and everyone else who was getting the information from me courtesy of my radio – Henry went one goal behind Shearer again, when Shearer pulled one back for Newcastle at Southampton. We were all overjoyed when Henry scored a second to tie things up once more but began tearing our hair out when Francis Jeffers came on as sub and Henry handed Franny a sitter when he could have completed his hat-trick instead. Especially when Franny fluffed his chance.

Arsène eventually brought on Stuart Taylor as sub for Wright in goal, because Taylor had played nine influential league games for us and it would have been outrageous if he'd missed out on a medal merely because he was one game away from the required ten matches. Jeffers finally managed to put away one of the many chances he was offered and to be honest, it wasn't really necessary for Franny to run over and taunt the Everton fans. When the final whistle blew, as far, as we were all concerned Thierry's selfless football had ensured he would be sharing the Golden Boot with Shearer.

So there was some surprise when Thierry was announced as the outright winner of the Golden Boot on the big screen. After much debate we finally discovered that the programme had listed Shearer with one too many goals. Still it didn't belittle Henry's attempt to try and set a goal up for his team-mate Jeffers, when Titi didn't have a clue who was scoring elsewhere. It said a whole lot for the team spirit which is so evident amongst this squad. The players had trooped off at the whistle to allow time for the podium to be erected in the centre of the pitch.

My only complaint about these proceedings is that they are a little too stage-managed, all timed to perfection, with a backing track provided by the club DJ (are we destined now to be stuck with Queen as the soundtrack to such occasions for all eternity?). What transpired was that instead of the crowd being able to spontaneously pay tribute to each player in turn as they stepped up to receive their medal, we had the DJ blasting out the backing tracks to various Arsenal tunes. He must have been pleased with himself to have sorted out the music to Freddie's theme tune, but sadly the pace of the music for the Andy Williams original of this song is far too slow and so it only ended up preventing some of the communal singing which would have transpired – if it hadn't been impossible to try and sing above the sound blasting out from the speakers.

Nevertheless, it was wonderful when it came to the end of the line of players and Robbie Pires limped up to collect his medal. I imagine it was an organised stunt suggested by one of the players, but it was still a touching moment when the entire squad ran over and prostrated themselves before him and at least it appeared to add a touch of spontaneity to the presentation. As Tony Adams said in his programme piece after Leeds '99, Galatasary in Copenhagen and Liverpool last year, he was beginning to wonder what was going on. It might have taken four long seasons but the moment we were waiting for came along eventually with all the pyrotechnic trappings: Adams finally collected his fourth Championship trophy, only for everyone on the pitch to disappear in an explosion of ticker tape.

Plenty of looning around went on during the lap of honour; Wiltord and Edu wearing Elvis wigs and shades sticks in my mind for some bizarre reason. There were also some poignant moments, like Dave Seaman dragging the shy Bob Wilson over to walk around with the rest of the squad, a last chance to express our gratitude to the versatile Grimandi and the sight of Lee Dixon departing the Highbury turf after his last competitive game. Myself, I loved the plain white T-shirts worn by all Arsène's staff, Pat Rice, Gary Lewin et al. which had just the three years printed on them: 1971, 1998, 2002 – our three Doubles. For many Gooners, the most significant fact is that we have now won the Championship at White Hart Lane, Anfield and now Old Trafford. Some Treble that!

The pubs around Highbury were obviously rammed for the rest of the afternoon and long into the night. With huge crowds overflowing onto the pavement, it was as though there was one long street party the entire length of Blackstock Road. What pleased me most is that there was none of the aggravation that occurred in '98 which doubtless was related to the way the police started marching into pubs en masse and shutting them down. It seemed downright ridiculous that there were problems on both nights, after we won the title and the FA Cup, when we saw pictures of the losers partying peacefully on Tyneside. The majority of Gooners don't live in the immediate area around the club, but for those of us that do, it was my friendly Indian late-night shop that had their windows smashed and their car set on fire when it all went off around here. I found myself feeling obliged to apologise on behalf of all Gooners for at least six months after the way the shop was terrorised that night.

As boisterous as they were, this year's celebrations didn't turn nasty, although the only reason we know for sure is that we didn't find ourselves at home listening to police sirens blazing all night long, as we decided to get a fairly early night in order that we could be up with the lark for the parade the following morning. You know you are knocking on a bit when you need a good night's kip to guarantee getting up in the morning. Yet if I felt a sad old bugger going home to bed, just as the party was hotting up, it is nothing to how I felt the following morning when we overslept.

Over the years we've come to know the caretaker of one of the buildings opposite the Town Hall in Upper Street. Since I work for an Irish newspaper, so long as we cross his palm with silver he is happy to let us up on his roof with all the other media folk.

We knew we had to get there early as you just cannot imagine how completely rammed Upper Street becomes by the time around 100,000 people are squeezing their way down, to try and get a pitch near the Town Hall. We only just made it to the building by the skin of our teeth last time, getting there around 10.30, to wait until noon for the open-top bus to arrive. Even then I had been sure I was about to get hit at any moment by those who'd arrived there hours earlier and who weren't happy about Ró pushing past but if they couldn't have a pop at her, they sure could give me a dig. This time around, after oversleeping, we ended up leaving the house at 10 a.m. and I made my second mistake of the day, as we decided to try and make up for lost time by driving a little closer. However, with all the main streets nearby closed, the congestion on narrow side roads meant that we soon found ourselves trapped in the car, no more than five minutes nearer the Town Hall, but after wasting quarter of an hour.

We just dumped the car and started walking as fast as possible until we got to Upper Street. Then we walked along side roads until we came to the stretch of Upper Street that we had to negotiate our way along if we were going to reach the building. It was already impossible to move, but being a brave sort of guy (and because fellas are far more likely to let a female pass) I let Ró go in front as we tried to force our way through. After about half an hour we had made it to about 20 yards away from our objective but by now the nearer we got to the Town Hall the more impossible it was to get any further. In plain sight of where we wanted to be, we were forced to give up for fear of starting a riot.

The problem now was that we were completely stuck where we stood, with a great big tree obscuring our view of the balcony on the front of the Town Hall where the team would eventually appear and with thousands of tall folk, waving flags and with kids on their shoulders, who would obscure Ró's view of even the bus when it passed. If I thought it would be easier to go back we would have done and found somewhere more comfortable. Meanwhile, we were staring at the people sitting on our roof, remembering how we had commented the previous time, quite how much we would have hated to be stuck like sardines in the crowd below. It was lucky it wasn't as warm a day as four years ago, as I feel sure it could have been dangerous. Mind you, even if someone passed out, there would be no possible way they could collapse. We had about a 90-minute wait before the bus would arrive, during which time we managed to manoeuvre into a slightly better spot where Ró might at least see something if she stood on tiptoe.

We were dripping with sweat and dying of thirst when the bus did eventually pass and we caught a fleeting glimpse of the players and the trophies, in between all the obstructions. We see all the players live on the pitch all season, but one of the reasons I have enjoyed the parade in the past is because we get a chance to hear the players, albeit briefly, when they each say a few words on the balcony of the town hall. So having stood there for hours you can imagine we were more than a little disappointed when the team appeared at the balcony to enormous cheers, only for us to quieten down to a hush in the hope of hearing our heroes, only for their voices to be inaudible to all the crowd. I couldn't understand: four years ago the PA was perfect and we heard every player in turn, had a little sing-song for each. It had been great fun.

This year, though, they had over a week to organise this parade and they ended up with hundreds of thousands, crammed into Upper Street to the point of being dangerous, and most of these people, if they were lucky, got nothing more than a glimpse of the players and the trophies on the bus. We gave up on standing there as it was frustrating watching the players speak without hearing a word. The doors of the pub behind us opened and we were just glad of the sanctuary, to get out of the crush.

Far be it from me to end up on a gripe about what is supposed to be a wonderful occasion, but these parades have just become too popular.

If there was too much organisation for the trophy presentation, then there is too little for the parade (there's no pleasing some folks!). However, with thousands of parents bringing their offspring along on the day why couldn't the Arsenal simply open the ground up, have the team do a lap round the pitch before leaving on the bus and then show the whole thing on the Jumbotron screens?

Monday, 13 May 2002

Stepping outside the door last Thursday, it was the morning after the night before. The Highbury dustmen were clearing up the debris from the previous night's delirium. Arriving back from Manchester in the wee hours, to the residue of all that rapture, it felt like we'd foregone that scene straight out of *Fever Pitch* in the streets around the Arsenal a few hours earlier.

Yet far from missing the party, we'd been amongst the fortunate 3,000 Gooners who were its very life and soul. A seat in the 'Champions Section' of Old Trafford was the hottest ticket of the whole season. My cousin had motored north along most of the 200 miles of motorway, when he was mortified to be told: 'The bad news is that Tony Adams is injured and there's no ticket for you!' Coughing up a mere £150 outside the ground, he wasn't clobbered quite so badly as the poor bugger who had blown £175 each for his two tickets. Obviously with more money than sense, this particular flibbertigibbet failed to open his envelope until the morning of this momentous match. Whereupon he must have been more than a mite surprised to discover the scalper had sold him tickets for the previous Saturday's FA Cup final!

The recent red-letter days of these milestone matches have been ruinous to my reputation. The climax to the season had me in such a state of excitation that even I have managed to set out in good time to get to the last three games. Yet the Arsenal's success was so entwined with my tardy timekeeping that I was terrified we would come a cropper in The Theatre of Dreams. Nothing to do with the absence of Adams, Pires, Bergkamp and Henry, or United's determination to delay the almost inevitable day of retribution, but on account of my early arrival. We managed to miss most of the usual motorway madness, until we finally slowed to a stop around Stoke, surrounded by Scousers and various other supporters' sorties, including the mythical vast majority of United fans travelling from all points south of Manchester.

This was the contention of a partisan pantechnicon driver, who as a City supporter couldn't abide the fact that he was left floundering in the traffic, caused by his enemy's southern cohorts, every time United played at home. We would've been inching our way along until midnight if, while offering the Arsenal every encouragement, this gregarious Good Samaritan hadn't suggested we forsake the main road and follow in his slipstream. His lorry thundered through some of the northern metropolis's most solvent suburbs. The squeals of surprise from our somewhat parochial passenger suggested the sight of so many gargantuan gaffs didn't quite sit with his mental image of a Manchester entirely made up of 'mad for it' house-party hobos. No amount of double glazing could guarantee the occupants an early night, as a queue of cars miles long crawled homeward a few hours later. The whole of Lancashire must have been left wide awake by a barrage of horn-blowing and hollering Gooners, hanging out of their vehicles, having a high old time in the traffic.

Our scintillating success was all the sweeter because it was so unexpected. No team turns up at Old Trafford with such a threadbare front line and sits in their own half, inviting the Red Devils to do their worst, without suffering severe damage. For some time United tried to kick us off the park and it was remarkable that Durkin made it to 90 minutes without producing a single red card. Although after this reckless red-rag plan failed to provoke any retaliation from our brave bulls, it was United's impotence in attack that was most amazing. At the back the Arsenal might have matured into an indomitable defence (without a decidedly iffy Igor) but Man United were a pale imitation, a complete metamorphosis from the marauding machine which mullahed us so majestically on our last traumatic trip to Manchester.

Mind you, it may be many moons since I last put on a pair of boots, but I do recall being far too focused on our own game to have the foggiest how well anyone else performed. Outnumbered on Wednesday night, we Gooners were so totally committed to our 12th-man role that apart from those scything tackles and the wild eruption with Wiltord's winner, most of the match is a muddled blur, culminating in the multi-orgasm of 30 minutes of magical celebrations.

After watching a recording of the highlights the following day, I wallowed in every word of all the wonderful tributes in the papers and on TV. No matter how much pleasure I took from all the sycophants, sucking up to Wenger, as if his side was the best thing since sliced bread, I couldn't swallow their tall tales of how we had eventually accomplished the toughest task with such style and panache. Arguably, this side is capable of the most attractive football ever seen at Highbury, but the truth of the matter is that we haven't shown this fabulous form since Easter. In his programme notes on Saturday, Arsène was entitled to crow over the fact that prior to playing Everton, we hadn't conceded a goal in 15 and a half hours of open play. During a run-in where we've battled to break teams down for long periods, struggling to reproduce the guile and craft of earlier conquests, we've had to rely on odd inspirational flashes of Freddie's brilliance. Above all, during the last few weeks, our stunning success rate has been a direct result of a cumulative number of clean sheets, which will have even conjured up a smile on George Graham's merciless mush.

I adore the fact that Arsène has accomplished the incredible task of turning 'Boring, boring Arsenal' into the country's most exciting entertainers. However, it is the terrific team spirit, guts and grit necessary to consistently maintain clean sheets that are the traditional values which first attracted me to the club as a kid. It is 31 years since I watched Ray Kennedy score at White Hart Lane, in a '1–0 to the Arsenal' to take the title en route to our first Double. The reflective glory of giving the goal-scorer a lift in my old man's motor rubber-stamped a relationship which has been rock solid ever since. Yet in an age when loyalty has a shelf-life of your average club kit and successful teams are a multinational hotchpotch of stars, there have been times when I've wondered if the famous Arsenal spirit was permanently on the wane. It is therefore extremely gratifying to see its gradual regeneration in recent months to the point where I am now able to believe in a bond that exists in our squad.

Similarly, of all the countless collection of records clocked up in such a sensational season, it was the undefeated away-match record which made the result at Old Trafford so significant for me. Not only has this stood for 113 years (way back when only 11 away games were played), but it could well be a feat that will not be repeated for another century. It is in the enemy's lair where the mettle of our panoply of star players is really tested. They have consistently proved they are 'up for it' in the face of adversity away from home and, in our own small way, it is wonderful to know that the travelling faithful have played our part.

Moreover, taking the title at Old Trafford confirmed the Arsenal as true Champions, rather than opportunists cashing in on United's dodgy season. It enabled us to look forward to a weekend which was one big party, without any of the hair-raising tension that would have remained if a win was required. Hardly anyone noticed the score against Everton. We were all focused on willing Thierry Henry on to win the Golden Boot. Even more icing on an incredibly sweet cake.

Sunday's parade was an opportunity for hundreds of thousands of Arsenal fans of all ages to catch a rare glimpse of their heroes in the flesh. It must have made for an incredibly colourful, cacophonous scene. If only we could have seen more between big heads and huge flags, or heard something of what each of the players said. Being crushed to death in such a dangerously packed crowd is perhaps not the best way to celebrate. As my aging bones begin to buckle with all that barging, in future I might well admire such an occasion more comfortably from my couch! Hopefully we'll have an opportunity to express our gratitude to Grimandi, Dixon and Adams at tonight's testimonial, as no one really wanted to put a downer on the day.

Our delight may be beyond all description, but it is tinged with a deal of sadness, to think we might have seen the last of two of our defensive dinosaurs. Accompanied by his loyal lieutenant Dixon, Adams is the only man to captain a Championship-winning team in three decades. They certainly don't make them like our Mr Arsenal any more.

Arsenal FC: 2001–02

Honours

Premier League Champions
FA Cup Winners

Barclaycard Manager of the Year: Arsène Wenger
Barclaycard Player of the Year: Freddie Ljungberg
Premiership Golden Boot: Thierry Henry (24 goals)
Professional Football Writers Association Player of the Year: Robert Pires
Capital Gold Sportstime Player of the Year: Robert Pires
U-19 Academy League Champions
FA Women's Premier League Champions
Groundsman of the Year: Paul Burgess

Records and milestones

Unbeaten away from home all season (W 14 , D 5, L 0) – not achieved since
Preston in 1888–89
Club record for scoring in consecutive matches (39 currently) – previous best of
31 set in 1931
Premiership and club record for consecutive victories (13 currently) – previous
club best of 10 in 1998 and 1997
Premiership and club record for consecutive wins away from home (8 currently)
(joint league record) – previous club best of 6 in 1977
Consecutive away league matches unbeaten (19 currently) – previous club best of
13 set in 1990
Wenger: first Arsenal manager to win FA Cup twice
Wenger: first Arsenal manager to win the Double twice
Most points in the league 87 points – previous best in Premiership 78 (1998, 1999);
league best 83 – 1991
Adams: first captain to win Championship in three different decades
Adams: captain of three Championship sides: 1989, 1998, 2002
Dixon: played in Championship-winning sides: 1989, 1998, 2002

Three Doubles: 1971, 1998, 2002
The Treble: White Hart Lane 1971, Anfield 1989, Old Trafford 2002

Postscript: The Full Monty

Monday, 13 May (Tony Adams' Testimonial): Celtic (H) 1–1
Dixon (68)

Testimonial matches are a bit of an anathema these days. They used to be a means by which a distinguished period of loyal service to a club could be rewarded, by providing the respective player with a lump sum of cash with which he could buy a pub, or some sort of business to guarantee him a little financial security in retirement (providing he didn't drink all the profits!). This may still be the case in the lower reaches of the football hierarchy, but it hardly applies these days to the multi-million-pound stars of the Premiership.

However, I still like the idea of a testimonial, in as much as loyalty is such a rare commodity in the modern game that I appreciate the opportunity for us fans to express our appreciation to any player who has served our club proud for many years. Yet when you consider the exorbitant cost of following our team, it doesn't seem right that we should be asked to fork out even more, in order to put money into the pocket of someone who is more affluent than we could ever dream of being. So the best solution seems to be the one found by Niall Quinn, where his testimonial ensured the fans got an opportunity to show their gratitude and any money raised went to charity.

Meanwhile, you would struggle to find a Gooner who would begrudge Tony Adams a testimonial. Not only was he donating up to £500,000 from the money raised to further the aims of his own Sporting Chance charity, but anything that remained would be only a small recompense for all the millions he has missed out on over the years because of his decision to remain a career-long, one-club player. Personally, I was delighted because it gave us all a chance to set the record straight, after the shameful episode of the shambles that passed for his initial testimonial eight years back. If I remember correctly it was organised for a time when many Gooners were away on holiday and, of those who remained, most had just shelled out a tidy sum to watch the Arsenal play glamorous opposition in the Makita tournament the following week. This wasn't helped by the choice of Crystal Palace as opposition and the turnout had been poor.

ARSENAL ON THE DOUBLE

There was a bit of a contrast this time around. I remember first hearing about his testimonial on a Monday evening and then running around to the box office first thing Thursday morning, having been flabbergasted to hear the previous evening that it had already sold out. The fact that the opposition arranged for the night was Celtic was not irrelevant. They completely sold out their allocation of tickets for the entire Clock End. It was a great choice, because it guaranteed a great atmosphere on the night. We'd had Rangers down a couple of years back for Merson's testimonial and, while they also ensured a good atmosphere, there wasn't this fraternal feeling which has always existed between us and the Celtic contingent.

I can remember Ró had commented that night on the bellicose-looking Rangers boys milling around outside before we got to our seats. Then we found ourselves sitting with a boozed-up Rangers fan who was screaming a disgusting invective at an Arsenal side comprised largely of French protestants. He didn't stop fuming with his foul-mouthed racist claptrap about Fenians and the Pope and I could see Ró was quietly seething beside me. I thought she was going to get me into trouble when eventually she couldn't resist leaning over and tapping him on his shoulder to inform him that this was a friendly game of football, not a political rally.

I assume the Celtic connection with the Arsenal stems from the days of our Irish triumvirate of Brady, Stapleton and O'Leary, when we had such a huge Irish fan-base. One of the guys who sits in front of us at Highbury still wears his hat from that era, with the Arsenal colours on one side and an Irish tricolour on the other. Or perhaps it dates further back than that because I recall as a kid that if you were Arsenal, you were automatically Celtic as well. Whatever the case, on the night of TA's testimonial, they certainly didn't turn up just to pleasantly play the patsy.

The fact that they exist permanently in the shadow of the English Premiership means that Scottish sides can't resist any opportunity to try and put one over on an English team. I think the Hoops' intensity must have surprised one or two of the team in Arsenal shirts who were expecting a gentle run-out. It was without doubt worth the price of admission alone just to see the Arsenal fab back four of Dixon, Adams, Bould and Winterburn line up for the kick-off of a match with John Lukic minding the goal behind them for one last time.

To see them all step forward with Tony Adams in that infamous pose – his arm pointing skyward, in what has become since that movie (in my mind at least) the Arsenal defence doing the *Full Monty* doing the Arsenal offside trap (if that makes any sense) – was such a poignant moment. It might have brought a tear to my eye, if I wasn't saving them all up for later. Celtic had an African youngster Mohammed Sylla playing up front. His fleet-footedness was impressive all night long but for a while there Martin O'Neill's side were in danger of putting a complete dampener on Tony's party, by taking it all far too seriously. Thompson thumped a free-kick into Lukic's net to take the lead after half an hour (although it was the sort of effort that I am sure Lukic would have dealt with a few years earlier).

Richard Wright replaced the ageing goalie in the second half, but we were all pleasantly surprised to see our favourite back four still in place. Though there were flashes of Bouldie's brilliance with beautifully timed tackles, it was obvious they were all intent on saving their legs, as they kept a line high up the pitch. It was like old times, as the linesman duly obliged to the traditional Arsenal request to stick his flag up and as they all stood there with their arms up in the air, you could see them have a little chuckle amongst themselves about the comfortable familiarity of this scene. This was an image burned into the consciousness of every Gooner and the rest of British football over a decade, but I would take home this happy reminder of it on the night.

We did not get a goal from Tony Adams, as is often contrived by the two teams on such occasions, but we were treated to a magical moment from his loyal lieutenant of such long standing. It was all the better due to the spontaneity of the move and the fact that Winterburn was able to share in the glory. Nige hit a ball from wide on the left, which hung in the penalty area just long enough for Lee Dixon to come steaming in and head it home. Injuries had prevented Lee spending too much time on the pitch during the season, but whenever he did get on, he was always striving to land himself at least one goal and was inches away from succeeding on several occasions. So it was fabulously fitting that he should close the book on his brilliant Arsenal career by opening his account for the season.

Stevie Bould had departed minutes earlier to a standing ovation from the crowd and Nigel followed him soon after to similar heartfelt applause. However, probably the biggest cheer of the night was heard at the introduction of the inimitable Ian Wright. Wrightie remains such a popular figure that he had previously stolen the show at Lee Dixon's testimonial. He is so much larger than life that he just can't help it. I imagine the organisers were mindful of this when considering Ian's introduction. It was obvious from his big entrance how much Wrightie has missed the Highbury limelight. As the cameras focused on his beaming face, the crowd were treated to a cunnilingual tongue twister on the big screens. It was a reminder to us all that while Wiltord might be the current joker in the pack, he can't touch the Gooners' favourite goon.

Having appeared on the pitch before the start, with his hands full of kids – Oliver and Amber – and cups – the Premiership trophy and the FA Cup – Tony Adams trotted off the turf alone with a minute to go. The whole of Highbury, including the Hoops fans, resounded to the tune of 'There's Only One Tony Adams'. After 19 years and 659 appearances, he returned at the final whistle for a hard-earned lap of honour. We had all read how our captain intends to consider his options during the summer and see how his body holds up before making his mind up about whether to retire or not. After so many years of loyal service, Mr Arsenal's decision will not be disputed by his devotees. Yet, when Adams sauntered over to the North Bank, he could be in no doubt as to the fans' strength of feeling, as thousands rose as one, singing as loud as we had sung all night, imploring him to defer his departure for just 'One more year!'

English football might never see the like of Tony Adams again and while they say no one player is bigger than the club he plays for, this is almost true in Adams' case. Ever since George Graham installed his 'colossus' as captain of our club 15 years ago, Tony Adams became synonymous with the Arsenal. Despite the fact that such a fitful season for Adams this term has given us all time to come to terms with the reality, it is still hard to imagine Highbury without him. As he ambled around the pitch, absorbing the adulation of his adoring fans, I suddenly found myself devastated when the possibility dawned on me that we might never again see the great man lead the Gunners out in a competitive game. I was grateful he was at the Clock End saluting the Celtic fans and I was able to hide behind my binoculars, because this thought caused a lump in my throat and I found myself choking back the tears as I welled up with all the emotion of the moment.

The whole night was a tremendous tribute to the Arsenal life and times of Tony Adams. Whether or not it was the curtain call of his playing career remains to be seen. His eventual departure for the sanctuary of the dressing room was our cue to exit Highbury for the last time until the whole beautiful business begins again in August. Standing in the North Bank amidst all the Gooners bidding their pals farewell for the relative purgatory of an Arsenal-free summer, I was amazed to be able to do likewise with Ray, my neighbour from the West Upper. Coincidentally, he was standing only a few seats away with his wife. Although Jennie might not be such a regular visitor to Highbury, after she beckoned me over to have a few words it was evident that she'd been reading my weekly missives.

A lending institution would usually be my last option in any attempt to obtain the astronomic sum of the nearly three grand required to renew our season tickets. Yet Jennie kindly advised me of an offer by a building society, where I might be able to obtain an interest-free loan, on production of merely my season-ticket book, instead of resorting to a pair of Róna's stockings and a sawn-off shotgun. Having said our farewells and bid adieu to assorted other familiar faces, I lingered for a few moments, as I'd been extremely fortunate to lay my hands on a precious pass for the players' bar after the match. Usually I am the person least likely to make the most of such a marvellous 'ligging' opportunity. Yet my disappointment over the parade meant that I was determined that this should be the perfect finale to a fabulous season.

The usual pleasantries were exchanged in the player's bar in the Clock End complex. Arsenal's vice-chairman David Dein thanked the players and staff of Celtic and the match officials for their participation on the night and presented each of them with a small memento. Martin O'Neill accepted some silverware to take back to Scotland with Celtic's own Premiership trophy which had been on parade that night, before waxing lyrical with a few words about Adams' wonderful career.

Standing beside Dein, Tony looked decidedly embarrassed to be the centre of so much attention, as the Arsenal's head honcho heaped high praise upon the Club Captain with his own tremendously touching tribute. Unlike some of the faceless suits behind various publicly listed Premier League conglomerates, it was so reassuring to hear the words from the man at the helm of the Arsenal, which confirm that below his corporate head there beats an irrepressible red and white heart.

Having being presented with his own silver souvenir of the occasion, Tony responded to Dein's deification with a simple but extremely emotional speech which moved everybody in the room. Amongst a largely masculine audience, I was far from alone in trying to limit my lachrymose reaction. Runny noses were blown and tired eyes rubbed, as many did their utmost to disguise a dreaded public display of emotion in such macho surroundings, while Tony told how proud he was to have his dad present and hoped his mother, who had passed away a year prior, was there on the night in spirit. His father was an unrecognisable figure, sitting in a wheelchair some yards away. The ravages of terminal cancer and the torture of his treatment seemed to have left him on the very cusp of this mortal coil.

Only the most stone-hearted stoic could have remained dry-eyed as Adams went on to describe how we were standing directly above the old indoor playing surface, where he'd shared so many laughs in the company of his close pal, poor David Rocastle. Ever since this true Gooner was taken from us in such an untimely tragedy, Arsenal fans have been paying their respects to poor Rocky at virtually every game. Although it sometimes feels as though our motives are less altruistic: we holler the name of this footballing god, in the hope that he might have some heavenly influence over the Arsenal's fate. Yet of all people Rocky would appreciate the importance of the result and to this day I still find myself choking up during this chant.

It had been a year since he had buried his good buddy and it was with regard to fate's sudden twists and turns that Adams referred to Rocky. His reflective mood suggested an awareness of his own mortality which might influence whether he decides to continue playing. Thankfully he kept his speech short and sweet, stopping before the tears were actually streaming down my face. However, after O'Neill and Dein had both described him as an extraordinary player, before Tony sat down he made a point of directing our attention to the fact that he had been privileged to play alongside some great players. Adams then invited up the current and former cogs who had combined in the Gooner gearwheel on the night, in order to express his gratitude with a small gift (only after he'd pulled Ray Parlour's leg by suggesting he put his pint down first!).

My only slight grievance was that our French contingent couldn't make it on the night. I can't overstate how grateful I was to be able to slink into this post-match shindig, as I had long since craved an opportunity to express my heartfelt appreciation to the defensive dinosaurs who'd done us so proud this past decade.

I also like to think of myself as a founder member of the *Allez Gilles* fan club and it would have been great to be able to express my gratitude to Grimandi before one of the Arsenal's more unsung heroes hoofed it out of Highbury's marble halls for the last time. Nevertheless, I could hardly complain when most Gooners would gladly give their right arm to get into a room with Dixon, Adams, Bould, Winterburn and Ian Wright to boot.

I latched onto Lee Dixon first. In the light of Dixon's imminent departure, I was desperate to hear Lee lauded a little louder by the Arsenal fans during the nonstop jubilation of the last few weeks of the season. No doubt it is simply because he doesn't have a better song, but while our other stars stole all the limelight, it often felt like Lee was the forgotten man (at least he'd heard his name sung at long last, when he scored the equaliser earlier that evening!). In my desire to set the record straight on behalf of Gooners everywhere, it might appear little more than a token gesture, but I wasn't going to let Lee leave without shaking his hand and letting him know quite how much we valued his enduring loyalty and his age-defying stamina.

Having dealt with my diffident nature in talking to Dicko, I was on a roll. I managed to waylay a nattily attired Wrightie, in his pinstripe jacket, black and white brogues and his foppish French beret. Seated beside him was a weary-looking Stevie Bould, who, when I suggested that he looked as fit as ever, pulled an extremely pained expression that suggested otherwise. Sadly I wasn't able to corner Nigel Winterburn as he spent the evening chatting and I couldn't find an opportune moment to interject. Yet I finally managed to collar our captain just before he crept out of the door, off to continue his sober celebration at the Dover Street Wine Bar. As with the others, I made a somewhat feeble attempt to express what a privilege it had been to watch a myriad of marvellous performances over so many years. Yet I didn't want to sound too obsequious to the point of embarrassing him and in truth words are so inadequate when it comes to expressing how fortunate we have been to witness some of the greatest players in the club's history. With his customary sincerity, Adams actually thanked me before leaving and so this proved to be the perfect end-of-term party. Arriving home a little later, as I turned the key in the door I found myself reluctant to use the hand which had just shaken those of Adams, Wright, Dixon and Bould, wondering how long I could get away without washing it!